Return To Chewelah

Return To Chewelah

A Story of Innocence and Loss

by

Janet G. May

Storm Peak Press
Seattle, Washington

To Mel

"Goodbye," said the fox.
"And now here is my secret, a very simple secret: It is only with the heart that one can see rightly; what is essential is invisible to the eye."

— Antoine de Saint-Exupéry

All rights reserved under International and Pan-American Conventions, including The Berne Convention, under international copyright, under which terms no copies of this material may be made by any means whatever. Reproduction or transmission by any means including photocopying, sound recording, or electronic file prohibited without written permission of the publisher. Exceptions permitted for brief quotations in reviews. This book conveys the experiences of the author and is not to be construed as a critical assessment of medical rehabilitation programs.

Excerpt from THE LITTLE PRINCE by Antoine de Saint-Exupéry, copyright 1943 and renewed 1971 by Harcourt Brace & Company, reprinted by permission of the publisher.

Storm Peak Press
157 Yesler Way, Suite 413
Seattle, Washington 98104

© Copyright 1997, Janet G. May
ISBN 0-9641357-5-2
Library of Congress Catalog Card Number: 97-12093

Library of Congress Cataloging-in-Publication Data
May, Janet G., 1952-
   Return to Chewelah: a story of innocence and loss /
by Janet G. May
     p. cm.
   ISBN 0-9641357-5-2 (pbk.)
   1. May, Janet G., 1952- . 2. Quadriplegics—Washington (State)—Biography. 3. Quadriplegics—Washington (State)—Rehabilitation. 4. Quadriplegics—Washington (State)—Family relationships.
RC406.Q33M39 1997
362.4'3'092—dc21
[B]   97-12093
                                                      CIP

PROLOGUE

The hospital where she worked was widely known as the best in the region, and its reputation was well-deserved. Yet she found herself thinking, "If things like this can happen in the best hospitals, what may happen in the worst?" Looking back, certain experiences began to make sense.

Who was ultimately responsible for the welfare of the patient? Certainly not the patient, especially when under anesthesia or unconscious. Not entirely the physician, who must be able to rely on staff to communicate accurate information. Probably not family members, who are often uninformed or perhaps lack knowledge of a situation. And not solely the bedside nurse, who may care a great deal, but goes home at the end of her shift.

In this lies the biggest flaw of the hospital system, staffed by regular human beings of all different types and personalities, some intelligent and compassionate, some judgmental and lazy. The chain is only as strong as its weakest links, with the weakest links spread randomly throughout the system . . .

She was waiting outside the hospital for a ride when she saw the car approach. It was traveling much too fast as it pulled into the horseshoe turnaround at the main entrance. It stopped quickly and one of two black women inside threw open the passenger door. That's when she saw the blood. More blood than she could ever have imagined — brilliant, fiery red — splattered up onto the windshield in thick drops and collecting on the floor mats.

One of the women was completely soaked, the front of her blouse sticking crookedly to her skin as the blood had already dried and caked. A young black man lay slumped on the seat, blood spurting from a gaping hole in his neck. He had been shot repeatedly in the head and chest.

The women were hysterical. "Get help, please help us," they screamed as they held his head.

She rushed into the deserted lobby and found only a security supervisor. "There's a man outside who's been shot!" she exclaimed frantically, pointing to the car. "Can we get somebody to help him? He's bleeding like crazy."

The supervisor sauntered over to the double glass doors and peered outside. Then he turned and walked slowly back to his station in the lobby.

"Aren't you going to do anything?" she demanded, "They need help! Can't we get a doctor or something?"

"It's not a security matter, ma'am," he replied in an official tone of voice. "It's a police matter."

"This is a hospital!" she screamed. "Somebody needs to help them!"

"It's not our responsibility, ma'am," he replied coldly.

She looked around the lobby, but it was late and most of the employees were gone. She returned reluctantly toward the entryway, wondering what to say to the women.

"Oh my God, somebody please help us," one of them screamed as she returned to the car. "He's dying."

She ran back into the lobby and reached for the phone to call the nurses upstairs. The security supervisor took the phone from her hand and placed it back on the hook.

She raced down the hall and pushed the elevator button for the second floor ICU. As usual, it took the elevator forever to arrive. "C'mon, c'mon," she muttered, hitting the button repeatedly. Finally, the light came on and she hurried inside.

When she arrived at the ICU, the day nurses were giving report to the night shift, but she interrupted them.

"A man is dying right outside the lobby," she explained frantically. "Can't we call a code or something?"

After asking a few short questions, the nurses called the code team. They bypassed the elevators, running down the stairs and out the door to where the car was waiting. By now, about fifteen minutes had elapsed from the time the car had arrived at the hospital.

The gunshot victim no longer had a pulse by the time the

code team reached him. They worked on him for about fifteen minutes before pronouncing him dead.

Later, she asked another security supervisor what he would have done in the situation.

"It was a judgment call," he replied. "It could have gone either way. But they should have gone to the emergency room entrance. They came to the wrong door."

She awoke to a warm, comforting room with her orange tabby, Buster, curled against her shoulder. He stretched and purred as she pulled back the covers and, again, checked the clock.

"What a terrible nightmare," she murmured, rubbing her eyes.

It was just before one in the morning and she knew, before turning off the light, that it would be another sleepless night.

ONE

When I can't sleep at night, I lie in bed staring up at the old saddle hanging above me on the cedar bed frame, and it takes me back to the dreamlike childhood days spent on Grammie's farm.

I'm standing next to a towering copper cattle-horse. The blanket is on straight and I'm gathering my strength to swing the heavy western saddle up onto his back. I have one stirrup looped over the horn like Grammie showed me, so that it won't get caught underneath the saddle when it lands.

Once the saddle is on, I have to tighten the cinch, but the powerful horse puffs his belly up with air so that I can't cinch it tightly. I try elbowing him in the stomach, but he swings sideways and raises one hind leg as a warning. I remind myself to tighten it again later, hoping the saddle doesn't slip as I mount.

I usually use the fence, but this time I manage to reach the stirrup with my foot. I wrap the leather thongs tightly around my fist, push off the ground with my boot, then swing the other leg high into the air and over his back. I'm on, and the ground is now a long way down.

Sundown is anxious to get going and takes long rapid strides as we head up to the woods. The other cattle horse follows along on the opposite side of the fence, whinnying in protest at being left behind. The two horses have been together since they were colts, and are nearly inseparable.

We ride through the pine forest, startling deer and angering chipmunks who scold loudly. I keep my eye out for baling wire which can easily entangle my horse's hooves and spook him.

Chapter One

Broken wagons, left by settlers who came to live in this Washington valley sixty years earlier, lie deserted in the brush, wooden spokes parched and splintered. I watch the ground for fragments of enamel-coated cookware which lie rusting at the old sites of settler campfires. The enamel is turquoise with white speckles, like a robin's egg, and I've hoped someday to find a piece whole.

The woods once belonged to the Indians, who gave the place its name: Chewelah, or "Water Snakes" in their language. They were peaceful Indians who brought families to pick huckleberries alongside the settlers. They lived in tipis heated only by fire, performed ritual dances by moonlight, and spoke to their god in dreams.

I grew up proud in the knowledge that my grandmother was part Indian. She was kind, brave, and strong, and a master of cattle, horses, gardens and all living things. As an adult I learned the painful truth that my grandmother had often denied being part Indian. There were no Indian families in Chewelah. Greedy settlers had stolen the best of their land and herded them away to reservations where the soil was dry, rocky, and infertile. In exchange for their autonomy, they were offered meager monthly checks similar to welfare payments. Some made their way in this hostile world, rising like bright stars in the fields of art and literature, but many others lived in poverty and squalor, their spirits broken or pride extinguished.

We reach an abandoned road through the forest where we can gallop: a breathtaking experience like bumpy, lurching flying. The ground passes by in a blur and a cool wind whips my face. I'm careful not to let the horse run too fast, because he's part thoroughbred and I'm not yet strong enough to stop him if he decides to run away with me.

At the edge of the woods, I slow the horse to a walk, and he steps out onto the road. I love the clip-clopping sound his shoes make on the hard ground. I stand up in the stirrups a little to stretch my legs, and listen to the creaking of the leather as we travel along. I could never be happier than at this moment, alone with the most magnificent creature on earth.

The sun is already hot, and I have to be back for dinner

at noon. Farmers eat their biggest meal midday, after rising early to bring in the hay during the coolest part of the day.

We sit down at the table with eight dusty men, and Grandpa says grace. The table is laden with fried chicken and roast beef, corn on the cob and peas from the garden, mashed potatoes, gravy, homemade bread and jam, and apple pie. It's considered rude to send the haying crew away from the table hungry.

My big sister and I always help wash the dishes after dinner. I wash and she dries, and we sing the corny songs we learned in Brownies. Grammie loves to hear us sing.

Later that night, I draw a bath, wadding up my filthy jeans and setting them on the little table by the sink, so they don't drop hay and dirt all over the floor. There are puffy red chafe marks on the insides of my knees from the saddle, and when I slide into the hot water, the sting brings tears to my eyes.

The bathroom has its own special smell, the lingering scent of the aftershave Grandpa buys from the Watkins man, mingled with the faint scent of hay. I lie back in the tub, peaceful and content, until the water starts to get cold. I wrap up in a towel, take my wadded clothes and climb the stairs to bed, exhausted and looking forward to the next day.

That summer spent on Grandma's farm was thirty years ago, but it feels just like yesterday. Since then, I've hung up my spurs, sold my horse, and returned to the city.

I remember every detail of the gloomy winter day that changed my life. The house on Vashon Island was quiet except for the chickens crowing outside, and soft rain was falling. Mel had already left for work and I was sleeping in.

I awoke that day feeling exhausted and depressed, and didn't even want to get out of bed. Since moving from the house in Magnolia, I had been having nightmares, and one bad dream kept repeating itself. I was sleeping in the master bedroom at my father's house, in his big double bed, alone. Mel was gone, and I didn't know where he was. I had telephoned everywhere, but couldn't find him. I couldn't reach him; he wasn't answering my calls, which

Chapter One

was very unlike him. An impenetrable wall seemed to have formed between us, for no reason that I could understand. We had been married for over five years, and always kept in close touch with one another when we had to be apart. The dream left me feeling abandoned, anxious, and confused. I awoke perspiring and filled with panic, as though I had almost drowned. Sighing deeply, I pushed back the covers and stepped out onto the rough burlap floor covering.

"What will I do if something really awful happens?" I wondered. "What is the worst experience a person can have?"

Visions came to mind of Mel involved in a fatal car accident, of his being diagnosed with leukemia or an inoperable brain tumor. I thought living alone would be unbearable. I would have to become a nun and disappear into a convent, never to speak again. Or perhaps I'd go crazy and be sent to a mental hospital.

Maybe we were just too lucky. Maybe God didn't like it because we had everything we wanted, except kids.

Mel's mother always said that "things of the earth" weren't supposed to be important. Did that include people, too? I didn't think so, that wouldn't make sense . . . God wanted women to love their husbands. I knew I loved Mel more than anything on earth, and that to be with him was all I really wanted; the other stuff I could easily live without. The farm, the horses, even the Porsche, I could stand to lose. I couldn't live without Mel, though.

"Better drink some coffee," I thought to myself, walking barefoot toward the kitchen. "I need to work outside again today."

The kitchen was cold, damp, and muddy. It had been the rainiest winter in memory, and the ancient farmhouse leaked like a sieve. The gritty linoleum on the kitchen floor made me curl my toes in discomfort, but I decided to ignore it long enough to get the coffee going, then I would go back to the bedroom to get dressed.

I put on my most rugged clothes, because I knew I would be getting dirty. I chose my sturdiest, most unattractive pair of underpants, my wafflestomper boots, a flannel shirt with a sweater underneath, and, of course, my Levi's.

Since the beginning of the week, I had been trying to clean up the orchard, a job actually much too difficult for one person. It wasn't safe to ride a horse there with all the dead branches on the ground. We had pruned some of the trees and never gotten around to hauling the limbs away. Jesse was a little spooky already, and the last time I rode her in the orchard she got her hoof caught, just the type of thing that might cause a serious accident.

It was a nasty day, typical of mid-February. The wind blew gustily, the skies were dark, and it was sprinkling from time to time. In spite of the weather, I didn't feel like spending the day in the house. We really needed to get our place cleaned up.

My only tool was a large, dull handsaw, and it turned out to be completely inadequate for sawing up green tree limbs; they seemed made of iron. I tried to pull them apart, and they just pulled back. If they weren't sawn completely through, they were impossible to break apart. I jumped on them, bent them, twisted them, and nothing worked. I finally settled for dragging the long, tangled pieces away from where we rode. It was discouraging and just too much work for one person alone. I had already worked at it for three mornings in a row and had made no noticeable progress.

By the time I got back inside, it was close to noon. The phone rang as I walked in the door. It was Mel. "Hey, Gretch, whatcha doin'?" he demanded loudly over the scratchy long distance line. "I've been trying to call you all morning. Mack wants to come out and go riding."

I was completely out of breath, and paused a minute before answering.

"Well, he's going to have to go riding by himself," I replied. "I'm way too tired. I've been cutting up trees all morning."

We talked for awhile, and he told me that Mack had already left Seattle and would be there in about an hour.

We didn't know Mack very well. He was a friend of a friend, and he was rather eccentric-looking, with long, frizzy hair, an untrimmed beard, and wire-rimmed glasses. I also didn't know whether or not he could ride. I would

Chapter One

offer to let him ride Mel's horse.

After working in the orchard, I was cold and covered with mud, but there was plenty of time to take a bath before Mack arrived. I made some fresh coffee and went in to soak in the tub.

The hot bath felt wonderful to my sore muscles. I closed my eyes and slid into the bottom with my face underwater. I liked to imagine I was floating in a big warm lake when I took a bath. After adding more hot water a few times, I heard someone pounding on the front door. It was the company already.

"Have I been in here that long?" I thought to myself. I shouted for him to come in, then jumped out of the tub to dry off.

"I'll be right out," I yelled through the door. "What a drag," I said aloud. "Right in the middle of my bath."

Still feeling worn out, I thought about what to wear. There was no point in putting on clean clothes if we were just going back outside. Besides, the clean clothes were in the bedroom, and I was in the bathroom with nothing on. I was reminded that the laundry was stacking up again.

"I hate not having a washing machine," I bitched to myself as I put on the same jeans and underwear I had worn earlier. "I don't feel like going riding. I'm really tired."

Finally, I decided to go, whether I felt like it or not.

The horses hadn't been ridden for at least a week, and they were acting more unruly than usual. They fought me from the second I took them out of their stalls. This type of horse behavior was not new; sometimes, when I was younger, our cattle horses had to be pinned into a corner of the corral before we could catch them. When I was very little, Grandma taught my sister and me to hide the bridle behind our backs as we approached the horses.

Mack stood a good distance away while I jerked the obstinate animals over to the hitching post. He looked a little apprehensive. I saddled George, tightening the cinch twice after kneeing him in the stomach. He was one of those horses who loved puffing himself up while being cinched. He knew every trick in the book.

There was a bar lock on the inside of the barn where

we kept the hay, and George was able to fit his oversized nose through a small hole in the door and turn the bar with his teeth. More than once we discovered that he had pulled a bale of hay down from the middle of the stack, and dragged it out into the rain to eat it. George was not my favorite horse at times. He was stubborn, smelled terrible, and looked pathetic. Mel was really proud of him though, which showed how much Mel knew about horses.

I always wished for a good saddle for Jesse. I was stuck with a brand-new one that didn't fit, and I could never decide if I should just keep trying to use it, or give up. Mom had spent a lot of money for the saddle, and it wasn't returnable.

Grandma said it was better to learn to ride bareback, because then you knew you could really ride. It was also safer without a saddle, because your foot couldn't get caught in a stirrup and drag you to death if you fell off. That happened once to a girl I knew in Chewelah, and her father later found her dead in a field.

Jesse had a very comfortable riding pad I had made by quilting pillow-stuffing and white cotton fleece onto a regular saddle pad we'd bought at the feed store. It looked just like a soft, white English saddle with no stirrups, and I used it most of the time. She was a very pretty horse, and I thought she looked dressed up in it.

Jesse didn't like having her cinch tightened either, and I anticipated a reflexive kick from her hind leg every time I cinched up. She didn't kick hard, just enough to let me know she didn't like it. Today I didn't feel like dealing with any kicking at all. I would just ride bareback.

We both jumped on and headed toward the neighbor's field. Mack was holding George's reins too loosely, and both horses were tossing their heads and acting spooky. Jesse had a way of kicking her feet and leaping sideways that made me very nervous, and she was doing it now. About a third of the way up the field, Mack let George start to run. I knew it was a mistake instantly, and yelled as loudly as I could, "Don't let him run away, Mack!" My voice just blew back down my throat, and he didn't hear a thing. Jesse wanted to follow the other horse. She hopped sideways all the way

Chapter One

to the top of the field, tossing her head and pulling against the hackamore's restraint.

Mack was quite a distance away, and I saw him get bucked off. I tried to make Jesse stop completely and stand still, but she jerked hard with her head and gave a wild kick. I jerked back hard on the reins. They were already pulled up short, and when she kicked, I lost my balance and fell off over her front shoulder. My head hit the ground first because I didn't have time to break my fall with my arms. I heard a loud crunching sound as I landed in the field, and felt a pain in my shoulder. I looked around. George had already returned to where Jesse was standing, and his leg was right next to my head. "Oh, great. He's going to stand on me while he eats," I thought to myself.

My shoulder had a cramp in it and was actually starting to hurt. I had never had a broken bone before, but this seemed like something else. I wondered if my shoulder might be dislocated.

I felt weird. I couldn't breathe very easily, and now my back and neck were starting to hurt. Gradually, it dawned on me that I had probably been hurt very badly. A voice inside me seemed to be saying: "Be careful now, or you might die. Stay quiet and don't breathe too hard." The cramp had now become a strange vibrating pain which traveled through both shoulders, up my neck, and down my back. It felt like my legs had been drawn up into a sitting position and were pulling on my spine.

By now, Mack had returned to where I lay.

"Call for help, Mack," I told him calmly, "and bring me a chair. I need to put a chair under my legs so they'll quit pulling on my back."

My legs were actually flat on the ground. Mack's eyes grew wide with fright and he took off running for the house. I closed my eyes and rested, feeling resigned and calm.

The first person to appear was our strange next-door neighbor, of whom I had always been a little afraid. Soon I heard a siren, and other people appeared, wearing ambulance coats.

"Don't pick me up," I warned them. "I think I broke my neck."

TWO

1957 was a big year for me. It was the year that I turned five years old, which meant I was no longer little. I started school, learned to read, and quit sucking my thumb. It was also the first time I rode a horse by myself, and, even though I fell off, I never let anyone lead the horse I was riding again.

My dad was in medical school, where he learned to stand on his head and play the banjo. He taught me how to read chords and play the ukulele, so I could play along with him. We played popular tunes from my *Bing Crosby's Greatest Hits Ukulele Songbook*, such as "Just Friends" and "All of Me."

I took the words to the songs literally and seriously. As we sang "Take my arms, I'll never use them . . ." I envisioned a person whose lips, arms, and heart had been surgically removed and given to someone else. As we played "Just Friends," I would become teary-eyed at the thought of my parents parting ways. However, I thought that if they ever had a serious fight, I would just sing them one of my most sentimental songs and they would be obliged to reunite.

In the evenings we wrestled on the floor with Dad, and had contests to see who could do headstands the longest. Sometimes we played hide-and-seek and Dad jumped out the bedroom window and disappeared completely. On our turn to hide, we asked Mom to pull up a chair and we hid on top of the refrigerator, crouching back against the wall where we were sure he couldn't see us. To our great disappointment, he always found us there.

I loved both reading and spelling, and could sound out big words, so Dad let me read *Williams Obstetrics*. I liked the black-and-white pictures of the babies coming out, but

Chapter Two

they didn't look anything like the bodies of real people I had seen. I already knew what boys looked like, because my best friend, Bobby, and I used to play see-how-fast-you-can-pull-your-pants-down in the bathroom at his house. His mom always made us come out when she heard us laughing. We played doctor, too, listening to each other's hearts, and sometimes I would pretend I was having a baby, moaning and groaning like the ladies on TV.

My sister Marie was in the first grade and we had a baby sister named Julie. We were poor when we were little, but we didn't know it. Sometimes Mom would cook sausage every day for a week, but she was such a good cook that we thought it was something different every night. Our dad saved his meal tickets from the hospital where he worked, and then he took us out for dinner. Mom dressed us up in lacy dresses she sewed by hand, and curled our hair tightly in pincurls. Dining out was a very special occasion, and sometimes we were allowed to have 7-up.

I always chose Ry-Krisp crackers and a colossal, fresh orange to go along with the roast beef dinner served every Sunday at the hospital. The cafeteria food tasted heavenly, and we thought we were dining in the city's most elegant restaurant.

I was still sucking my thumb at the age of four, but I was trying to quit in order to please my parents. They could always tell when I had been slipping, by checking my thumb where the skin was puffy and white. While I sucked my thumb, I liked to stroke the shiny part around the edge of my blanket. Mom wanted to get rid of the blanket because it was full of holes, but I resisted for a long time. I finally threw it in the fire on Mom's birthday, but then realized I couldn't do without it, and had to hide in the closet to suck my thumb with my sister's blanket.

I ate weird things when I was little: gravel from the driveway, which Mom would find in my diapers; and, later, the beads off our Indian moccasins. I chewed all the beads off my pair first, and then started on my sister's, again hiding in the closet so as not to be discovered.

I was potty-trained at a very young age, and my mother claims that when I learned to talk, I didn't start with single words, but amazed her instead by rattling off complete sentences. I was fairly bright, though there were some areas where I could have been better.

In the evening, my two sisters and I took a bath together, all lined up in a row with floating toys and bubble bath. For some reason, I sometimes pooped in the bathtub. I never realized I was doing it, but there it would be, floating around and clouding up the water. The inevitable tattling would bring a displeased parent running in to change the water. At first it was considered an oversight, but one evening it happened once too often for my father's patience. I was hastily plucked from the water by one arm and given a hard slap on my bare bottom, which I still remember clearly. Worse, I had to stay out of the bathtub and go to bed. I was very humiliated by the spanking and by not being allowed to finish bathing with my sisters. When Dad came in later to say good night, I tearfully apologized, and he gave me a kiss and a reassuring hug. I promised I would never poop in the bathtub again.

Marie started school first, then it was my turn to go to kindergarten. Mom went with us at the outset, because it was far away, but eventually we grew big enough to walk there by ourselves. All we did was play in kindergarten, though some of the children were very shy. We played with huge blocks, and those of us with a penchant for hiding used them to build forts. We had lime Kool-Aid and Graham Crackers for snacks and sat in a circle on the gritty floor while the teacher read us stories.

Sometimes we had show-and-tell at kindergarten, and Dad would let me take the monkey skull, a real monkey skull that he had cleaned and preserved as a project in medical school. A few of the teeth were missing, but otherwise it was all there, about the size of an orange, perfectly smooth, and very waxy to the touch. There were oversized holes where the eyes had been. We had to be very careful with the jaw, as it was quite fragile. We packed the skull cautiously into its special box, and I carried it like a treasure, warning other children to handle it gently.

Time passed quickly that first year at school, and before I knew it summer had arrived. It was time to go see our grandparents.

My Grandmother May was born in 1890 in the tiny gold-mining town of Republic, Washington, an Indian reservation until 1898. In that year, the land was made public and she was the first white baby born there. She grew up in Republic, and later met my grandfather while attending nursing school at St. Luke's Hospital in Spokane. He was a medical resident. They married soon after they met. After living in Idaho, and Mt. Angel, Oregon, they returned to Republic in 1927.

Grandpa May was a doctor and owned a tiny hospital; he was also the mayor. They had a large, comfortable home in Republic, and my father remembers many very happy years there. During World War II, however, a shortage of doctors prompted the Army to tell Grandpa he had to move to a more populated area, where he would be of service to more people, or be drafted. He made the logical choice to move, which was difficult for the whole family. When my dad was thirteen, they moved to Chewelah and Grandpa set up practice as the only doctor in town.

Grandpa May was usually in his office when we came to visit. It was located in an old-fashioned brick building at one end of Main Street. I remember the arched doorway and a cool, sterile atmosphere, with wood-paneled examining rooms equipped with bottles of tongue depressors and rubbing alcohol. Grandpa always had a sucker to give us, and usually an interesting story or two. He was soft-spoken and conservative, like a doctor using his bedside manner, and we never got to know him very well as children. As a teenager I finally had many long visits with him and found him to be kind, intelligent, and humorous.

Grandma May was a little cool toward small children. I remember, in particular, a fancy brocade couch which she was protective of and a generally formal atmosphere in the living room. Fortunately, the upstairs and basement were endlessly intriguing with a deep attic and many hidden closets to explore. The medicine cabinets contained mysterious potions which smelled like menthol, and dramatic red lipsticks and rouge which could only have been worn by

Grandma May. Our favorite uncle, Uncle Robbie, would hide in the closet and play bogeyman. Every time he jumped out at us we were hysterical with laughter. We begged him to remain in the closet, all the while giggling in anticipation of his bogeyman attack.

It was quiet in the yard and usually extremely hot, so we cooled off by jumping through the sprinkler, which was always turned on. As there were no real horses to ride, we straddled and pretended to ride the banisters in the old colonial-style home. Sometimes we entertained ourselves by playing on large boulders in the backyard that were surrounded by thorny berry bushes.

My mother's maiden name was Hafer. Her parents, George and Jesse Hafer, were some of the first farming settlers in the Chewelah Valley. My great-grandfather, Eli Hafer, was a pioneer who moved to Chewelah from Shannon, Iowa, in the early 1900s. He married a woman named Mae Kendrick and they had five children: Ralph, Mae, Kenneth, Clarence, and my grandfather George.

I always called Grandma Jesse Hafer "Grammie." She was originally from Montana and her Indian blood was evident in her appearance. Grammie's hair was long, thick, straight, and jet-black streaked with silver. She had high cheekbones and a thin, pointed nose. Her skin was silky and flawless, almost completely without wrinkles. Except for my mother, I thought she was the most beautiful woman in the world. She was also an accomplished horsewoman with an independent nature. In her younger years she was much more inclined to be out riding than tending house. She was a very special person in my life, and I acquired my love of horses from her.

Chewelah is a small town situated 350 miles northeast of Seattle, over the lofty bridge of the Cascade Mountains and completely past Central Washington's expansive stretch of rolling wheat country and desert. The eight-hour drive to Chewelah from Seattle was like torture when we were small. Crammed tightly into the back seat, we squirmed, fought for space, and tattled on one another over inconsequential things.

"Mom, Julie's kicking me," one of us would whine.

"Mom, Marie won't quit looking at me." And finally: "How many more miles till we get there?"

The answer to the last question was always enormously discouraging, always in the hundreds, and we would groan in unison at the thought of many more hours cooped up in the stuffy car. By the time we really were close, we were too tired to ask. Dad usually tried to break up the monotony by singing old cowboy songs like "Home on the Range," and funny songs of unknown origin.

Here are the words to one peculiar song, at least the way I remember them: "There was a man, now please take note/There was man, who had a goat/Bill Grogan's goat, when feeling fine/He ate three red shirts off the line/Bill took his goat, gave him a whack/And tied him to the railroad track/Bill Grogan's goat, though in great pain/Barfed up the shirts, and flagged the train."

After driving for six hours, we finally reach the other side of the endless desert. Pine trees sparsely dot the bleak, sagebrush-covered land as we near Spokane, the only large city on the east side of the state. From there we turn directly north, with only fifty miles to go. The trees become thick on both sides of the highway between Spokane and Chewelah, forming high walls unbroken except by the white thread of pavement stretching before us. Eventually, farms begin to appear, and one notices signs of nearby lakes, overturned boats in people's yards, and creeks dissecting fields and turning them vibrant green. A faded billboard proclaims:

Entering Stevens County, The Sportsmen's Paradise
Fishing, Hunting, Boating, Swimming

The mood in the back seat of the car turns to excitement bordering on hysteria as we break through the pines into the valley. Now we're about to turn off the pavement onto a dusty lane which stretches across the small end of the valley and leads directly to Grandma's. We can see the white frame house nestled against the base of a mountain a mile away, and we are springing up and down on the car seat, clamoring to see out the windows.

"We're here, we're here!," we scream together, and the last few minutes are unbearable. Finally, the car stops, the doors fly open, and we catapult into the yard. Grandpa and Grandma are waiting, and we all take turns hugging them. The long-awaited greeting is anticlimactic. We run through the yard while the grownups talk, and, at last, we are finally at Grammie's house.

At the age of five, since I had become so big, it was decided that I should be allowed to ride a horse all by myself. I think it was partly my idea and partly Grammie's. She usually took my side in such matters. My mother was disdainful of horses, perhaps because she had been forced to spend so much time ironing and doing other household chores while Grammie rode at county fairs and parades. In defense of Grammie, horses were work animals in those days, and she was a successful cattlewoman.

At my age, riding an animal the size of my grandparents' cattle-horses was equivalent to a man riding an elephant, but I thought I was ready. I was very tired of being led by my big sister, and anxious to try it by myself.

My sister and one of my cousins took the horse up the driveway and across the road to the bare hayfield above the house. The hay had been cut the week before and lay in bales on the hillside. The weather was typical of Chewelah in midsummer, an uncomfortable ninety degrees before noon, and dry pine cones cracked under the horse's hooves as he walked.

The older girls had instructions to hand over the reins and let go of the bridle once things were in order. Mom and Grammie were keeping an eye on us from the yard below. I was riding Scooter, the black roping horse, who was trained to stop instantly if the rider dismounted. He was very calm and careful, and Grammie felt confident that he could be trusted with me.

"Hey, Mom, are you watching me?" I shouted down to the house.

"Quit hollering, you'll spook the horses," Grammie yelled back. "I swear, you kids don't know from nothin'."

My seating was wobbly and unstable as the giant animal started down through the stubbly alfalfa field. I struggled to hold the reins and saddle horn, at the same time feeling strangely out of control because of the slope of the hill. My legs were much too short for stirrups, and I kept slipping off to one side and then to the other each time the horse took a tentative step forward. I couldn't remember the saddle being so slippery.

By now I had let go of the reins and was clutching the saddle horn with both hands. The hill had become steeper, and for some reason the horse began to trot. With each lurching stride he took, I flew up into the air and landed off-balance. The next thing I knew, I was tumbling the remarkably long distance from the saddle to the ground. After I was off, the well-mannered horse began to leap in circles and kick wildly, the loose reins and stirrups flapping dangerously. Soon all the adults in the house were running up the hill, some to protect us, and others to restrain my horse.

Once Scooter had been caught, everyone could see that his stomach and legs were covered with angry hornets. They had even crawled up under the saddle blanket, and were stinging him viciously. I was badly frightened by the long fall, but not too badly hurt. My arm had an angry red scrape from the sharp stubble in the field, and I had bumped my head on a rock, which upset my mother more than me. We had to put the horses away after that, and spent the rest of the day bored, and suffering from the heat.

"Hornets are just plain mean," Grammie explained as she unsaddled Scooter and the other horse Sundown. "There's nothing you can do when they decide to sting your horse. If he starts to buck and act up, you just tie him to the nearest tree and stand back where he can't hurt you."

For the rest of the summer, we were not allowed to ride up on the hill, but were confined to a dirt road which connected the house to the barn and milkhouse. I had to be lifted onto the horse, but once mounted I was able to ride unaided from the bottom to the top of the road. The horses became irritated by our short trips back and forth, and our constant bickering over whose turn was next. They misbehaved often, usually by veering off the road into the tractor shed. At times we had to get off in order to regain control. Considering what they were putting up with, the cattle-horses were actually quite patient After a few hours of giving rides, they signaled irritation by laying back their ears and raising a hind leg in warning. There wasn't much point trying to ride them after that. We were never actually kicked, but we did get bitten from time to time.

The following summer, my grandparents moved to a ranch on the opposite side of the valley, leaving the old place to my uncle. The two ranches were connected by a short stretch of paved road and a mile-long dirt lane which served as a shortcut to the main highway. A creek ran through the middle of the valley, over which a wooden bridge was built. Cattle were kept in the fields on either side of the creek, restrained by the inevitable barbed-wire fences which kept us from being able to cross the valley on anything but the lane. The wooden cattle guard on the bridge served as a constant test of the horses' moods and our riding ability. Often we had to get off and lead the horses over the bridge.

At the new ranch, there was a flat corral where we could practice riding. We rode up and back on a curving trail which led past the barn and to the end of the corral. The horses liked coming back the best. With a little coaxing, we usually got them to gallop. The corral was a good place to learn, because it kept the horses from running away with us. They were both half thoroughbred, half quarter horse, and loved to run.

Sundown was our favorite of the two horses, and we fought over him constantly. He was a muscular, bright copper-colored animal who was both powerful and graceful. Scooter was the same height, and jet-black in color. Scooter had been used to pull a snowsled in the past, and trotting was his favorite gait. It was also his roughest gait, and could not be tolerated long.

Sundown was so huge that I had to climb up on the gate to get my foot in the stirrup. When he didn't feel like being ridden, he stepped away from the gate and laid his ears back. Then we had to get Grammie. She took the reins in one hand, gave the stirrup a jerk, and slapped him on the shoulder. Grammie didn't put up with any guff from the animals; she didn't seem afraid of anything, a trait I greatly admired.

There were snakes in Chewelah, as the Indian name implied, but, unlike water snakes, there was nothing little

Chapter Two

about them. Occasionally, Marie and I saw a four- or five-foot snake slither across the road toward the woods. This caused a great commotion and we screamed as though we were being pursued. Every time, Grandma assured us it was just a bull snake, and not poisonous. Then she awed us with a story from her own childhood in Montana, where, attracted by the shade and moisture, rattlesnakes lurked in the vegetable garden. When startled by an unsuspecting hand rustling leaves, the snake coiled to strike. Grandma said she then calmly located a large stick and clubbed the snake to death.

Grandma and Grandpa were Jehovah's Witnesses, and every Sunday before meeting she put on a pastel-flowered dress and let me fix her hair. It took dozens of pins to hold up her hair in a bun because it was so heavy, and I can't imagine that I did a very neat job, but she always acted pleased and wore the hairstyle I fixed for her. Sometimes she wore lipstick and a little makeup, but she didn't need very much.

At a very young age, I remember being fascinated by the texture of my grandmother's skin. It was as soft as the finest silk, especially her face. She didn't use anything on it but Pond's cold cream, and claimed that her skin was pretty because she had always kept it out of the sun. Later, I realized that she was probably avoiding the sun so that she wouldn't get a suntan. My mother tans so darkly that she is often mistaken for Spanish, particularly when she travels in Mexico.

The town of Chewelah had virtually no black residents; most of the people living there had never even seen a black person. Discriminatory remarks and insulting jokes were, instead, made about the local Indians. Being part Indian was not something one was supposed to be proud of; it was hushed and hidden.

I wouldn't have been able to understand or accept this type of thinking had I been aware of it as a child. It seemed to me that Grammie knew everything about everything. When we talked to her, she listened, and she always understood. She had a way of settling things that was reasonable and fair, and whenever we stayed with her, I felt special and important.

Along with his three sons, my grandfather formed the Hafer Land and Livestock Corporation. Uncle Glen was in charge of the cattle, Uncle Carey ran the dairy, and Uncle Rodney helped Grandpa in the fields, where they farmed oats and wheat.

The corporation owned a great deal of land in the mountains east of the valley. Beef cattle were kept at Craney Camp, a clearing with a creek running through it, and higher up the mountain, at Bett's Meadows.

Each summer my grandparents would load us into the car and head up a narrow, snaking road that led back into the mountains where Grandpa kept the cattle. The road was unpaved, and thick clouds of gritty, choking dust filled the air around us as we drove. It was 20 miles to the secluded meadows, but the trip up the treacherous dirt road took almost an hour.

As we traveled up into the mountains, the sides of the hills became steep, sheer cliffs of loose shale. Sometimes the rock would slide into the road, making it impossible to continue. The road was so narrow that it was impossible to turn around, and when it was blocked we had to back the car down the mountain until we reached a spot intersected by another road. There were alternate routes we could take to reach the meadows, but they took much longer. Near the top, you could look out the car window and see straight down into a bottomless canyon filled with tall trees. At this point, the one-way road was literally carved into the side of a rock cliff.

After about fifteen miles, we began to see an occasional stray cow. When we reached a clearing with a flat place and a stream, we had arrived at Craney Camp. From there, it was only about five more miles to the meadow.

Bett's Meadows seemed like the top of the world. It was a field so wide you could barely see to the other side, and one end of it disappeared around the side of a tree-covered mountain. Water came from natural springs which fed the lush, knee-high grass. In the spring the meadows were inaccessible by road because of the mud, but by early summer

Chapter Two

the road was easily passable. It was as hot as a pistol in July, and in August the heat was torturous.

The main purpose of our trips to the meadows was to take salt to the cattle. The salt came in blocks which the cattle licked. When we arrived at the meadows, there were no cattle in sight. Then Grammie would call them by hollering, "Souee, soueee," and one by one they started mooing back until hundreds were calling out to her. The shrieking moos and cries echoed off the sides of the canyon as the animals slowly emerged from every corner of the meadows and ambled eagerly toward the salt licks. Gradually, entire herds appeared, complete with bulls and calves, and they all seemed to remember Grammie.

When the cattle had to be moved down out of the meadows towards Craney Camp, we were allowed to help herd them on horseback. Looking back, I wonder if we were really helping, or if the cows just knew the way. Either way, I felt like a genuine cowgirl.

We wore leather chaps to protect our legs from the sharp, brittle pine needles and carried a switch to chase strays out of the woods, not always an easy job. The horses knew what they were doing, but cattle are dumb and easily confused. Occasionally a cow got tangled up in the brush and you couldn't get behind her with a horse. When this happened we had to throw rocks until she turned one way or the other and got moving again. I once threw a handful of rocks at a particularly obstinate cow which turned out to be a huge, very hostile-looking bull. The hanging-down thing I'd thrown my rocks at had not been an udder. I left him there as a challenge for one of the grownups.

There were cougars and bears at the meadows, and once Sundown and I ran into a shaggy brown bear climbing out of a tree. He was coming down fast and taking a lot of branches with him. It spooked Sundown, and he ran away with me. I was riding bareback at the time, and he ran all the way back to the cabin with me clinging onto the mane. I was terrified all the way home that he might step in one of the deep gopher holes and break a leg. Maybe he was smarter than I was. It was my first sighting of a wild bear and I lamented not having had a closer look.

Return To Chewelah

Unfortunately, summer always had to end, and Mom always picked us up in the station wagon to take us back to Seattle for school.

THREE

During first grade I showed signs of being a good learner and was praised highly for my budding intelligence. I learned to read sooner than the rest of my class and was allowed to sit in the hall and help a little boy learn to read.

The lessons got harder, though, and by third grade I had slipped back from A's to B+'s in some subjects. I overheard adults in deep and serious conversation about my grades. "Perhaps she's become overconfident," they whispered conspiratorially. "Things were too easy for her at first, and now she thinks she doesn't have to try."

The truth was that I was trying. Some things were just harder to learn than others. This led to a new label for me, which I liked even less: underachiever. I decided school was not so much fun, after all, and became discouraged. I developed a policy of trying hard in the things I cared for, and not so hard in the subjects I considered boring, like arithmetic and history.

In our backyard we had a chokecherry tree and a swing set. We also had two small gardens; one for my sister Marie, and one for me. One spring some flowers came up in Marie's garden, but none in mine. I felt very left out and started crying. She was such a good sister that she picked some of her flowers and dug a little hole and stuck them in my garden. The adults laughed over the gesture and remarked that it was cute. The flowers stayed alive for weeks, a tribute to genuine sisterly love.

My favorite pastime was collecting balls of pitch off the chokecherry tree. It oozed out in many different colors. Collecting pitch was an exact science. It was very important that the pitch be in the right stage of dryness before it could be moved. The outside had to be hard and the inside gooey. Picked too soon the pitch stuck to my skin and made a terrible mess, which my father had to remove with gasoline.

I tried to save specimens of all different colors, from clear to dark-brown. Amber was the prettiest. I arranged them in symmetrical lines on the part of the tree I could reach from the ground, placing them in order from the lightest color to the darkest. I was very proud of my pitch collection, and showed it off whenever I could find someone who was interested.

When I was in third grade, we moved to a new school so that Dad could be closer to the university. He was going to be a resident, which meant he would live at the hospital most of the time. He wanted us to live close by, so he could have more time with us.

When we moved I had to leave my pitch collection behind. There were new kids moving into our old house, and when I showed it to them, they just scoffed and said, "big deal." I had to leave it with people who didn't even care about it, and I've never since had one like it.

Music and singing were my favorite subjects at school. Mom and Dad decided to let me learn to play the saxophone, a gigantic, heavy instrument, which I had to pack back and forth from school each day in order to practice. We had a chart to mark when we practiced, and if I completed one hour every day I got an A. I liked the certainty that was built into this agreement, and practiced diligently for exactly one hour each day.

Spelling was my other favorite subject, and I was quite good at it, especially when it came to the long words. There was only one word I couldn't remember how to spell: friend. Even now I have to look at it twice before I'm sure it's right. So all through third grade I got a B+, instead of an A in spelling, reinforcing my opinion of myself as a pretty good, but not perfect, speller.

I was an awkward-looking kid, a fact well documented by scores of old pictures. I had a voracious appetite which resulted in a round face and tummy, and I grew out of my clothes almost as soon as I got them on. The kids at school

Chapter Three

invented a disease and named it after me — the mayonnaise disease — and teased me relentlessly. They would run up and touch me, cringe as though they had touched a slug, and then pass it on to someone else. I tolerated the teasing, but hated it. Most of the obnoxious behavior occurred on the playground, where there was little adult supervision, and there was nothing I could do to stop it. However, some of my frustrations were released by playing Sock 'em, a game in which we threw a ball at each other from opposite sides of a court. I could throw as hard as some of the boys and took pleasure in striking them out by hitting them with the ball.

By the time I was nine, there were four kids in our family, three girls and one boy. At the new house, Marie and I shared a bedroom and continued to do everything together, including getting in trouble. Mom lost a set of premature twin boys sometime after I was born, but I was too young to remember when it happened. She was very careful with the following pregnancy, and my sister Julie arrived three years after I was born.

Julie wanted and needed attention from Marie and me, but was often left out because we were older. She was a darling, chubby little girl with dimples, and pigtails that hung in perfect ringlets. Her presence in the family was further upstaged by the arrival of our only brother, Karl Joseph May III. We now had the perfect setup for genuine sibling rivalry.

Julie had her own bedroom and Karl slept in a tiny den. My parents had the master bedroom upstairs. Once in awhile Mom and Dad let us sleep in the basement on cots, which we thought was fun because it was different. The first day we moved in, Marie and I decided to make a tent in the basement with old sheets. We tied them to the light bulbs. When Mom smelled smoke and came down to investigate, the sheets were about to ignite. She got there in enough time so that we didn't burn the house down, but she was still a little upset.

Marie and I also considered sleeping downstairs a perfect opportunity to "sneak out," a term we used to describe escaping from home and discipline, as though as we were being raised in a concentration camp. The trouble was that there was absolutely nothing to do once we were out. Everyone else was asleep. Besides, we always got caught by our parents and, once caught, were severely reprimanded and automatically grounded, a fate worse than death. It was not fun to have either Dad or Mom mad at you, as both could be extremely unpleasant when tested. Mom was usually distant and impatient when angry, but Dad had a way of yelling at us that made us feel one inch high, an experience we referred to as being "bawled out." It usually took a few days to recover from being bawled out by Dad, but eventually we got over it and tried something sneaky again.

As my dad didn't like carrying his lunch to work (he thought it looked like he was carrying a purse) I rode my bike to his university office in the summer to deliver it. I was very proud of the fact that he had become a real doctor, and I felt important walking down the sterile halls.

The residents were working on artificial heart valves, and one day Dad brought some of the valves home to show us. They were made out of translucent white fabric and fine silk thread, and had three chambers. He explained that sometimes the real valve stopped working, and that by replacing it the doctor could save the patient's life. We regarded the clover-shaped creations with amazement, deeply impressed by the importance of our father's work.

We were adventurous girls whose favorite pastime was exploring. The university campus was a fascinating place to ride bikes, and provided us with endless opportunities for discovery. The university was involved in research, and many of the buildings and laboratories near the hospital were unlocked. Marie and I investigated them thoroughly, discovering white mice in cages, and dark, silent basements where jars of unidentifiable organs were kept preserved. In one part of the basement, an ancient fish lived in a large, cylindrical cement tank with windows. We could crawl under the tank and stand up in the center and watch him tirelessly pass by. His skin was crusty and marked with scabs, as though he had been fighting. I felt sorry for the pathetic creature, and wished he could be let go. We visited him often, in hopes it would keep him from being lonely.

Chapter Three

We found the white mice impossible to resist, and took them out of their cages to play. We always attempted to put them back, but they were lively and difficult to hold. We returned them inevitably to the wrong cages because, once loose, they were impossible to tell apart. I've often wondered what types of experiments we botched up by switching the mice, or if anyone ever knew. We were never discovered causing mischief in the laboratories; they seemed completely deserted, which added to their aura of mystery and suspense.

Our new house was so close to the university that football traffic clogged the streets in our neighborhood whenever there was a game. We discovered that, by standing on the corner and yelling, we could sell parking spaces in our driveway for a dollar apiece. We had a comical-looking basset hound named Charlie Brown, after one of the football players. Mom made him a coat in purple and gold, the colors of the university's team, and we used him as our mascot. He was great for business; he stopped cars with his long, droopy ears, short legs, and fancy jacket. People didn't seem to mind not being able to get their cars out immediately after the game, so we lined several of them up in both our driveway and in the driveway of the house next door. On a good day, we were able to make eight or nine dollars, which was a lot of money for a couple of kids.

At halftime, the gate at the stadium's end zone was unlocked and we were admitted for free to watch the last half of the game. The university was the biggest in the state, and the stadium was packed with fans. Cheering fans could be heard all the way back at our house, and inside the stadium the noise was deafening. You could literally feel the ground shake when our team made a touchdown.

After the game, Mom and Dad usually had friends over for drinks, and then we entertained the neighbors with a flag-lowering ceremony. The idea for a flag lowering ceremony had come about in stages. First, we had a nice white flagpole erected on the strip of lawn next to the driveway. Sometime later my dad was given a miniature cannon that made an extremely loud boom when fired and shot a little flame out the end. My little brother, who was five, attempted to play taps on his trombone. He was so skinny that his pants were always slipping down and they usually slipped partway off by the time he was finished with taps. Marie and I folded the flag according to tradition, careful not to let it touch the ground, and as a finale Dad shot a few cherry tomatoes across the street at the neighbor's house.

We loved the new neighborhood. Every weekend Marie and I packed lunches, took off on our bikes, and returned just before dinnertime. We were always required to be home for dinner; it was important to Mom and Dad that we always got together as a family once during the day.

A few years passed after moving to the new house before Mom got pregnant with her last child. This time I took great interest in the process, asking questions and watching her stomach grow. I needed some clarification about how the baby got out of the belly button, but wasn't entirely satisfied with the answer. Apparently, there was an opening somewhere else, which I had not been aware of and to which I chose not to give much further thought.

Mom seemed quite miserable with her stomach sticking out, but then also had to have some wisdom teeth pulled, which caused her cheeks to swell up like a chipmunk's. My father seemed amused by her appearance, and made her sit down on the front porch so he could take a picture of her. She did not share this amusement and refused to smile for the picture.

The new baby was another girl, and they named her Lisa. I remember vividly the day she came home from the hospital. She arrived after an eternity, so my expectations were high; then she was not what I had imagined. She was tiny, nondescript, and quiet, with fuzzy, black hair. I had expected something, perhaps with pigtails, like Julie. In spite of the disappointment, I took responsibility for caring for Lisa, learned to change diapers and hold her properly. Soon she was waving her arms and laughing like a real baby. I played with her every day after school and packed her around on my hip long after she was big enough to walk. While she napped, I practiced my saxophone softly, so as not to wake her. I was the only saxophone player chosen for

Chapter Three

the school orchestra that year, because I didn't "honk" on my instrument.

I was nearing the age of puberty, but had no idea what it meant or what I was in for. One day after returning home from a rough game of Sock 'em, I ran into the kitchen to greet Mom and Lisa. Mom stepped back and informed me that my armpits stank and that I should go upstairs and wash. Not understanding the true nature of body odor, I put perfume under my arms and returned to the kitchen. This time she completely lost patience and started yelling, then sent me back upstairs to wash thoroughly with soap and water. I stayed upstairs until it was time for dinner, feeling confused.

In the fifth grade, I learned I needed glasses. Marie had worn them since the first grade, but till now I had escaped them. I chose white frames with large points in the corners, adorned with rhinestone corncobs. I considered them the height of glamour. The ear pieces never matched because people on the playground kept hitting me in the side of the head with balls. It was not easy to locate replacement parts for fancy glasses like mine. My hair was cut short in a stylish "bubblecut," and I often wore an elastic headband because it was also in fashion. The combination of all these things created a look which was quite ridiculous, but so far I was spared the misery of being aware of it.

My growing streak continued until I became the tallest student in the sixth grade. When we all lined up at the door to go out for recess, my head towered over everyone else's. I stood and stared at our reflections in the window, feeling awkward and self-conscious. Mercifully, time passed quickly and summer came before I knew it. Soon we all headed to Grammie's again.

FOUR

Returning to Chewelah was always the same: the heart-pounding anticipation on the last strip of highway before the valley appeared, the suspense of drawing near and discovering whether the horses were in the corral or out in the field, and the last-minute decision of whether to hug Grammie or the horses first.

Since Julie was old enough to stay all summer at Grammie's too, my grandparents bought a Shetland pony so that we could all ride together. He was an obstinate little beast with an incredibly short, thick neck and a very strong set of teeth which he frequently used to nip. Although he was rather unpleasant, we named him Freddy after an imaginary friend Marie and I had had when we were little. It was very rare that Freddy felt like being ridden, and his favorite trick was to run underneath the clothesline in order to scrape us off. He was also carnivorous, a fact we discovered one day by accident. Freddy used to snatch sandwiches out of our hands when we weren't paying attention. One day a little cousin of ours discovered a nest of mice and was carrying around a dead baby mouse to show everyone. Suddenly Freddy's neck shot out and he snatched and devoured the baby mouse in one bite, swallowing without even chewing.

Once at Grammie's we were transformed, and life became as perfect as it could possibly be. All the insecurities of growing up were lifted away by the magic of the farm.

Cowgirls could be any age, as long as they were wearing jeans and a pair of boots. Straw cowboy hats hung waiting on the front porch, steeped in the aroma of hay and tractor grease.

Chapter Four

Genuine wooden wagon wheels flanked each side of the porch. Flowers interspersed with aromatic dill burst wildly from the narrow strips of soil bordering the white frame house, and a gigantic flower garden flourished beneath the kitchen window. To the left of the house, Grammie grew all her vegetables, including cucumbers for pickles, sweet corn, gigantic beets, squash, cauliflower, cabbage, and peas. While we sometimes helped her pick peas, we weren't really that much help, because we consumed the sweet tender peas, shell and all, right there in the garden.

Chamomile blanketed the entire corral, and Marie and I loved to collect the tiny flowers. With a thumbnail, we slit the stem and threaded the flowers together to make bracelets and necklaces.

After spending days in the summer sun, my skin turned brown, and my hair became as white as sun-bleached stalks of wheat. We had huge family picnics with twenty-five cousins at Bett's Meadows. They were joyous get-togethers lasting from noon to dusk. The adults brought potato salad, watermelon, and cake, and we quenched our thirst with spring water from a sink in the tiny cabin that sat next to the road. At dinnertime, we roasted hot dogs and marshmallows over a crackling bonfire of dry pine branches and needles that was sometimes difficult to keep under control. We dodged large popping sparks and embers, and most of our marshmallows flamed into black crust.

We rode horses until our legs were wobbly and rubbed raw from the saddle. We fed calves and fished with homemade poles in creeks at the back of the meadows. We found tiny wild strawberries that were so intensely flavorful that I was willing to search at length just to find one to eat.

Returning home to Grammie's, we crawled upstairs to knotty pine-paneled bedrooms and slept under intricate handmade quilts sewn by our great-grandmother. Every year the palomino-horse clock on the dresser greeted us, and it was customary to unsaddle and saddle it back before pulling off jeans and getting into bed. The crickets lulled us to sleep and we woke at the crack of dawn, ecstatic to find ourselves still at Grammie's.

In the morning breakfast was waiting: the inevitable gummy oatmeal, pancakes, bacon and eggs. Grandpa had gotten up long before us to cut hay during the cool morning hours. Grammie firmly believed in starting the day with breakfast, and we knew better than to try to skip. After eating we usually tried to ride the horses, but were soon stricken with sideaches from the jogging motion that disrupted digestion.

Sometimes we went off to town with Grammie to buy penny candy from the musty little variety store on Main Street. We liked to feed strawberry caramels to the horses and laugh at the faces they made when it stuck to their teeth.

When I was about eight, we were allowed to take the horses down the five-mile back road to town to ride in the Frontier Days parade. There were bands with noisy horns that marched down Main Street, floats with Miss Chewelah and her princesses, antique cars, clowns, covered wagons, and Indians.

I felt extremely proud riding the spirited black cattle horse down Main Street. He was excited by the long ride to town and all the commotion. He pranced sideways, tossed his head, and snorted. I sat up straight and held the reins perfectly, convinced I was the best rider in the parade. By the end of the day, we were too tired to ride anymore, and had to go home in the car. Grammie brought the horses home, riding one and leading the other.

We never wanted to leave Grammie's house, but eventually summer would end and it was time to go home. We were always glad to see Mom and Dad, but Seattle was a different world, one that didn't feel as safe or as comfortable. In many ways, the city felt less like home than the ranch.

My new junior high school was quite a distance from our house, in a very rough neighborhood. We took the bus in the morning, and walked home at the end of the day. The school was racially mixed, with twenty percent white students, sixty percent black, and twenty percent other groups, mostly Oriental. We quickly learned that there were good and bad people of all races, and the only generalizations that really could be made were that the girls fought

Chapter Four

more than the boys and the Oriental students got most of the A's. I genuinely believed that the Chinese and Japanese students were smarter than the rest of us, and gave up any hope of competing with them for grades. My report cards now came home with mostly B's, and only occasional A's.

The one subject I seemed to excel in was music. I was encouraged to switch from the saxophone to the bassoon, a double-reed instrument said to be hard to learn. I learned to play quite well, and Dad decided I should take private lessons at the university. The hour-long lessons, very intense and not at all enjoyable, were conducted in the basement of a prestigious-looking, ivy-covered brick building. The music professor often asked me to play the same few notes over and over again, listening for something that might be too slight for me to detect. He offered little encouragement and was very distant.

During the second year of junior high, a big concert came up at school and I was required to play a fast, complicated solo. It consisted of four or five lines of classical music filled with sharps and flats. I practiced it constantly until every note was deeply ingrained in my memory.

The day of the concert, I looked anxiously for my parents in the audience. The music started and the concert was going well. Then, somehow, I lost my place in the music, became confused, and missed my entire solo. I'll never forget the look of frustration on the music teacher's face as he stood in front of the orchestra, futilely conducting a piece of music that wasn't being played. In a short while I gave up the bassoon.

Meanwhile, I was beginning to discover The Mirror. Most of the girls at the new school wore lipstick and nylons and looked quite a bit more grown up than I did. I became so preoccupied with my appearance that I wouldn't come out of the bathroom when my friends came to visit. Mom tried talking to me about it, but that did nothing to resolve my insecurity. I was caught in the awkward time between childhood and adulthood, and was hopelessly uncomfortable. I was too old to be a child, and too young to be an adult.

Marie already had a voluptuous figure, but my chest

was flat. I copied Marie as much as possible, hoping to look older, but nothing seemed to work. We experimented endlessly with makeup, and simulated sexy looks by combing our hair down to cover one eye and holding our heads certain ways. Marie tried to outfit me with a bra stuffed with socks, but it looked very obvious and I didn't have the nerve to wear it. Our father was disgusted with us and had no qualms about letting us know. We were entering into the stage he has since referred to as the "hateful-ungrateful" stage, when hormones take over the child's thought processes and the parent loses control, despite all effort.

I began to hate spending time with my parents. I sat in the backseat of the car and cried when they *made me* go skiing with them. I developed lengthy infatuations with boys I hardly knew, pouting because I rarely saw them. We talked about sex at school, and, while the truth about reproduction gradually became inescapable, it remained distinctly unappealing. I received my first kiss on the lips from Tony, a boy down the street, and that was as much as I cared to experiment with the opposite sex.

Until now, our family had only owned one car, a heavy old station wagon dubbed "the killer car" after an incident in which my mother literally flattened an Austin-Healy Sprite with it. She accidentally drove over it while attempting to park in front of the house. Its owner, one of my dad's best friends, was inside visiting at the time. The accident caused my mother great embarrassment and ruined her driving reputation.

Somewhere near the end of seventh grade, Dad brought home a surprise: an elegant old Jaguar sedan that somewhat resembled a Rolls-Royce. I had never seen a car anything like it and was mesmerized when I climbed inside. The seats were genuine black leather, and the dash and interior door panels were made of rosewood, a richly swirled, mahogany-colored wood. There was a purple light set into the dash which illuminated the gauges at night, and the motor rumbled deeply, setting it apart from ordinary American cars.

Every Sunday Dad took us for a ride, seeking out winding, tree-lined roads and quiet neighborhoods away from

Chapter Four

the traffic. Every second of the afternoon drive was pure bliss, and I was even able to forget that I was with one of my parents. With the arrival of the Jaguar, I was introduced to my second greatest passion in life: foreign cars.

The Jag, as we referred to it, attracted a lot of attention, and one afternoon, as I was idly staring out the upstairs window in my parents' room, a white Jaguar similar to ours pulled up next to it on the street. Two teenage boys were in the car, one driving and the other apparently a friend along for the ride. They noticed me gaping from the upstairs window and asked me who owned the car.

They introduced themselves as Dave and Donny, two football players from the high school near us. They began stopping by once in awhile, and were popular with me, as I really liked their Jaguar.

Having discovered cars and boys, we embarked on a phase of childhood unlike any other. My appearance became more of a worry to me than ever. Marie had a steady boyfriend. And just as our alarmed parents attempted to tighten the reins on our behavior, we became more devious than ever. Our social lives were all-important. We were willing to risk any punishment rather than miss a dance or party, and when a certain engagement or event was forbidden, we tried to sneak out to it, saying we were spending the night at a friend's or going someplace we thought would be acceptable to them. As our parents had learned long ago not to trust us, the probability of our getting caught was determined only by how badly they wanted to catch us.

Somehow a positive change occurred when our friends discovered they were welcome to stay and have fun at our house. Our parents didn't seem to mind how much company we had, as long as we stayed home. Our house became known as a place for impromptu parties. Sometimes we had seven or eight people over at once to dance on the hardwood floor in the living room. We played stacks of 45s, our favorites: The Temptations, The Impressions, Ike and Tina Turner, Smokey Robinson and The Miracles. The parties were allowed to last until just before dark; then Mom would let everyone know it was time for the rest of the family to get ready for bed.

Donny became my first real boyfriend, although it was a strange relationship. He knocked on the door on Sunday afternoon and asked for me. Then he went straight to the living room, took his shoes off, and lay down on the couch. While his eyes were closed, it was obvious he wasn't sleeping. I played records while he napped, occasionally sitting on the edge of the couch beside him. This suited me just fine because I was still just thirteen, and I still slept with my stuffed donkey. Eventually, Donny acquired the nickname of Donkey, which he didn't seem to mind. I don't think he ever knew he had been named after my favorite stuffed animal.

Dave and Donny belonged to a boys' club called The Revelers, whose members were considered extremely cool. I managed to talk Donny out of his Revelers' sweatshirt, which had already been worn so much that it had a hole in the stomach. I felt it was a tremendous honor to have it.

My best friend in the seventh grade was a girl named Kevin, and it was through her that I became aware of a closely guarded secret. She had been told the secret by her sister's friends, who were in their early twenties. In slow, cautious stages, it was explained that some of the words in the Beatles songs had double meanings, and that the phrase "turn on" meant to smoke marijuana, or grass, as it was called. It was my understanding that the popularity of the drug had originated in Britain, and was just beginning to take root here. Use of the extremely illegal drug was limited to very secretive groups who lived in the University District. I listened to the strange news with a moderate amount of interest and curiosity.

Kevin's sister usually had a cigarette hanging out of her mouth, and yelled at Kevin. "God, you're so uncool," she shouted impatiently, as she ran through the house leaving a trail of cigarette smoke behind her. "Quit buggin' me, Kevin," she screamed, as Kevin attempted to talk with her.

I was not anxious to imitate her. At any rate, we were still little kids. Since I wasn't supposed to know about the secret, I didn't ask any more about it.

FIVE

I was in my bedroom, watching afternoon soaps with Lisa, the day we learned that Mel had died. As soon as we saw it on the news, I had a sickening, gut-wrenching feeling that it must be him. Reluctantly, I phoned the secretary down at the shop, explaining that a light plane had crashed on Vashon Island, and I asked her if Mel was all right.

"No," she replied sadly. "They think it was Mel."

It had happened the night before, but they still hadn't been able to identify the body. The details on the news were sketchy, but my sister Marie was a firefighter on the island and she had been the first one to respond to the call.

He hadn't informed anyone that he intended to go flying that night, but it was not unusual for him not to. He had attempted to take off in the dark on a bumpy, uphill field which was the island's only runway. Nearby residents said they remembered hearing a plane's engine sputter and fail, and then the crash. Apparently, when he realized he wasn't going to clear the trees at the end of the runway, he made a fatal error in pilot judgment and attempted to turn back. Lacking sufficient airspeed for the turn, the plane spun and dove straight into the ground, exploding in flames on impact. There was very little left of it by the time the fire trucks arrived: just the suggestion of a frame, a broken tail, and smoldering embers.

We had been divorced for four years at the time of his death. He had remarried and fathered three children, the second youngest a girl he named Jesse. He loved his family, but was at times uneasy and restless, and would spend weeks and months away from home, traveling alone on his motorcycle.

If things had ended differently between us, the circumstances of his death would not have troubled me. I knew what we'd been put through after I broke my neck, and I wondered if he might still be alive if he hadn't had to live with the guilt.

Marie, Karl, and Lisa went with me to the funeral. I started crying as soon as we entered the chapel, but everyone else was crying too. Hundreds of people were there, and I wondered who they all were. After the service, I saw Mel's only brother, and held him as he sobbed in my arms. After that I didn't want to stay any longer. On the way out, we ran into the young, blonde, divorced woman who lived next to us in Magnolia, the one I had long suspected of trying to seduce Mel.

"What are you doing here?" I blurted out rudely. I felt like saying, "I always knew you were after my husband." That was the only drawback in being married to Mel, the fact that he was so attractive to other women.

The end of our marriage was very hard to accept, largely because it was sudden. It was one month after our fifth wedding anniversary when I was snatched away from my life and imprisoned in the hospital; it would be nearly a year before I was allowed to return home. And when I finally did return home, things were different, very different.

For our anniversary Mel had given me a black velvet suit, high-heeled black boots, and a light blue silk scarf. I gave him a pair of Tony Lama cowboy boots with riding heels; they were the color of Sundown.

We were never able to talk with one another about the accident, or the reasons we had for separating. I do know that neither of us did the things we did out of choice. One day I was his wife, and the next day I was clinging to life with a severe fracture-dislocation of my neck. It would be weeks before I would even know if I'd live.

At the time of Mel's death, I was working in a large Seattle hospital. My job was to watch heart monitors and interpret heart rhythms for the nurses. I was very dedicated to providing quality patient care after having been a patient for so long myself. I took my responsibilities seriously.

Chapter Five

It was both stressful and rewarding and would have been easier if I had gotten more sleep.

During the night Mel would return to hold me in my dreams, and I would wake up thinking he was next to me in bed. Then he vanished when I opened my eyes, leaving an unbearable emptiness and I would drive to work in tears, struggling with the memories.

His death was also difficult because people did not seem to understand why I still loved him. Friends, my parents, and the psychologists all essentially said the same thing: he treated you badly, why don't you hate him?

The only person who genuinely understood was Lisa, for she still loved him as much as I did, in a different way.

I buried my feelings, and during the day I was relatively all right on the outside. Deep inside, and in my dreams, I was indescribably sad.

In the eighth grade things got tough at school. There were violent fights among girls in the lunchroom. They stood up on tables, tore each other's clothes off, and bit and ripped out hunks of each other's hair. The school was so undisciplined that there were virtual stampedes to the lunchroom when the bells rang. Those who didn't run were in great danger of being pushed down and trampled in the halls.

The bathrooms were terrifying. They provided meeting places for gangs who congregated to smoke cigarettes and cut class. The girls were hateful and nasty to anyone they considered an outsider. They hung dirty sanitary napkins on the water faucets in order to drive unwanted company away, and made threats if one attempted to linger. We were often followed outside by groups of kids who wore sharp cleats on the toes of their shoes. They followed us home and sometimes kicked us in the calves, causing nasty, painful cuts and ruined nylons.

Academically, the school was average. I had some good teachers and was doing well in my classes, but the administration simply did not have the type of staff necessary to curb violence.

On one occasion, as Marie and I walked home from

school, I was sexually assaulted by an eight- or nine-year-old boy who was passing us on the sidewalk. He jammed his hand between my legs and then went running off, leaving me to stand in a pile of dropped books with my mouth open. Required to wear skirts to school, we were easy targets.

I got picked on much more than my older sister, so my parents finally talked to a school official about the problem. They were told that my blonde hair and blue eyes probably incited the problem.

It got so bad that by the end of the year we were afraid to walk home from school. Our parents finally decided that, while it would be expensive, they would send us to a private high school the next year.

The public high school we normally would have gone to was Garfield, a multiracial school in the Central Area of Seattle. The students were extremely loyal, knit together primarily by a very successful football and basketball team. The teams usually remained unchallenged for championship titles except for Ingraham, a rival, all-white school in Seattle's North End. It was common for fights to occur at playoff games between the two schools.

During eighth grade I developed a close friendship with a very polite, reserved Japanese boy named Kay, and was allowed to go out with him whenever I wanted. He drove a silver Malibu Supersport with mag wheels, and we both loved soul music. Kay played the drums in a band which practiced in his basement. There were good musicians in his band, some white, some black, and I spent a lot of time with them.

Kay also introduced me to a Filipino family with whom we became very close. All five children were extremely talented musically, and some of them jammed with Kay's band. The oldest boy was a fantastic guitar player who eventually became so well-known that he was asked to record with Quincy Jones. The second oldest boy, Chick, had a singing voice like Smokey Robinson and played alto saxophone.

I liked Chick as soon as I met him and we saw each other whenever we could. We were first attracted by our

Chapter Five

mutual fondness for the alto sax. He also had a great sense of humor.

The absence of the chaos of the public schools was at first a shock. The private school seemed like a convent in comparison. Students were required to wear itchy blue wool skirts and jackets, and prim white blouses with rounded collars. The skirts were to be no shorter than one inch above the knee, a stipulation I considered ludicrous. No makeup was allowed, another of the conditions I found difficult.

The school was run on an honor system. Violations of rules were handled by a student court with a jury and judge that passed out sentences like a real court. Students who fell behind in studies were required to attend study hall on Saturdays. Talking in study hall was also punishable by the court. Infractions were reported by other students to a member of the court, and the guilty party was asked to appear for trial.

One of my biggest shortcomings was the length of my skirt; the other, telltale signs of makeup. My skirt had been sewn to the proper length, but I couldn't stand the way it looked, so I rolled the waistband a few times every morning after I left home. More than once, a member of the court stopped me in the locker room to measure my skirt. After getting caught, I unrolled it for awhile, then rolled it back up later when I thought interest in my disobedience had chilled. For my hem-length violations, I was given warnings and let go.

I was required once to appear in court for wearing makeup to school. I was informed by a court member that the other girls could see traces of mascara which remained from the previous day. I avoided a sentence by claiming that, if there was indeed makeup left on my face, I had taken off all of it that would come off. This wasn't exactly true, however. So much for the honor system.

Courses at the new school were college preparatory, and each class required an hour's homework each night. The English class also required that a composition be turned in once a week, in addition to the grammar lessons. I took French, English, Biology, Math, and the mandatory Physical Education. Although the academic requirements were higher than the public school's, I found to my surprise that my grades improved considerably. I was able to earn A's in French, Geometry, and English, and I began to enjoy the schoolwork. Geometry, in particular, was easy, though I had previously disliked math. It seemed more like solving puzzles than counting numbers. The English teacher was rigid, puritanical, and demanding, but she liked my writing and often rewarded me with A's for compositions.

Most of the girls who attended the school were from extremely wealthy families. Some lived nearby, in the exclusive neighborhoods nestled above the shores of Lake Washington. Others lived in a boarding house which was part of the school. I felt sorry for the girls who boarded at the school, because they didn't get to see their families and seemed lonely.

When dances were held, students were allowed to invite friends from the public schools. Almost overnight, instead of competing for grades, I found myself also competing socially with girls who were not only pretty, but filthy rich. One girl in particular had such a reputation for being beautiful and rich that she was a legend among our friends. Her father owned a nationwide shipping line and was rumored to be the richest man in Seattle. The girl was blond, had a fantastic figure, and looked like Brigitte Bardot. She drove a sophisticated foreign car, had her own ski boat with a dock on Lake Washington, and was a champion waterskier. Dave and Donny mentioned her a few times and often were invited to parties at her parents' mansion. She was three years older than I was, so I never met her, but Dave had a picture of her in a bikini, which he showed everyone. My heart sank when I saw the picture. She looked just like a movie star, and I was certain Donny would fall in love with her and never speak to me again.

In the tenth grade, our school had a dance in the gymnasium. Some of the older girls invited Dave and Donny, so I was pretty excited about going.

In the sixties, the height of fashion was to be as skinny as a rail, a fad started by the model Twiggy. This was lucky for me, because that's how I was built naturally. I ate very little for a few days before the dance, so my hipbones would

Chapter Five

stick out, then I wore a knit minidress. Donny asked me to dance several times that night, and afterwards we drove around with Dave and his date. Donny and I kissed in the back seat of the Jaguar the whole time we drove, and I felt so happy that it was like being in a dream.

Rumors of our romantic encounter spread around the neighborhood after the dance, and Donny avoided my house for awhile. I was still far too young for a serious relationship, and I knew he didn't want one either. It had been a very special night, and that was all that mattered to me. One of the rumors that surfaced after the dance was that people thought I was beautiful, perhaps even as pretty as the legendary rich girl. I was surprised to hear this, and inspected myself in the mirror. I saw the same roundish face I had always had and a very unremarkable, straight-up-and-down figure. At least I had been allowed to get contact lenses, so was minus my pointy glasses; otherwise, I was just me.

The sixties were very difficult years in which to grow up. Many college-age students were being drafted because of the war in Vietnam. Those who escaped the draft protested the war and created a strong anti-establishment atmosphere where drugs flourished. Peace symbols, psychedelic posters and clothing, head shops, beads and long hair were so commonplace that we accepted them as normal. In addition to the war protests, the riots in Watts in 1965 incited violence and unrest on campus and in our neighborhood.

By the end of our second year at private school, both Marie and I had been turned on to pot by friends. We were acutely aware of the social attitudes on the university campus because of our proximity to it, and it was difficult not to be influenced. I learned quickly that wearing peace symbols and sunglasses was unacceptable at home, but as time went by even our parents became used to the changing styles.

They did not know we smoked grass. Although smoking grass was illegal, we didn't consider it harmful. We considered it great fun, and it set us off on laughing sprees that continued for hours. It also made food taste really good, especially candy bars, ice cream, and cheeseburgers. Once one started eating, it was difficult to stop. It was hard sometimes to locate marijuana, therefore the pursuit of it became a form of entertainment in itself. Friends from the public high school especially liked to get stoned; pot use was less common among girls in the private school. Many came from highly conservative families and had lived very sheltered lives.

After we attended the private school for two years, Mom and Dad announced that we were moving back to the old neighborhood in the North End. Marie and I were to attend Ingraham, Garfield's rival school.

We were extremely reluctant to leave friends and the neighborhood, but fully understood that the private school was expensive and that our parents could not afford to send us all there. We were consoled by the fact that soon we would both be able to drive and could then visit our friends easily.

The new house was a sprawling, unattractive split level. It had originally been a small home, but room after room had been added. The upper yard had been completely neglected. Broken sinks and an old toilet seat lay strewn about in the overgrown, dry and tangled grass and blackberry vines. The home was, nevertheless, a good investment and situated in a nice community. There was an outdoor swimming pool at the end of the block, which our family would share with nine other homes on the street.

The first day we moved in, I decided to walk to the end of the block to check out the pool. I was barefoot and dressed in jeans and my treasured, holey Revelers sweatshirt. I was partway down the street when a screen door opened and two faces popped out.

"Hey chick, wanna a beer?" one of them shouted.

I waited until I got a little closer before I replied. Both guys looked about seventeen and appeared fairly harmless.

"O.K." I answered, a bit uncertainly.

They opened the door wider and let me in.

The boys were cute in a way and looked like greasers from the 1950s. One had curly blond hair and the other was very tall and awkward-looking, with brown hair. They introduced themselves as Wayne and Mel. They inspected me as if I were a specimen from another planet.

Chapter Five

"Why are you wearing that shirt with a hole in it?" the gangly one demanded obnoxiously. "Can't you afford anything else?"

"This is my favorite shirt," I answered in defense, and proceeded to explain why it was special. Their manners definitely needed improvement. They asked me if I would like to go out with them sometime.

"Maybe," I answered noncommittally. They were beginning to make me uncomfortable; I excused myself and left to continue my walk. I wondered which of them I would end up liking best.

We hated the new school from the very first day, a shabby, tunnel-like building with narrow halls and fluorescent lighting. I immediately felt claustrophobic there, and the feeling never went away.

Most of the male students were jocks. It was rumored that the football coach encouraged them to beat up hippies, and there was evidence it was true. The school vicinity was completely segregated. There was only one black student and he was treated like an oddity, even though he spoke and acted like the other students.

The classwork was routine and boring. We spent our breaks in the parking lot, smoking cigarettes, and sometimes pot.

The only class I felt to be worth attending was Art. The teacher and I hit it off right away, and he gave me special encouragement, claiming that I was talented. One of our projects in Art was to produce a drawing without looking at the paper as the pencil moved. This was called contour drawing. I started by copying the Northern toilet-paper girl, a small girl with a bow in her hair and holding a rose. We were required to repeat the drawing several times. By the time I finished, the bow in the girl's hair had become a devil's face in profile. I named it "Devil Girl" and won honorable mention in a citywide art contest.

Moving to the North End was like entering a time warp. The area had so far remained completely untouched by the social change of the '60s. The hamburger stand's parking lot was packed with hot rods that burned rubber entering and leaving. Bottles of beer were passed freely from car to car, and occasionally a pickup truck would drive into the lot with a keg tapped in the back. The girl's restroom at the A & W reeked of urine and vomit, the toilet and sink clogged with putrid paper towels. We completely avoided the restroom.

After getting completely drunk, the hot-rodders headed for a long stretch of road at the nearest beach to race. There were so many kids out on the streets in fast cars that the police were outnumbered. It was not at all uncommon for the hot-rodders to race the police and attempt to ditch them, and often they succeeded. The unlucky ones were given a ticket or arrested, but appeared back on the street the following day.

We observed this behavior with great interest, but stayed with the more sedate crowd getting high on pot. After hearing of the racing at the beach, our parents forbade us to go near, especially at night.

The first time I went out on a date with Mel was an experience unlike any other. He showed up with his buddy Wayne and a case of Heidelberg beer. Mel drove a burgundy El Camino with bucket seats and a four-speed transmission. I was required to sit on the console between the two guys, so that we would all look cool. The console was a raised, hard plastic box, and extremely uncomfortable. Mel burned rubber all the way up the street, passing every single car that got in front of him, whether he could see to pass or not. He drove sixty miles an hour wherever the speed limit was thirty, taking every corner at breakneck speeds. It was terrifying. I wanted to get out, but had no other way home. I begged him to slow down, but it only seemed to encourage him to become more reckless.

About a mile from home, he attempted to pass a car full of teenagers who raced him instead of letting him pass. He gave the other driver the finger and swerved towards them. They stopped their car right in front of us, smack in the middle of a busy two-lane road. The car doors flew open, two boys stepped out and headed aggressively toward Mel's car.

Mel and Wayne were both wearing white fishermen's-

Chapter Five

knit sweaters, which they tore off and threw on the seats as they jumped out of the car.

"Move the car," Mel yelled to me as fists began flying.

I didn't know how to drive a car with a four-speed transmission, so I did nothing.

An old lady was standing on a nearby curb, shouting in a feeble voice, "Oh, boys, please stop!" I watched with alarm as another car pulled up with two more guys who appeared to be friends of the enemies. Mel and Wayne were outnumbered four to two, and soon both were pinned against the side of the car. They were punched repeatedly. Realizing they were clearly outnumbered, they jumped back in the car and we continued on our hair-raising, death-defying drive through the neighborhood. As soon as we reached my driveway, I got out and faced Mel angrily.

"I am never getting in a car with you, ever again, as long as I live!" I screamed. "You're crazy!"

"Ah, she'll get over it," Mel's buddy shouted from the car. "Let's go!"

"Shut up, you asshole," Mel hollered back at his friend. For best friends, there was not a whole lot of respect between them.

"I'll call you tomorrow," he said to me. Lights were beginning to come on inside my house, and we both sensed the presence of disturbed parents right inside the door.

"I've gotta go," I answered over my shoulder as I ran for the house.

The neighbors hated Mel and Wayne. Our street was in a constant uproar with their car racing and fights, and sometimes police cruised the neighborhood hoping to find them. My father threw rocks at them from the deck when they squealed around the corner by our house. The police knew them by name and awaited their appearance at the beach each night, ticket books in hand.

Mel honked at the police just to irritate them, and once received a ticket for "excessive honking of horn." Despite the tickets, the hostile parents, and the occasional black eyes, they remained undaunted in their mission to behave as wildly and recklessly as humanly possible.

In July I went to Chewelah to get my driver's license.

My Uncle John was the driver's education teacher at the high school there, so he was going to give me lessons and help me take the test. I was a fairly good driver from the beginning, so the lessons went quickly. I visited Grammie and Grandpa briefly, and Grammie told me I was getting too skinny. The horses were up in the mountains, so I didn't get a chance to ride that summer.

One night as I was getting ready for bed at my uncle's, I received a long distance call from Seattle. I answered it anxiously, wondering what could be so important to warrant a call from all the way across the state. It was Mel, just wanting to visit. I was flattered that he thought so much of me. In spite of his wild behavior, there was something about him that stirred my interest. He had a pleasant voice and could be sort of sweet when he wanted to be.

I had taken the train, and he offered to pick me up at the station when I returned home. During the long train ride, I fantasized about what Mel would do when he saw me. I would step down from the platform into his outstretched arms and he would hold me closely. This must have been programmed into my psyche by watching too many old movies. I played the scene over and over in my head, anticipating the romantic moment with enthusiasm.

When the actual moment came, I stepped down from the platform alone. I searched the crowds until at last I found him, standing there waiting for me with his hands in his pockets. As soon as I approached, he turned and headed for the parking lot. I followed with my suitcases.

"Are you glad to see me or what?" I thought silently as I tried to catch up. Once we reached the car, he warmed up a little. To my surprise, he even drove like a normal person that night, slowly and carefully the way a parent would drive. I was impressed; I didn't know he could drive that way.

I actually don't know why I continued to date Mel. There were times in his car that I was certain we would never make it home alive, that I would be dismembered in a fiery crash or arrested by the police and detained in jail. He seemed to possess an insane, immortal attitude that defied authority and knew no fear, an attitude I didn't share.

Chapter Five

But there was some unidentifiable quality that appealed to me, and with each date that passed without disaster, I became less fearful.

Even my father developed a grudging respect for Mel after an incident he witnessed from the deck above our garage. Mel and Wayne had been having a pushing and shouting match on the corner and Wayne was losing. He was also crying, in a whiny, sniveling manner very unbecoming to an eighteen-year-old boy.

"C'mon, hit me, you son of a bitch!" Wayne shouted, in a voice loud enough to be heard all over the neighborhood. Mel's long muscular arm shot out and caught Wayne squarely in the face, knocking him down and shutting him up. I guess Dad decided that although Mel was awfully rowdy, at least he wasn't a wimp.

We continued to see each other quite a bit after I returned home from Chewelah, particularly since I lived right between Mel and his best friend. Often I was able to talk him into walking down to the beach, and then I didn't have to worry about getting into his car.

Mel was not what I considered great-looking. He was tall and skinny and had the worst set of crooked teeth I've ever seen. When he was just a child, his mother had taken him to the dentist for a root canal and it had been so painful that he passed out. From that time on, he stubbornly refused to return to a dentist. As a result, he reached adulthood with six too many teeth in his mouth, all crowded for space and protruding unattractively when he smiled. He was self-conscious about his breath and didn't ever really learn how to kiss well. He expressed his affection mostly by touching, and I learned to consider his amiably groping hands a hazard when I was alone with him.

Mel spent most of his time under cars, and often came to see me greasy, filthy, and reeking of gasoline. His hair was naturally oily and was usually in great need of a shampoo. I tactfully encouraged him to take a shower before coming over, which he sometimes did. I was able to bribe him by telling him I would wear his favorite dress, a short white mini-dress made of fishnet. He knew he couldn't touch me in that dress with grease all over his hands. It wasn't a secret to me why he liked that particular dress. He could see partway through it. I always wore a beige slip underneath, or my mother never would have let me out of the house in it.

Mel was trying to grow a mustache, but it was so thin and fine that it looked silly. After a lot of persuading, Marie and I talked him into letting us fill it in with brown mascara. It worked quite well.

I loved going to the park, and there was a convenient trail through the neighbor's yard at the end of our street which led to the upper part. Mel always carried his traditional case of Heidelberg under one arm, ready to toss it over the Cyclone fence bordering the railroad tracks at the first sign of police. We knew that if we were caught in the park with beer, they would ceremoniously open every bottle and pour it on the ground, a humiliation to be avoided at all costs. It was better to throw the beer and break it all than let the cops pour it out.

The park was intimately familiar. Our father had taken us there every weekend when we lived in the house with the chokecherry tree. Now we lived so near that we could smell the salt water from our backyard. Everything was exactly the same as I remembered it. In the semi-darkness, Mel and I would descend the steep stairs from the lofty overpass to the rough, rocky beach, walking close together, his arm wrapped protectively around my waist.

Each time I returned to the park, my mind flooded with the memories of our trips to the beach as children. When the tide was in, the seawater came all the way up to the railroad tracks, limiting the distance one could travel on the sand. To continue walking north we climbed the rocky bulkhead and walked down the tracks to a spot where the beach was exposed. If a train came at the wrong time, it was necessary to escape by clinging to rocks below the tracks. The trains were thunderous, ground-shaking, deafening masses of metal that took five or ten minutes to pass. Eventually, the last car would disappear around the curve to the south and leave a vacuum in its wake, a welcome silence.

At low tide, long sandy stretches of beach were exposed, and the traveling was effortless. We walked and ran for

Chapter Five

miles through shallow tide pools full of tiny crabs. The low tide exposed large black rocks covered with kelp, mussels, and Chinaman's hats. At the base of the rocks lay pools full of brightly colored sea anemones, giant starfish, and other little fish trapped by the receding tide. The beach was full of moon snails, beautiful tan snails with shells as big as oranges. We carried buckets for our treasures and saved room in them for the butter clams we dug at the far north end of the beach. We returned home wet, sandy, and exhausted, with buckets full to the brim of salt water and live sea creatures. After a few days, they inevitably died and began to stink. Then Mom collected them and threw them deep into the canyon behind the house. My fondness for being at the beach stayed with me as I grew older.

At night the beach was illuminated only by the moon and occasional bonfires smoldering in the crevasses of weathered logs. Mel and I lay on the cold sand together, listening to the waves. I liked the feeling of his arms around me; I rested my head on his chest, and the softness of his t-shirt against my face was comforting. His kisses were pleasant but brief, and I wished he would kiss me longer. After lying there awhile, the unavoidable would happen: his hands would wander. First they found their way inside my blouse, and, encountering no resistance, they headed for my jeans. At this point I always had to push him away.

"I don't feel like doing this tonight," I protested, trying not to sound mean.

"O.K., baby, I'm sorry," he would reply contritely. After this the mood was ruined, and we got up to go home.

It was bothersome always to be approached for sex. There were people on the beach who might see us, and anyway, I was only fifteen and didn't know the first thing about it.

One afternoon, as I came downstairs to investigate the suntanning weather, the front doorbell rang and a large box was delivered. Mom said it was for me, and we took it to the kitchen table to open it.

Inside the elegant white box adorned with red ribbon were a dozen red roses. I had never seen such a spectacular bouquet of roses in all my life. The stems were a yard long!

Excitedly, we opened the card which read simply, "To Janet, Love Mel."

"Oh," I groaned with disappointment. "I wish they were from someone I liked."

We set them on the picnic table outside and took a picture of them.

"They really are beautiful," I murmured absently as I snapped the picture.

Once in awhile we still saw our friends from the old neighborhood. This always reminded me of the contrast between the two areas, and renewed my boredom with North End people.

Chick, Kay, and Rod had formed a band and were playing in a nightclub near our house. Marie and I gained admission with the help of some outstandingly lousy, phony ID cards. I wore a white satin halter dress so short that it barely covered my underpants. Something about the looks I received from the people at the door gave me the distinct impression that it was the dress, not the ID, which convinced them to let me in. Chick and I were still infatuated with one another, and after a night of dancing under romantic subdued lights and listening to him sing, I was convinced that this was how I wanted to spend my life: dancing and listening to my friends play music. However, the mere physical distance between our two neighborhoods kept us from getting together as much as I would have liked.

Mel hated to dance. He listened to a blaring, all-white radio station when he listened to music at all, and as for dancing he simply didn't know how. I offered to teach him, but he emphatically refused. At times like these, I felt we had absolutely nothing in common. All he cared about was cars.

It bothered Mel that I couldn't drive a car with a stick shift, so one afternoon he decided to teach me. We headed up the hill in an old Chevy pickup he used when he wasn't driving his fast car.

We switched places a few blocks from my house and I prepared to drive. He showed me how to shift and how to use the brake and clutch. We were going to drive down a short, steep hill and around a corner. The truck's steering was stiff and hard to get used to after the power steering in Mom's station wagon, and I really didn't have any idea what I was supposed to be doing. As we headed down the hill, I tried to step on the brake, but got it mixed up with the clutch. As we started to pick up speed, I panicked and my feet froze. There were cars lined up near the curb all the way to the bottom of the hill and we were going too fast to make the corner at the bottom.

"Turn!" Mel yelled, grabbing the steering wheel and cranking it sharply. We careened around the corner on two wheels and narrowly missed crashing into the parked cars. After that we decided it would be better if I learned on my own, which I managed to do later in a car of my father's.

I always thought Mel was a little spoiled. His mom acted strict, but he got away with things I never would have dreamed of doing. And even if he did get caught, his parents didn't stay mad. His dad always lent him his car, though Mel could wreck a whole set of tires in one night burning rubber outside Dick's hamburger stand. As long as the tires were replaced the next day, his dad pretended it hadn't happened. I couldn't tell if Mel's mother liked me or not. I noticed that she always stared at my clothes when I came to the door, but she was always polite.

In late summer Mel's parents left town and he and his brother threw a party in the basement. Most of the guests were crowded into a low-ceilinged room with a pool table. There were very few places to sit. The party was rowdy, noisy and unpleasant, and I wanted to leave. Mel convinced me to stay and led me away from the racket into a plain wood-paneled room where he slept. I naively lay down on the bed with him and we started to kiss. As usual, I was soon being separated from my clothing, so began the familiar struggle to stop before sex was inevitable. My desire to resist had been worn down with familiarity and time, and I did little to impede the advances.

Being touched all over felt strange and uncomfortable, but I knew that sooner or later I would have to survive "the first time." I reluctantly allowed him to continue, and sex for the first time was difficult, painful, and embarrassing. I couldn't believe how unpleasant it was. Soon afterwards I told Mel I had to go home. He wanted to take me in the car, but I didn't let him. I walked the short distance, wondering if my mom would be able to tell by looking at me that I had gone all the way.

Nobody had told me making love was going to hurt the first time. My curiosity was thoroughly quelled and I decided unconditionally that I hated sex. I vowed to myself never to go out with Mel again.

The Vietnamese war was in full swing, and during a one-year period almost every one of my male friends received a draft notice. My Japanese friend, Kay, escaped because he had braces on his teeth. Some of the less fortunate, including Rod and Chick, were drafted and eventually sent to Vietnam. Mel's older brother also was sent, and the following year Mel was drafted. Mel was to be stationed at nearby Fort Lewis because his brother was already in Vietnam. This was a generous stipulation made by the Army so that all the males in one family wouldn't get killed.

I didn't realize at the time how devastating the war would be on the individual lives of those sent. I viewed their situation with an air of detachment and with a self-centeredness unique to teenagers. It wasn't until later, when they returned home, traumatized and changed, that the effects of the war were felt on my life, too.

I received many letters from overseas and most of them spoke about the great drugs in Vietnam. Once in awhile a letter would contain a sample of potent marijuana, or some Thai sticks: bamboo sticks with buds of marijuana fastened to them like Fourth of July sparklers. The grass from overseas was so strong that, after smoking just a tiny bit, a person was in such a stupor it was practically impossible to do anything but sit and stare. Normal activities like driving a car or going to the store were completely out of the question. My friends were being dumped out of helicopters into dense jungles under full enemy fire, and all the while stoned out of their minds. Most of the time they couldn't see who was shooting at them, or who they were killing when they returned fire. It was common knowledge that many Americans were being shot by Americans, and Asian-Americans or Americans of Filipino descent like Chick were particu-

Chapter Five

larly at risk of being mistaken for Viet Cong.

I lost touch with most of the young men who were drafted in the year that followed and didn't see them again for years.

Tension had been building between my mother and father, and after our first year at the new school they decided to separate. My father had been spending less and less time at home, and when he was home a cloud of anger, like a thick fog, seemed to settle in the house. My mother felt the need to get completely away and decided she would take the three youngest kids and move to Chewelah to be with her family. Marie had already moved out and was living with her boyfriend. I wanted to stay in Seattle with Dad. I couldn't imagine leaving him completely alone, without someone to help cook and take care of the house.

I don't know exactly where the problems originated; as children, we simply witnessed the results. The coming apart of their marriage was like the unraveling of a twisted knot. There were accusations and denials, indignation and lies until it was impossible to tell who was being unfair. I loved both my parents, and hated the notion of having to take sides, so I avoided the issues, thereby avoiding the painful truth. I watched them retire grimly to the bedroom in the evening, and observed the frowns deeply etched into their features as they rose the next morning. In the back of my mind, there was a weak realization that they were still sleeping together. The intricacies of adulthood disturbed me.

Dad traded the old Jaguar in on a different one, a long, sleek XK 150 convertible, and we continued our tradition of Sunday drives. We used our drives together to talk, mostly about my life, but one particular Sunday he seemed depressed, as if he wanted to talk about his own problems but didn't know how. Finally, when the ride was over and we were sitting in the driveway, he said without looking at me, "There is something I want you to know. If I ever do anything you don't understand, it's because I'm confused."

"O.K. Dad," I answered quietly.

Later that night I told my Mom that I thought Dad was going to try to kill himself. When I repeated what he had said, she looked angry. I couldn't understand how she could be angry with him for being confused or depressed.

I was glad when they finally decided to separate. I thought it meant that the gloom would leave the house and we would all be happy again.

With my mother gone, I plunged headlong into the role of housewife, planning meals and cleaning obsessively. The house was huge, and keeping it in shape was exhausting. I mowed the lawn, cleaned the cupboards, and mopped the floors, keeping busy with housework from the beginning of the day until my father returned home from work. I wanted everything to look just perfect.

I spent most of the summer that way. All my friends were gone, so there was nothing to distract me from my compulsive cleaning. It was very quiet in the big house, and with Mel gone the neighborhood too was silent. Often Dad had to stay late at the hospital, and his dinner would remain on the stove untouched. It was becoming very, very lonely.

The last day I attended Ingraham is a day I remember clearly. It was one of those times in life when a decision states itself so plainly and undeniably that one feels compelled to act immediately and without hesitation.

It was a warm day in September, and would have been the first day of my senior year. I entered the artificially lighted, tunnel-like hallway, and felt as though the walls were closing in on me. I turned and bolted for the door, as though my life were in danger. Glancing furtively behind me to be sure I wasn't getting caught, I hurried for a bus stop a few blocks down the street and caught a bus which took me all the way to south Seattle. My destination was Beacon Hill, as far away as I could get from the dreaded school without leaving the city completely.

I couldn't attend that school for one more day. I had barely made it through the junior year, and now I didn't even have Marie as company. I couldn't think of a single person there that I considered a friend, except maybe the Art teacher. I hated it too much to continue just for that one relationship.

That night I talked with my father a little and told him

Chapter Five

how I felt about the school. He said he thought it would be a good idea if I joined my mom and the others in Chewelah. He told me that he had noticed how I seemed lonely and that he'd been worried about my spending so much time in the house by myself. I had to agree that I really did miss the little guys.

Suddenly, the thought of getting away filled me with elation. I had always wanted to live in Chewelah. I could finish high school there. It would be perfect. I made plans to leave as soon as possible.

SIX

The air in Chewelah has a scent all its own. It crackles with the intensity of its dryness. It is deeply perfumed with pine and chamomile and free of the dulling smog caused by too many people and too many cars. I loved the solitude of the wheat fields and cherished the sounds of nature. Amidst chirping grasshoppers, scolding chipmunks, and the faraway calls of cattle, I felt peaceful and at home.

My mother had moved to a large two-story house in an isolated area called Wright's Valley. The house was nestled against a hill at the west end of the valley and faced out toward expansive wheat fields separated by a single narrow dirt road. The fields to the right of the house were bordered by birch trees which turned fiery shades of yellow, orange, and scarlet in the fall. In an opening in the line of trees, there was a shallow creek where my brother fished for hours, catching tiny silver trout on a homemade pole.

The house was unfinished upstairs, but spacious and comfortable. Julie and I were given a large area to share, divided by a curtain. Bare lumber was exposed in many places and I pounded in nails wherever I chose; for the first time in my life, there were no walls to ruin.

My previously stifled creativity flourished in the undisturbed beauty of the valley, and I began to surprise my mother by producing imaginative artwork on canvas with acrylic paints. My mom was very creative, but had never painted, and my seemingly inborn talent was a pleasant discovery. Soon Julie began painting, too, and the unfinished upstairs was transformed into an art studio. Our ability was eventually attributed to Grammie Hafer, who had painted with oils. Her favorite subjects were herds of buffalo and

Chapter Six

haunting scenes of Indians riding bareback, hunting with wooden spears.

When school started, Julie, Karl, and I walked up to the road and waited for the old yellow school bus which carried grades one through twelve. I felt awkward boarding the bus for the first time, but the other students didn't seem to notice me. They jumped up and down in their seats and acted like monsters, oblivious to the fact that there was a sophisticated city girl right in their midst. Peer pressure and the desire to grow up were concepts that didn't at the time seem to exist in Chewelah.

The school was quaint and incomprehensibly old-fashioned in its educational standards. Actually, the whole town seemed to be untouched by modern progress. Perhaps more important, it was also untouched by status and wealth. There were no visible signs of prosperity, no fancy cars, no mansions on the water. Everything was covered with dust; the whole town appeared to have been asleep for the last twenty years.

On the first day of school, I was called into the principal's office and informed that skirts as short as mine would not be tolerated. The principal was a hateful, nasty man with a reputation for being unduly strict and unfair. I ignored his warning and eventually gained the dubious title of "outside agitator," a phrase he'd evidently picked up from the newspaper while reading about war protesters. I decided I liked the title, and to live up to my image, I occasionally wore a meaningless white armband on my high school sweater.

Many of the junior and senior boys were pimply-faced members of Future Farmers of America. And social life centered around the 4H Club, an organization which taught farming skills, such as the proper raising of livestock.

Home Economics was the focal point of education for the girls. On the first day of my Home Economics class, it was apparent that the senior project would be to make a tailored coat. Everyone in class seemed to be an accomplished seamstress. Embarrassed by the fact that I couldn't sew, I confessed the problem to the teacher and requested that I be allowed to transfer to a different class. With amusement, and perhaps a little sympathy, she responded that she would teach me how to sew. She told me I could work on something much easier than a coat, and she would be more than happy to help me. I was unaccustomed to this type of personal consideration and kindness after attending public schools in Seattle. I fought back grateful tears as I thanked her.

The English teacher was an older man with an albino complexion, and he appeared to be nearly blind. He wore Coke-bottle glasses which made his eyes look ridiculously crossed, and he squinted terribly in an effort to discern what was going on in class. The students teased him relentlessly, taking advantage of his poor vision to pass notes and throw spitwads. There was constant commotion and giggling, and he never seemed to have control of the class. I felt sorry for him as he spluttered ineffectively at the rowdy students, and I wished they would stop tormenting him.

Part of the problem with the English class was that the teacher's approach to grammar was archaic and intensely boring. Recalling a project I had enjoyed in private school, I suggested to him that the class might enjoy actually producing a book of poetry and other writing. He agreed immediately, and most of the other students liked the idea, too. Many contributed writing to the book, even those whose primary interest appeared to be farming. I was assigned the job of editor and my function was to collect the writings.

When it came time to publish the book, the principal wouldn't let us have any paper to print it on. Only after a tearful and bitter struggle and with help from the English teacher were we finally able to acquire some cheap paper. We produced the book and it turned out to be a delightful project that renewed student interest in the subject of English. After we won the skirmish with the principal, the English teacher became regarded as a friend and ally, and those who had teased him stopped.

During the first week of school, I was introduced to a group of girls who called themselves "the gang." I was warned, "You'll either really like these girls, or you'll really hate them." As it turned out, I fit right in. They were hilarious and welcomed my uninhibited addition to the group.

Chapter Six

The gang's leader was a very overweight blond girl named Cheryl. But in spite of her chubbiness, she was full of energy and had a bubbly, infectious laugh.

Cheryl's mom lived in a trailerhouse with an old geezer named Pete. They were an eccentric couple who made a huge vat of sauerkraut and stored it under their kitchen table each year. The stench and fumes from the fermenting cabbage inside the hot stuffy trailer made visiting for more than a few minutes next to impossible. We paid them a visit occasionally, but could never stand to stay long.

Cheryl stayed in a small two-bedroom house, near the trailer, which was owned by her mother. Since the house was just a few blocks from school, we walked there for lunches of canned string beans or whatever else we could dig out of the nearly empty cupboards. We spent most of our time sitting around the living room in a circle smoking and gossiping, or sharing each other's makeup in the bathroom. At times I ended up with so much makeup on my eyes that I could barely blink. Then we all walked back to school together, reeking of smoke, and spent the rest of the afternoon goofing off.

After school we all loaded into Cheryl's big black vintage auto—nicknamed Harriet—and cruised town and the back roads. There wasn't much to do but drive around, and the gang was always ready for excitement, in whatever form it could be found. It wasn't long before they discovered that living in the city had made me even crazier than most of them. Then we really started having fun.

The first thing they wanted to know was whether I'd ever tried pot, which surprised me. I assumed that Chewelah was so far removed from civilization that no one would have heard of illegal substances. Apparently I was mistaken; they knew all about pot and were anxious to try some. I had brought a small amount with me from Seattle and agreed to share it with Cheryl and one other girl.

On the day we were to smoke the pot, we ran into a slight problem. After parking Harriet in a secluded gravel pit several miles from town, we discovered we'd forgotten cigarette rolling papers. Unwilling to abandon our plans, we racked our brains, searched our purses, and suddenly came up with what we thought was the perfect solution: a Tampax wrapper.

After removing the tampon from its flimsy cylindrical wrapping, I carefully poured in the coarse marijuana and tried to form a small cigarette. The joint came out loosely rolled, and small pieces of stem punctured the paper, leaving tiny holes. The other girls giggled in anticipation as I held the makeshift joint to my lips, lit it, and inhaled. What happened next came as a total surprise and was a grave disappointment to my friends. The paper ignited instantly from end to end in a poof that singed my lips and fingers. The precious marijuana crumbled in smoldering pieces onto the floor of the car, impossible to retrieve. After picking at the grimy worn carpeting for awhile and coming up with nothing but dirt and rocks, we each dejectedly lit a cigarette and headed back to town.

A few weeks later we faced another grand dilemma. There was going to be a dance in a neighboring town on Friday night and we wanted to get some beer. All the seniors from the year ahead of us were gone, and there was no one old enough to buy any for us. We searched our minds for a solution, and, as usual, I came up with a perfect plan.

We would drive to Valley, a tiny town nearby, and I would disguise myself to look like an older woman. The regulars in the Valley tavern were widely known as the most comatose alcoholics anywhere, and the owners were also usually drunk. It was my guess that they probably wouldn't care how old I was, even if they could tell; I had visited the place once before with some older boys, and left with the impression that none of the people inside could see past the ends of their noses.

It was a schoolday when we planned the caper. I was dressed in a straight brown skirt that zipped up the back, and a plain blouse. My plan was to make myself look like a frumpy housewife in her mid- to late-twenties.

We parked a few blocks from the tavern while I prepared my disguise. The others laughed hysterically as I wiped off most of my eye makeup, applied bright red lipstick, and tied a scarf around my head. I climbed out of the car and partially unzipped my skirt, pulling it down until it

Chapter Six

almost reached my knees. I untucked my blouse to cover the open zipper, waved goodbye to my friends, and headed down the street toward the tavern.

It was a bright autumn day and I had to stand and let my eyes adjust for a moment after I entered the dusty tavern. The tavern was pitch dark and the small windows were caked with dust. Fossilized pickled eggs swam in jars on the counter, alongside peanuts that had been packaged a decade or two earlier. The air inside was stale and reeked of cigarette smoke. Three or four of the regulars sat hunched over glasses of beer, talking. Their voices were deep and gravelly from years of continuous smoking and drinking.

"Say, she don't look more than about eighteen years old," one of them remarked as I approached the bar.

"Oh, yes, she do, Frank, she looks to be around twenty-two to me," another argued, peering at me through the haze.

The man behind the bar was unshaven, and wore strange-looking glasses with tinted lenses.

"I'd like a case of Heidelberg, please," I stated boldly, setting my purse in front of him.

He looked me over and decided to accept the money.

"We don't have Heidelberg, miss, just Rainier and Buckhorn," he said.

"O.K., Rainier is fine," I answered, trying to suppress a triumphant smile.

He went to the cooler and brought back a case of Rainier, swinging it up on the bar and sliding it toward me.

The one thing I hadn't anticipated was how much a case of twenty-four bottles would weigh. I nearly dropped it as I lifted it from the counter. No one offered to help me with the door.

I was again momentarily sightless as my eyes tried to adjust to the glaring sun. It was around four in the afternoon and seemed to have gotten hotter during the time I was inside. My legs were sweating in my nylons, and my wool skirt began to itch. The gang was waiting in Cheryl's car, which they'd parked two blocks away. Peals of laughter rang from the open windows as I struggled down the uneven sidewalk, scratching my knees and struggling not to drop the beer or my purse. Cheryl got out and took the

Return To Chewelah

case from me, stashing it in the trunk. We didn't want to take the beer to Cheryl's house, so we hid it in the bushes on a hill outside of Valley.

Unfortunately, buying the beer was more fun than the dance. No interesting people came, that is, no good-looking boys, and the local band was so bad that very few people stayed once inside. Someone had discovered our stash of beer, but had left a few bottles for us. We drove around town from Main Street to the hamburger stand and back, but could find no excitement anywhere. It was simply dead in town, a boring Friday night. We never bothered to return to the tavern for another case of beer.

When winter came to the valley, it was spectacular. Light, dry snow fell, deeply blanketing the ground. The temperature dropped to ten degrees during the day and below zero at night. The powdery snow formed ice crystals on every dry blade of wheat in the fields and turned the trees to sparkling ice sculptures. The sun shining on the ice created the illusion of a billion dazzling diamonds, and the sky was deep, azure blue.

Despite the extreme cold, we never felt chilled, because of the aridity of the air. The only indicators of how truly freezing it was were the tiny stinging crystals that formed around the edges of our nostrils as we breathed.

Soon after I moved, I met an older boy named Randy. He was twenty, had thick blond hair, mischievous blue eyes, and an outgoing personality. My mom thought he was a smart-aleck, but I dated him anyway, and eventually we became known around town as a couple. He frequently kept me out too late, and we began sleeping together, which I think my mother suspected.

One night we fell asleep in his bed and didn't wake up until three in the morning. When I got home I was locked out of the house. Hoping I hadn't been caught, we pried open a small window in the living room, so that I could sneak in. My mother caught me as I was climbing in, with one foot on the TV set. Dressed in an old nightgown, she was in the foulest mood I'd ever witnessed.

It was very unpleasant. I tried to tell her we had a flat tire, which she didn't believe. I didn't attempt to offer any

Chapter Six

other explanation; I certainly didn't want to tell her the truth. That evening did nothing toward improving our mother-daughter relationship.

Randy and I usually double-dated with his best friends, Gary and Sue. They had already finished school and were planning on getting married. At Christmastime, the four of us crowded into Randy's vintage pickup and drove high into the mountains to find Christmas trees. Randy was full of Christmas spirit and affectionately picked me up and lifted me onto the truck seat, giving me a kiss before closing the door. Partway up the mountain we stopped, and the two boys hopped out and disappeared down a steep ravine into the incredibly deep powder snow. While we were waiting in the truck, I confessed to Sue that I was in love with Randy and hoped that we could someday get married, too.

A few weeks later, as I was using the bathroom at Randy's house, I overheard him talking with his friend on the floor above me. "The Army wants my ass," he confided to Gary. "I've got to do something about it pretty soon. I think I'm going to join the Air Force."

I felt hot and weak with disappointment. Even here the draft was ruining everybody's life.

A few weeks went by after that evening, and Randy didn't call. Later I began to hear rumors that he'd been seen dating a notoriously cheap, unattractive girl from a nearby town. I was crushed when I heard the news; I was positive he had been in love with me.

After a few months we ran into each other at a going-away party for another draftee. We had a loud fight and I called him an asshole. I took a swing at him, hit a fish tank instead, and broke a beautiful opal ring. Randy left the party, and the guest of honor and I sat up until late in the evening, talking about the war and comparing sob stories. The guest of honor was later killed in Vietnam.

The night following our fight, I saw Randy in town and we had a tearful reunion. He told me he was leaving the States and that he didn't know how to say goodbye. He'd enlisted in the Air Force and was going to be sent to Korea. After I saw him that night, he didn't call again and I didn't see him for several more years.

After we had attended school in Chewelah for two quarters, Mom decided to move back to Seattle and try to reconcile with my father. I definitely did not want to go, and neither did Julie. Miraculously, my uncle (the driver's education teacher and coach at the high school) said we girls could stay with him to finish out the year. There was room for us in the upstairs of the roomy white house he had inherited from my paternal grandparents.

Julie had not found as many friends as I had in Chewelah, and seemed lonely and insecure. I tried to reserve time for her, hoping it would ease her unhappiness. We began a ritual of walking to town together each Sunday for lunch at the Busy Bee Cafe. Sitting as close as possible to the window facing Main Street, we drank cup after cup of bracing coffee served in thick, cream-colored ceramic mugs. We always ordered the same delicious thing to eat: a bowl of homemade soup or chili and a hot butterhorn. The butterhorns were gigantic, steaming sweet pastries served dripping with melted butter. An old lady baked them fresh every morning in the back of the restaurant.

There were old-timers in each of the establishments in town, some in restaurants, some in taverns. They were human landmarks, content for the rest of their lives to sit on the same stool in the same place every single day, amidst the comings and goings of other townspeople. Customarily dressed in plaid shirts and denim overalls, but too old to farm, some of them retired to town to spend their time amidst the cheerful clatter of plates at the Busy Bee. They sat lined up on stools at the counter, each stooped forward, propped up by elbows to read the paper.

We loved the town for its backwardness and the fact that it never changed. We took pleasure in visiting the shops full of outdated ladies' apparel, western jeans, straw cowboy hats, and plastic jewelry. The mannequins wore knee-length girdles, and bras with pointed foam-pads. There were two soda fountains in town, one at each drugstore. If you ordered a banana split, you were asked to wait while someone ran to the store across the street for a banana. Our favorite soda was a Green River, a fluorescent green soda with a somewhat indefinable flavor.

Chapter Six

When I was not with Julie, I walked downtown to meet classmates to play tennis on a weedy court near the bowling alley. I was in good shape and had enough energy to run all day. My legs became tan early that year, and my figure felt more shapely. Maybe I was just happier. Anyway, I liked myself better when I looked in the mirror.

Since Randy's departure, I had started dating a new guy named Steve. He was smart and good-looking, but our romantic encounters were miserable failures. I enjoyed the attention and companionship, but he couldn't replace Randy.

That spring an old friend of Grammie's moved his best horse to a field close to town and told me I could exercise her. She was a sleek, dappled gray thoroughbred named Sugarbabe. Her gaits were as smooth as a rocking horse's. The owner's only stipulation was that I had to promise never to let Sugarbabe run. At a full run she was so fast it would have been dangerous. I took the warning seriously and rode her at a safe, sedate pace. We usually went to the track field, where the football team practiced, and loped around the perimeter. Her graceful form caused heads to turn as we passed; her thoroughbred breeding allowed her to lope for mile after mile without ever breaking a sweat. She was the only horse I had ridden that was comparable to Sundown, and riding her filled me with the same sense of elation. To have this horse all to myself was indescribably pleasurable. It was a time I'll never forget.

We celebrated the last few months of school as though they were the last days of our lives. Many of my friends planned to go away to college, and we faced the eventuality of never being together again.

For me, the year had been almost a second childhood, a much needed respite from the pressures of the city and the strain of my parents' failing marriage. I had experienced more joy in just plain living during that short period of time than some people do in a lifetime. Unfortunately it had to end, as good things usually do.

At graduation time Mom sewed glamorous satin halter dresses for Julie and me and sent them ahead in the mail. They were perfect: mine was pink crepe and very short, the way I liked it; Julie's was an exquisite lavender. Chick was home from the war temporarily and he and Kay came east with Mom for the ceremony. They delivered my father's car for me to drive home later.

The graduation ceremony was farcical and embarrassing. The school's perpetually off-key orchestra played, and we fumbled through a poorly rehearsed program in gowns and caps which were much too big. I received my high school diploma with the Class of 1970, Jenkins High School, Chewelah, the same high school from which both my parents had graduated twenty years earlier.

A few weeks later I drove through town to say goodbye to my remaining friends. Many of them had already left for the summer, and the streets were silent and deserted. I didn't want the year to end. My future was filled with uncertainty and second choices. My first choice would have been to stay in Chewelah to live the rest of my life as happily as I had that year. Of course, that was impossible.

I had been accepted by the state university in Bellingham. I chose to go to that school primarily because a few people I knew from the North End of Seattle were already students there. They were not favorite friends, but they were the only ones I knew who had not been drafted.

Upon returning to Seattle I made the dismal discovery that my parents were no happier. My mom was going to start real estate school so that she would have a way to support herself if they divorced. Meanwhile, their continued miserable existence together cast a resentful pall over the home.

I had lost contact with most of my friends in Seattle during the time I was away. Mel was stationed at Fort Lewis, a few hours south of town, and only got away once in awhile. Chick was between tours to Vietnam. He had returned home thin, nervous, and shell-shocked. None of us realized how badly he had been affected by the fighting until we went to a park on the Fourth of July. Every time a firecracker went off, he dove to the ground and covered his head. We had to take him home almost immediately. It scared us and made us sad to see him that way, clearly traumatized. There seemed to be nothing we could do to help him, and he just wanted us to leave him alone.

Chapter Six

I visited Mel at his apartment at Fort Lewis, and he, too, was thin, gaunt, and unhappy. He had received a traditional boot-camp haircut, which did nothing to enhance his tall, awkward appearance and crooked teeth. He was living in a large, two-story apartment with several other GIs his age. There was very little furniture, and no food. The large, empty rooms were used exclusively for wild parties, and they smelled like urine and stale beer. The fort was saturated with every type of illegal drug on the market, and nearly all the GIs used drugs. Mel opened a drawer and showed me hundreds of pills, some black, some red. They were uppers and downers, and were often taken simultaneously.

I felt uncomfortable around the other GIs, so we went upstairs to Mel's bedroom for privacy. It was furnished with a waterbed and dresser. It seemed unfair to me that he had been taken away from his home and family and was being detained in a sickening place like this. I thought of his mother and how she would feel if she could see the way he was living. Only nineteen, he was being deprived of decent food before he was even through growing.

He wanted to make love, so I tried, hoping it would make him happy. The surroundings were not conducive to romance and the attempt left me feeling unclean. I took a hot shower afterwards, desperate to wash the rank, dismal atmosphere of the place off my body. That day I was grateful for the opportunity to go home.

I chose to attend an experimental college that was annexed to the state university. It claimed to offer more flexibility in learning than was available through a traditional education, which appealed to my creative nature. When I got there, I discovered it was so flexible that no learning was required at all. The students were allowed to go to their counselors and tell them how many grade points they deserved. Class attendance wasn't even required. The professors, some of whom were transplanted hippies from Berkeley, didn't even bother to find out students' names. Science classes consisted of foraging in the woods for edible plants and making homemade beer.

I wasted two quarters there before transferring to the

regular university. Once there I still lacked direction and a goal. It crossed my mind that I would like to be a doctor, but the tremendous time investment required caused me to shy away from a career in medicine. My broken relationship with Randy had left me with a vague, unfulfilled desire to be married someday, have a real home, and someone who loved me.

I was miserable living in the dorms, but shortly after I transferred to the university a girl in one of my English classes said she needed an apartment roommate. Greatly relieved, I moved in right away and began to decorate my first home away from home with colorful junk from the thrift stores in town and my own paintings.

Puttering around with domestic projects often took precedence over going to class, and I refined my bad habit of ignoring the classes I didn't care for and tried hard only in the ones I liked. I was too uninterested in my college career to bother dropping unwanted classes, and this was reflected in my grade-point average. I received a combination of A's and F's, which averaged out to a low C, barely passing.

My social life was a mess. I was constantly asked out, only to find that sex was the only object of the date. I became calloused by rude treatment and behavior, and treated disrespectful dates with reciprocal disrespect.

On one occasion I agreed to go to Canada with my sociology professor, who was unhappily married. Partway there, he pulled over to the side of the road and proceeded to attack me right in the car. I was nearly raped, but somehow convinced him to get off me. He promised to give me an A for the class if I promised not to tell anyone about the incident. I agreed, skipped the class for the rest of the quarter, and got an A in Sociology without ever opening the book.

I became so accustomed to aggressive behavior from men that it really surprised me if I met someone who didn't want to have sex. At times I got so sick of fighting off advances that I gave in just for the sake of convenience. This, in turn, left me feeling degraded and disgusted with myself. I was inadvertently becoming the type of person I didn't like.

Chapter Six

Psychology was one of my favorite classes, but the professor committed suicide in the middle of the quarter, leaving us feeling deserted and disillusioned. We were given no explanation for his death and were left with a miserably poor substitute professor who merely gave us a reading list.

All in all, it was a terrible year and a complete waste of my father's money. If he had known what type of education I was really getting, or how I was spending my time, I'm sure he wouldn't have agreed to keep paying for college. Bellingham was a long way from Seattle, and my father had plenty of problems of his own to worry about.

I returned home to my parents' house in Seattle to spend the summer, anxious to escape the sleazy men, far-out hippies, and the pressure of trying to decide what to do with my life.

One of our favorite places to go as children was to Grandfather May's log cabin deep in the woods at Swan Lake, a beautiful place near Republic. The cabin had been built for him during the Depression by his patients, many of whom were too poor to pay with money. When I was seven or eight, our family received a notice from the government, threatening to burn the cabin unless it was moved. Apparently it rested on government land, and the one-hundred-year lease my grandfather had was to expire in the next decade.

Dad began soon afterwards to look for a new piece of property, very anxious to preserve the original cabin. He planned to move it, log by log, and rebuild it in a safe location. He eventually settled on a seven-hundred-and-twenty-acre piece of land in a place called Aeneus Valley, which he purchased in partnership with three other doctors. They were able to get a good deal on the acreage because it was considered undesirable: dry, rocky, and infertile except for the low-lying area, which had a tendency to flood in the spring. For these reasons the region remained largely unsettled. Although the land was poor to farm, the windswept hills and mountains were covered with pines and crawling with wildlife, and it was a wonderful place to build a cabin. There was a spring somewhere uphill from the cabin site, and Dad planned to divert some of the water to the cabin.

We also acquired a small lake, although we shared ownership with Ralph, the man who had sold us the land. He frequently stocked the lake with hundreds of trout, then invited prospective real estate buyers up to his lake to fish. Many of them caught gigantic fish with amazingly little effort. Dad discovered later that when he and the other doctors had purchased the land, they'd not been sold the timber rights. Ralph still legally owned every single tree on our property, and about twenty years later had some of the property logged.

A long, flat stretch of land runs east and west through Aeneus Valley. Our property is used partly as an alfalfa field and partly as an airstrip. The infamous Ralph flew a small plane which he called *The Buzzard*, and my father purchased a Cessna 172 which he learned to fly. During the summer Dad often flew the plane to the cabin for the day, a flight which took him about an hour and a half. I rode along a few times, but small planes weren't my favorite way to travel. Flying to the cabin required roughly forty-five minutes of hanging suspended over jagged, ice-covered mountains where no human being ever sets foot, and I didn't trust the inexpensive, noisy little Cessna—just a machine—with my life.

The cabin was erected at the top of a gentle hill overlooking the lake. Moving the cabin was a lot of work, took several years, and Dad had to enlist the help of an old retired man who was an experienced builder. Although he turned out to be an invaluable asset, he was extremely opinionated and determined to do everything his own way. He and my father engaged in lengthy arguments, which were usually won by the old man's stubbornness. Despite the constant bickering, they became friends.

In July of 1971, just before my nineteenth birthday, I helped by hauling over one of the first loads of furniture. I stayed at the cabin for a few days alone, except for the company of my dad's crazy black Labrador, Elmer.

The isolation was deeply soothing, strong medicine for my ragged nerves. It felt good to let the silence and the smell of the pines cleanse away the disillusionment of the past year. Life here was delightfully simple and unspoiled: chop

Chapter Six

wood, light a fire, haul water, catch a fish and cook it for dinner. Feed the scraps to the dog. Go to bed and listen to the wind singing in the trees, the coyotes howling on the hill.

On the way home we stopped at a place called Vantage, one of the hottest, windiest locations in the state. We parked at a deserted boat launch and walked down the ramp into the Columbia River to swim. There are nothing but barren hills on either side of the river, and the only vegetation in the area is sagebrush. Most cars bypass Vantage, anxious to reach destinations east or west. The boat launch is always completely deserted, as though no one even knows it's there. But the river is beautiful, pristine, and icy-cold.

Elmer and I swam there, enveloped in dazzling cool water under a huge bright sky. We were two tiny specks, floating completely unnoticed and alone in the vastness of the universe. For a brief moment, my existence was drawn into perspective, and I felt connected with the true source of life.

The feeling disappeared as soon as we got back into the car and pulled out onto the freeway, heading for the city.

A few weeks later, Dad told me that the old man who had been helping him put together the cabin had lost his wife and that he was so lonely and depressed that he had stopped eating.

He asked if I would consider going over and cooking for him for a few days, and I agreed to go if I could take my little sister Lisa "for protection." The man lived in an old trailerhouse near the cabin. Lisa and I started the adventure off by going to the store to stock his refrigerator with food.

Things went well at first. He loved my cooking, and seemed to enjoy my company. At night I sat up talking with him at his dusty kitchen table, the room illuminated by a hissing kerosene lantern.

The old man was familiar with our family's fondness for ending the day with a glass of whiskey, and he began to produce a bottle whenever we sat down to talk.

He talked about a lot of things: his dead wife, our families. I felt very sorry for him, particularly because he seemed

Return To Chewelah

to hate getting old. He spent a great deal of time dwelling on the past. I let him hug me, and once in awhile his hand would wander a little too far up my leg, or he would accidentally slip a little and get too near my breast. I gave him the benefit of the doubt and let him get away with it at first; he was so old that I didn't have the heart to slap him or yell at him as I might have done with someone younger. After awhile he began to discuss his fantasy, or what I thought must be a fantasy, of our going to the cabin together for a weekend without anyone else around. When I realized he was serious, his accidental gropings took on new meaning and he began to give me the creeps. Lisa and I made plans to leave, and soon returned to Seattle.

I gave my Dad a shortened version of the events that had transpired, too embarrassed to fill in many of the details. He didn't act too surprised, was apologetic, and was glad we had come home.

SEVEN

It was a typical boring summer in Seattle and I was feeling restless. There was not enough sun in which to kick back and be completely lazy, yet I didn't feel like wasting what summer there was looking for a temporary job. Every time I put on my swimming suit to sunbathe, the weather turned cloudy. I was convinced there was a direct cause-and-effect relationship between my clothing and the weather.

One morning as I was standing in the kitchen pondering what to do for the day, a knock came at the back door. I opened it, wondering who might come to the back door instead of the front. My eyes fell upon a person in ratty cut-offs and an old t-shirt, unrecognizably thin. He was what I needed most in the world at that moment: a friend.

"Mel!" I shrieked. I then leaped toward him and threw my arms around his neck as though he had saved me from a fire.

He told me he'd been discharged from the Army and, because he was thoroughly disgusted with the United States, he'd been spending the past few weeks in Canada. His uncle had been trying to get him a job there without a work visa. He'd been unsuccessful.

Mel told me of his sojourn in Canada and how he had discovered a fantastic place for horseback-riding and swimming near Harrison. The town is on the edge of a beautiful lake surrounded by high mountains. There he had met a French citizen who worked as an assistant maître d'hôtel in the plush hotel at Harrison Hot Springs. The young man made Mel welcome in his apartment, gave him spending money, and stocked the cupboards with gourmet food, expensive wine, and liquor. Basically, it was an all-expenses-paid vacation with no time limit.

The more he talked, the more envious I became. Out of the blue he invited me to go back there with him. I ran into the house immediately and announced to Dad that I was going to Canada. My father, who had overheard most of the conversation, wasn't surprised.

When we arrived at Harrison, it was even more beautiful than Mel had described it, with one glaring exception. There actually were no horses. I let it pass and didn't complain.

The apartment was a tiny room with two beds separated by a curtain. At one end was a window which opened all the way to the ceiling, giving the illusion of open space. The kitchen was sandwiched in a hallway between the bedroom and bathroom. The place was spotlessly clean and quite comfortable. Mel's friend was at work when we arrived, and wouldn't be home until late evening. We opened an expensive bottle of rose wine, and toasted the beginning of our vacation.

I'm not sure if it was the wine or the situation, but soon I realized that I was in an extremely good mood and very happy to be with Mel. We decided to go over and lie down on the bed, and his skillful fingers began to pull up my blouse and unsnap my jeans as they had done so many times. This time I felt differently about it. After all the bad experiences with men at college and the distasteful encounter with the lonely old man, being with someone who really cared about me was like a breath of fresh air. I pulled him closer and let him finish taking off my clothes. For once, I really felt like making love to him.

"What happened to you, Janet? You've never been this horny before," he exclaimed, completely ruining the romantic moment.

"Oh, my God, why did he have to use that word?" I thought to myself. He seemed to have a knack for saying exactly the wrong thing at the wrong time.

A moment of embarrassment passed quickly and my feelings of warmth and desire returned. I kissed him deeply, overcome by a feeling I'd never felt before. He responded with energy and strength.

Chapter Seven

After about an hour we recovered our senses enough to realize where we were, and began to think about getting up. "You're a perfect fit," he whispered softly to me, and I thought that he was right.

The resort at Harrison was situated on the edge of a crystal-clear lake almost totally surrounded by pristine, snow-covered mountains. The only way back into the mountains was by plane. The Hot Springs gurgled naturally up from the rocks at one end of the lake and were thought to have medicinal qualities, despite their sulfurous, murky appearance. I found it amusing that rich people came from all over the world just to sit in them.

The town's main street was lined with European restaurants: French, German, Bavarian, and Swiss. The owner of the Bavarian restaurant held court each afternoon and played a graceful silver horn. The weather was clear and hot, so we swam every afternoon, then returned to the apartment for an afternoon nap, and later a walk downtown to eat.

Our constant lovemaking at night made Mel's roommate miserable, but somehow he endured. I gained the impression that my moving in had not been part of his plan. He still made every effort to make us feel welcome.

On one particularly hot afternoon, we packed a picnic lunch and went out with the Frenchman and his date. We hiked up a steep rock face which we reached from a park east of town. After a treacherous climb straight up, we reached a fast-flowing creek with carved rock pools, natural Jacuzzis with cascading waterfalls. It was like the steep waterfalls of Hawaii, except the water was ice-cold. We sat in the pools under the water and laughed like children. Later we climbed out onto the rocks to sunbathe. I recall gazing down at the lake, awed by its impressive beauty. How funny that life can change so quickly. I felt it was wonderful that Mel and I were so suddenly and unexpectedly brought together, and awed that fate had brought us away from our mundane existence to this fantastic place.

The longer Mel and I stayed at Harrison, the more attached we became to one another. We walked down the sidewalk with arms intertwined and sat on the same side of the table in restaurants, kissing openly. After a few weeks we called our parents to let them know we would not be coming home as soon as planned.

When our roommate's open-ended offer for spending money finally ran out, Mel went to work illegally in the restaurant as a busboy. He hated it and it wasn't long before he was let go. Somewhere along the line someone had discovered that he'd violated Canada's strict labor laws by working without a visa. Soon after, they discovered he'd tried to get a job through his uncle. He was picked up by local police and taken to a nearby town for questioning, then sent on from there to another town. When it became apparent to me that he was going to be detained for some time, I drove to Bellingham to wait. I was unable to contact him for about a month. By the time he was finally released, it was time for me to return to college, so I went to Seattle to pick up my things, then moved back to my apartment in Bellingham, where we finally reunited after about six weeks.

Mel returned to Seattle to work for his father. I registered for classes with much the same lack of enthusiasm and direction as before, vaguely wondering where English and Speech classes could possibly lead me. Before I had much chance to get started, Mel came to Bellingham. He had hitchhiked up the freeway with nothing but a large army overcoat. In it he had wrapped a gift.

"Here," he announced unceremoniously, stretching his long arm toward me. Clenched tightly in his fist was a scrawny, terrified Siamese kitten which couldn't possibly have been more than five weeks old. Its fur was sticking straight up, and its claws clung desperately to whatever it touched.

"I had to ball him up in my coat and throw him over the fence to get off the freeway," Mel said.

The terrorized kitten hid for the next four or five days underneath the stove, and the only way I could show him to anyone was by pulling out the drawer where he sometimes slept inside a kettle. The bed in my apartment was saggy and creaky, and sounds carried right through the walls in the old building. We made love in spite of the noise. Afterwards, Mel held me tightly as though he hadn't seen me for years.

"I can't do anything without you, baby," he whispered as he stroked my hair. "I don't want to be apart from you anymore."

Chapter Seven

"What do you think we should do?" I asked.

After considering options, I decided to drop out of college. I had already registered for fall quarter, and not all of the tuition was refundable, but I really wasn't happy there anyway. I knew my father would not be overjoyed at my plans to quit school, but I promised myself I would do something worthwhile after we got settled.

Mel went home to Seattle long enough to get a truck running. We packed up our things in Bellingham and moved to Seattle. He would work for his father in the maritime district of Ballard.

It rained the day we left and the truck got stuck in the yard. My roommate and I both fell on our stomachs in the mud trying to push it. By the time we finally got it free, there was a gaping hole in the lawn and everyone was soaking wet and covered with mud. But Mel and I were on our way, with the new kitten we named Tigger.

Shortly after arriving in Seattle, we rented part of a duplex in a modest neighborhood and proceeded to set up house. Neither of us had any furniture, but it didn't matter to us. We had dishes, a record player, a mattress, and each other. Who could ask for more?

Making love had become our favorite pastime, taking precedence over all other activities. The bed was upstairs, and we noticed that whenever we were in bed, the woman next door started sliding furniture noisily around her upstairs. It didn't occur to me that she might be able to hear us. Instead, we decided she was crazy, and watched her closely for other signs of eccentric behavior.

To decorate our bedroom we took Mel's old Army parachute and tacked it up over the bed. Tigger ran up inside the parachute, sending thumbtacks ricocheting about the room. Some of them ended up in our blankets, others we found with our bare feet in the dark.

I enrolled in a Medical Secretary course at a business college, which my father paid for, but only after he extracted a promise that I would pay him back if I didn't finish. I took the promise seriously, as the tuition had cost him over a thousand dollars. The course was supposed to take about nine months to complete and seemed a much more reasonable and direct route to getting an education than a four-year college.

So for the next few months we existed in our tiny, unfurnished home like children playing house. I dutifully attended business school, which was not as easy as I had anticipated. The classes lasted a full eight hours each day, and learning the skills required in order to finish the course was a time-consuming, lengthy process demanding infinite patience and hard work. The course included Business Machines, Medical Terminology and Transcription, Accounting (which I found particularly difficult), Speedwriting, and Typing. In order to complete the typing class, we were required to produce 100 perfect examples of statistical typing, 100 perfect business letters, and achieve a typing speed of 65 words per minute with three or fewer errors.

Mel went to work for his father as assistant manager of their shop, a thriving boat-propeller sales and repair business. Although we were much busier than I had anticipated, our first year together was blissful and fulfilling.

After we began living together, the rest of the world seemed to fall away. Mel became all-important to me, and most of my thoughts and energy were directed toward making him happy. We stayed in close touch by phone during the day, and at night we gratefully fell together, attempting to get closer to each other than humanly possible.

It was a late autumn evening and we were lying in bed together. Mel was on top of me, still inside me, and he said, "Don't move ... I want to stay just like this."

"Mel," I suggested impulsively, "why don't we get married?" I thought this would symbolically cement us together.

He didn't hesitate before he answered, "Let's start making plans." He held me close.

Later I called home to tell my parents the news, and my father answered the phone. When I made the announcement, he answered by clearing his throat and saying, "Uh, gee, Janet, I like Mel and everything, but I don't see why you need to get married. You're already living together and you've got everything else you need." I remember my mom saying that she thought it was just wonderful, but she claims now that she said she was horrified. Most of our friends were also shocked, and some told us we were crazy. I was still just

Chapter Seven

nineteen, and Mel was only twenty-two. We really couldn't have cared less what anyone else thought; we were hopelessly, completely in love.

I had a terrible time finding a white dress in November. We didn't want to spend very much money just to get married, so I was looking in small shops near home, which catered mostly to old widows. I found a black dress that fit pretty well, but when I told the ladies in the shop what it was for, they refused to sell it to me. "You can't get married in black!" they admonished, horrified that anyone could have such a lack of regard for tradition.

I finally ended up with pants made of ivory-colored crushed velvet, and a satin blouse. Mel hated my choice. He said he didn't like clothes made out of "that shiny stuff," but I was sick of shopping and wore the outfit anyway.

The wedding took place on December 10, 1971, in the county courthouse, the same building that housed the city jail. We were married by a traffic judge who remembered Mel for all his tickets.

Mel hadn't calmed down much since high school, and earned the dubious distinction of being the first person in Washington to be convicted under the new "habitual traffic offenders" law. He had received more than nineteen tickets in his driving career. His license was suspended for two years after enactment of the law, but he took chances and drove often anyway. It was uncomfortable to be in such close quarters with the authoritative figure who had sent Mel to jail more than once. He scowled as he read the wedding vows in the same tone of voice he used in court.

The ceremony was hasty and unromantic, with only my sister Marie and Mel's older brother as witnesses. I thought we should remain in the little room for a moment afterwards to let what we had just done soak in, but everyone took off down the hall and left me standing there alone.

"I'm married now," I announced to myself, as I hurried to catch up with the retreating wedding party.

When we got home we had a party. Our friends sat around on the floor and we served potato chips and beer. Our favorite wedding gift was an Elton John record, and the most practical gift was a set of dishes from Mel's parents.

Mel had been spoiled before we were married and was used to eating steak, and strawberries with real whipped cream. He hated all vegetables except lettuce and corn, and particularly despised broccoli. "If I ever smell broccoli cooking," he warned, "I'll leave and not come back until it's gone." He forbade me to keep onions and garlic in the house, but I succeeded in tricking him occasionally by using onion powder and garlic salt.

Another tradition of his I had difficulty upholding was making the morning pancakes he loved. I was not a morning person to begin with and was sleepy and uncoordinated at first rise, and all thumbs in the kitchen. The pancakes were tricky and there were many discouraging failures. Sometimes they were too runny, other times too thick. Mel repeatedly showed me just how the batter should look after the milk was added, but I could only get them perfect part of the time. When the batter was too thin, the pancakes stuck to the pan and spatula, creating a sticky, gooey mess that splattered and caked to the top of the stove. This inevitably made me grumpy and irritated, but I still tried, anxious to please my husband and convinced that cooking his breakfast was my wifely duty.

My father-in-law Robert—I called him Uncle Bob—was an easygoing, kind-hearted person and I liked him very much. When Mel was little, he worked as a redwood logger in Northern California. The work was difficult and the mortality rate extremely high. He once told us of a logger who was sitting next to a fallen stump eating his lunch, when the stump tipped over and crushed him to death. The constant threat of serious injury or death had been so hard on him that he became very ill and eventually lost half of his stomach to ulcers. They moved to the Seattle area when Mel was about ten years old and settled in a heavily forested area about an hour from the city. He then started a boat-propeller repair business with one old typewriter and a metal grinder. He was so sick and weak when he started that he carried the propellers around the shop in a shopping cart.

Their first home was on a lake, and Mel and his brother and sister learned to water-ski at a very early age. Mel's passion for water-skiing stayed with him as an adult, along with his passion for any sport involving speed.

As soon as the boys were ready for grade school, their parents bought them motorbikes so they wouldn't have to ride the bus. The school protested, claiming motorbikes weren't safe for boys that young. Of course, they didn't want the motorbikes to start a trend with other students. Mel's parents battled the school and won.

Uncle Bob met Mel's mother Norma while he was serving in the U.S. Air Force Search and Rescue Division. A native of India, she was attending a British boarding school near his station in Gaya. They met at a lake called Naini Tal while he was on leave. He courted her for nearly a year before they married and returned to the United States.

Norma had not learned any domestic skills when she was young. As Uncle Bob claimed, "she couldn't even boil water" at first. The adjustment was hard for her in the beginning, but by the time I met her, she had a beautifully equipped kitchen and was adept at producing American food and wonderful, tongue-searing Indian dishes.

At first Norma appeared rather plain to me. She wore glasses and always had her hair pulled primly into a bun. She dressed in simple skirts and blouses in accordance with her religion. When she let her hair down at night, however, she was strikingly beautiful. She had high cheekbones, blue eyes, and long black hair that hung in curls all the way down her back. She loved her children and defended them fiercely whenever necessary. Generally, she was strict and conservative in her approach to motherhood. By contrast, Mel's father was lenient and soft-hearted. Although they were so different, I never saw them have a serious fight in all the time I knew them.

Norma had a very direct way of speaking, which I was not used to, and I usually interpreted what she said as criticism. One day as we sat at the table drinking tea, she asked, "Why do you girls take all your eyebrows off and put that blue stuff on your face?" It was probably an honest question, but at the time I didn't see it that way.

I also got the feeling she didn't think I was a very good housekeeper. I loved pets and always let my animals in the house. Our pets were spoiled and allowed to sleep on the couch or bed, which she thought was unsanitary.

Underneath her reserved exterior, Norma was a kind, generous person and accepted me into their family like one of her own. We had one thing in common: we both loved Mel.

Bob's business flourished and grew into a successful corporation with about twenty-five employees, and by the time Mel was twenty-four he was managing the shop. The bulk of the work centered around repairing damaged propellers, but they sold new ones as well. Bob apparently had been in the right place at the right time, because they had enough business to keep Mel working overtime until nine or ten o'clock some evenings.

Mel worked primarily at the counter, waiting on customers who were frequently lined up all the way to the door. It was demanding work, but suited Mel's personality well. The customers seemed to like him and he was very knowledgeable about the business. Once in awhile his temper got out of hand when he was dealing with an unreasonable complaint, but generally he was very good with people. The shop was noisy and gritty and smelled like ground metal, but we spent a lot of time there and I soon got used to it. Mel liked to have me there when he worked in the evenings, and I always enjoyed being with him, even if it was just to watch him work.

Bob and Norma belonged to a very devout Christian sect called Workers for the Truth. On Wednesdays and Sundays, they had "meeting" in their home, and occasionally I attended.

I hadn't attended church much as a child, except for Jehovah's Witness meetings with Grammie and Grandpa Hafer. I found it interesting, and it was an effective way to please Mel's parents, something I wanted very much. I made a supreme effort to fit in, by putting on a skirt and not wearing much makeup, but my efforts to appear pious like the other women were futile.

Most of the people attending were quite old, and virtually all of the women wore skirts below the knee, flat black shoes, and their hair in buns. We perched uncomfortably

Chapter Seven

on folding chairs in little rows, clutching bibles and handkerchiefs in our laps. The meetings were long and solemn, and I was usually relieved when they were over. I tried not to show it.

Mel and I had now been married for almost a year. It was Wednesday night and I had promised Bob and Norma I would come to meeting. They had hoped that Mel would also attend, but instead he stayed home with the excuse that he had to help his best friend work on a car.

After the usual round of endless introductions, we all went to the living room to sit down. My pantyhose were sagging in the crotch, and they felt itchy. I was wearing a brown wool skirt, and although I considered it fairly conservative, it suddenly began to seem too short.

I glanced around the room at the others, who sat silently meditating on the teachings of the Lord, and realized they were unaware of my restlessness. A vague sense of guilt distracted me even further. There was no sound in the room except for the occasional rustling of pages. The air had become permeated with the smell of the old folks: a stale, musty odor, like a room that has been closed up for too long.

It was when I was very young that I noticed the peculiar smell of old age. When I was about eight years old, the husband of an elderly woman next door died suddenly. The woman was so overcome by grief and loneliness that she paid me fifty cents to come sleep in her house at night. I slept upstairs in the bedroom next to hers. The house felt deserted, with remnants of past life preserved in clusters of photographs and dusty keepsakes. During the night her tortured sobs echoed through the eerie, empty silence. In the morning she fixed me a dreary bowl of cereal and some dry toast which I dutifully ate before collecting my money and fleeing for home. Staying with her disturbed me a great deal, and after awhile my mother said I didn't have to go there anymore. After trying to fulfill our neighborly responsibility, we ultimately had to leave the poor old woman wallowing in grief.

I dreaded becoming old, afraid of what life would bring me toward the end. Perhaps I would be the last one left alive of all my friends? My hand involuntarily touched my face as I tried to visualize my skin, papery and thin, my hair white and brittle. Would I cut my hair short and wear it in tight little curls, or keep it long and tie it in a bun?

The lady next to me blew her nose and I snapped back to reality. I wondered what Mel was doing. Suddenly I couldn't wait to get home and put on some jeans. I discreetly checked my watch; it was still a half-hour from the meeting's end.

Norma had given me a nice bible, and I had read part of it without understanding a single word. However, I had a feeling there was something there to learn if one wanted to badly enough.

"There is no life unless all of the seed is planted," the wrinkly, white-haired man droned. The phrase seemed to come up often, and I realized it separated me from the rest of the people at the meeting. I wasn't willing to make their kind of total commitment to God. Sometimes I wasn't even sure I believed in "him." I suspected this was why Mel had also stopped going to meeting.

Certain passages kept surfacing in the presentation: "Lay not up for yourselves treasures on earth, where moth and dust doth corrupt, and where thieves break through and steal: For where your treasure is, there will your heart be also. . . . He that loveth his life shall lose it; and he that hateth his life in this world shall keep it unto life eternal."

What about other people? I questioned silently. Didn't God want one to love other people? Was it possible to love God more than one's husband? I didn't understand. And what about all the fancy stuff in Bob and Norma's house? What about the brand-new cars in the driveway? What about the twenty-dollars-a-yard wallpaper on their walls?

Well, count me out, I thought to myself. I love my life in this world. I wondered what God might have planned for me.

EIGHT

In Seattle the month of February is unbearably gloomy. Gray clouds hang low over the city, bleaching all color from the landscape. Water pours incessantly from rooftops and forms small creeks and rivers that erode the soil. Homes built too close to the beach slide off foundations and into Puget Sound. People stay inside and abandon outdoor exercise programs. Instead, they drink coffee and watch soap operas.

From the streets the city appears to sleep, with the only signs of life being endless processions of dirty cars and stinking buses. Residents have a peculiar habit of driving fast when visibility is poor, and this can create nasty pileups on freeways and hours of downtime from blockages. Cars are forced to take alternate routes that then jam up with irritated commuters.

We worked hard during the first year of our marriage, and the adjustment was difficult, particularly for the first few months. Mel was busy at the shop and I struggled through business school and wished I'd never started it. Each morning I waited for the bus in the rain, joining the miserable mob of wet commuters and staring with them dismally out foggy windows as we inched toward downtown. With household duties and eight hours of school a day, I sometimes didn't have time to shower before leaving the house. I was determined, however, to stick it out because of the deal I'd made with my father.

Desperate to escape the monotony of the rain and the nine-to-five grind of everyday existence, Mel and I decided to take a trip east of the mountains to Dad's cabin. We knew that the road conditions over the pass would be treacherous that time of year, and then we'd face deep snow and sub-zero temperatures in Eastern Washington. When my father realized that we were bent on going despite the weather, he suggested that we take his British sedan. The only vehicle we owned was the old Chevy van, which had proved itself unreliable on long trips. We eagerly accepted the offer, arranged for a few days off from work and school, and packed to go.

It was snowing on the pass as we traveled toward the ski areas, but the roads had been sanded and were not slick. The skies were dark and somber, but we proceeded without difficulty. It was cozy and warm in the car, and I rode alongside Mel with my hand resting on his leg. I gazed down at my ring finger adorned with two white-gold bands and a small but beautiful diamond. The gesture of the rings made me feel loved and cherished; our marriage had given me a sense of peace and belonging I had never before experienced. I felt that no matter what else I might choose to do with my life, this decision had been the most important. We had made a promise to each other to stay together, a vow we would keep forever.

The cabin was normally about five hours away from Seattle, but because of the weather the drive was much longer. A few times I leaned over to rest my head in Mel's lap, forgetting that we were in a car with bucket seats. In spite of its quirks, the old van was more comfortable. Occasionally I turned toward the backseat to check Tigger, who was riding safely in his cat carrier. At first he'd protested, but now was sleeping quietly.

It was midafternoon by the time we arrived in Tonasket, the last small town before the cabin. We stopped for gas, anxious to get out and stretch our legs. It was much colder east of the mountains, but the clouds were high and occasionally the sun broke through. Frost rose from our breath as we paid for the gas, returned to the car, and drove the last nine miles of paved highway. Finally, we turned onto a side road to Aeneus Valley, passed several small lakes and one large ranch, then turned left off the gravel road to a rocky, dirt-farming lane.

From the lane we could see the airfield covered with

Chapter Eight

snow. It was difficult to tell the depth of snow, but we decided to drive fast and make a run for it. We traveled about two car-lengths before the tires broke through the thick crust and we stopped like a beached whale, up to the windows in the snow and tipped to one side. We laughed and managed to get the doors open enough to get out. We let the kitten out of his box and set him down in one of the deep holes left by our feet. He bristled his fur like a porcupine and made it clear he didn't want to play in the snow.

Efforts to dig the car out were futile so we decided to leave it until morning. The cabin was visible, a short hike away. Without much difficulty we hiked up the hill and found a toboggan, which we used to haul our things up to the cabin. We took two trips through hip-deep snow and by the time we were finished, it was late afternoon.

As the sun dropped, so did the temperature. By four in the afternoon, the thermometer outside the kitchen window read ten degrees. Mel started a fire in the woodstove while I unpacked the things we needed for the evening. The double sleeping bags that usually served as covers for the bed had been hung from the rafters for the winter, so I got them down. While searching for more blankets, I came across a nest of mice in the dresser, all snuggled up in some of the filling from the couch. The baby mice didn't have any fur; they were pink, and smaller than my finger. I went to the other room and got a piece of cheese for the parents, which I placed near the nest before shutting the drawer. Overall, the mice were destructive and dirty inside the cabin; they left droppings in the cupboards and destroyed the furniture, but I did not believe in killing baby animals.

In order to preserve the rustic atmosphere of the cabin, Dad had chosen not to install electricity. Flickering kerosene lanterns and small candles provided us with our only light. Going to the bathroom required a cool trip outside or to the outhouse, so it was always delayed as long as possible. There was cold running water and a sink, but the pipes were frozen solid. We had anticipated this and brought extra water, but we knew we could melt snow if necessary. We sat in front of the wood stove and talked, sometimes just listening to the fire crackle in the silence. When it was time for bed, we were forced to leave the warmth of the fire and retire to the unheated sleeping porch. We huddled together for warmth underneath the icy blankets and Mel rubbed his feet together, a habit he'd had since childhood.

In the morning we awoke to extreme cold, the kind that makes you never want to get out of bed. The glasses of water we'd brought to bed were frozen on the window sills, and our breath rose like thick smoke from the covers. I wasn't looking forward to getting up, but I had to pee, and so did Mel. We reached for the suitcase at the end of the bed, and pulled on our long underwear and shirts while still under the covers. The long underwear clung to the flannel lining of the sleeping bags and made dressing difficult. Finally, I threw back the cumbersome covers and leaped for my jeans.

"Goddamn, it's cold!" Mel exclaimed as he buttoned his wool shirt and pulled on a navy stocking hat. His nose had already become red from breathing the freezing air. The fire had gone out during the night, so we started a new one and stood anxiously in front of the stove until the wood caught.

"You wanna try and go fishing today?" I asked eagerly.

"Maybe. We'll see." Mel answered. "We'll have to figure out how to get down there. We could take the toboggan, I guess. I'm starved. Let's make some breakfast."

We laid out stiff, partially frozen strips of bacon and watched them sizzle and curl on the black wrought-iron griddle. Then we added pancakes and eggs and ate until we were stuffed. After breakfast we hauled in snow to melt on the stove for the dirty dishes. The sun came out and brought the temperature up to about ten degrees. Within a few hours the fire was roaring and it was so hot in the cabin that we were able to remove some clothes. That afternoon we played in the snow and stomped down a toboggan trail that zigzagged around some large rocks and a few trees. Mel soon became bored with the traditional form of sledding, lying down on the toboggan, and stood up instead, holding the steering rope in one hand and using his other arm for balance. I watched him nervously from the top of the hill as he dodged the trees and boulders, barely missing

Chapter Eight

them. When we returned to the cabin, Tigger had caught his very first mouse, a specimen nearly as large as himself. We praised him and I went in to check on the mice in the drawer. Most of the babies appeared to have died, perhaps as a result of having been disturbed the day before, so I quietly shut the drawer and did not bother them again.

The following day we walked down to the neighbor's ranch to ask them for help in getting the car unstuck. They gave us a ride back and pulled the car out with a farm truck, shaking their heads in disbelief that anyone would have tried something so impulsive and ill-advised.

Mel had never seen Swan Lake, so we decided to take an afternoon drive so that I could show him where the cabin had once been. I hadn't been there for several years, but was sure I knew the way. We found the road easily and followed it for several miles. At each turn I was positive the lake would come into view, but each time I was proved wrong. The snow seemed to make everything look the same. The higher we went, the worse the roads became, and we were in danger of getting stuck again, this time much farther from civilization. I was so positive we were close to the lake that I convinced Mel to get out and walk. Finally, after several more corners, we gave up, returned to the car, and admitted defeat. Afterwards I was forced to suffer much teasing and humiliation about my sense of direction, and the incident was permanently recorded in the cabin's logbook.

In the spring we moved to another tiny rental home, a small white cottage right on a lake near our parents' homes. It had a dock for swimming, and the front porch was built right over the water. It was a beautiful location when compared with the drab neighborhood we'd left.

The day we moved, Mel just spread out a blanket on the floor and piled into it the contents of the kitchen, bathroom, and bedroom. He took it to the new house and deposited it in a jumbled heap in the middle of the floor. I cried as I sorted out the mess, because I always hated to move.

It was a long, difficult and crazy summer. My birth control pills made me so sick that I threw up every day as soon as I got off the bus. Business school was horrible. In order to graduate I was required to complete 100 perfect business letters, type 99 statistical examples centered on pages within a fraction of an inch, and pass 10 timed typing tests at 60 words per minute, with fewer than three errors. I did not comprehend the accounting class and repeatedly flunked the tests. Then, when I returned home from a grueling day at school, it was to a rowdy party of people throwing each other off the dock into the lake.

Mel was not totally insensitive to my struggle, however, and did try to cheer me up whenever he could. He knew how much I loved foreign cars and bought an old MGB that he completely rebuilt. He repainted it baby-blue, my favorite color, and put in a plush new interior. Once in awhile he picked me up from school, and one day, as I jumped into the car nearly in tears, he handed me a large white box. I opened it to find a delicate, full-length Mexican wedding dress, with a slender fitted waist and a high lace collar. It was made of sheer white cotton. I wore it often all summer and always felt like a princess in it.

About this time I decided that I would really like to have a baby, perhaps because some other girls at school had had babies with their boyfriends. I thought it was romantic, and deep down I hoped it would help settle our life a little. Mel wasn't nuts about the idea and said he wasn't sure he was ready. I stopped taking my birth control pills anyway, and every month I hopefully awaited the signs of pregnancy. The months passed by without a baby, and I told myself to be patient, that it would happen when it was time.

We lost our interest in the lakefront cottage after a tomcat came in through an open window and sprayed the wall and bookshelf. The walls of the cottage were damp and the odor lingered. It seemed to grow stronger when the doors were closed. It made the place barely inhabitable, and we finally both agreed it was time to move.

The next house we found was much larger, with a basement and fenced backyard. By this time I was twenty and had finally graduated from business school. I went to work for a temporary secretarial service so that Mel and I would have time to be together at home and to travel whenever we got the urge.

Chapter Eight

Mel, who was now twenty-three, had filled out and become strong and muscular. He had lost all the gawkiness of his teenage years and I had to admit that he'd become very good-looking. He was cocky, aggressive, and self-assured, and that year he even managed to overcome his childhood fear of dentists, agreeing to have his teeth straightened.

After working as a temp for about six months, I was offered a very good part-time job with an insurance company on the top floor of a downtown office building. The job was high-pressure and demanding, with heavy typing and perfection required in finished documents. Before I had time to settle in, however, everyone in the office was transferred to Portland. I was let go. After this discouraging experience I accepted a job as a hostess in a downtown seafood restaurant. The job ill-suited my temperament; I had no training or experience, and it made me nervous. Meanwhile, it also made Mel very jealous, as I was required to stay late and stand outside the bar on Friday nights to greet customers. Eventually I quit the job in order to keep peace.

Like all other married couples, we had occasional fights, but never anything serious, that is, until an incident that shattered my trust and very nearly ruined our marriage. We'd been married for three years when it all happened. All in all, it stands out as one of my most traumatic and unpleasant memories.

The trouble began when Mel and I decided to go on separate weekend vacations, something we rarely did. It wasn't my idea, but I went along with his plans willingly.

Through Mel's work we became acquainted with a young couple who had far too many children: four young rowdy boys, to be exact. Needless to say, they had been having a hard time raising the out-of-control youngsters, and their marriage was on the rocks. The mother of the boys was a cheap-looking, unintelligent woman named Jenny. She was desperate to get away from her family and proposed that she and I take off, without our husbands, to spend the weekend at the ocean. She said her stepfather had a place where we could stay, a bachelor apartment furnished with X-rated movies for entertainment. I didn't know her very well, because we had never had time to carry on a normal conversation. All she seemed to do was scream at the top of her lungs. I felt sorry for her and agreed to go. Mel planned to go to Lake Chelan to water-ski with Jenny's husband, who owned a very flashy ski boat with jet engines.

We left town on Friday night, with plans to stop at a small nightclub where Jenny's mom was a singer. The crowd consisted of a small group of men and women in their fifties and sixties who were totally looped and who had gathered around the piano to sing. Most of them needed to lean on the piano in order to stand. Jenny drank fast, switching types of alcohol each time she ordered. We stayed at the bar until quite late, and I was enormously relieved by the time we left.

When Jenny invited me to stay at a place by the ocean, I assumed she meant near the water. When we reached our destination, it was a rank smelling, sleazy two-room apartment located in a small town about twenty miles from the beach. As soon as we got inside, Jenny started throwing up, and she didn't stop retching until the next morning. She was absolutely no company, and I was very sorry I'd come.

I will never, in my entire life, forget the eggs she cooked the next day for breakfast. They were scrambled eggs to which she added Worcestershire sauce and half a jar of imitation bacon bits. They had a texture like cottage cheese and looked like coffee grounds. After listening to her retch all night, then tasting the eggs, I became a little sick myself.

The X-rated movies must have been the filthiest films available on the black market. They were completely unedited pornography, with no talking and no plot, just graphic, repetitive sex acts filmed from far away or extremely close. I found the extreme closeups particularly offensive.

I had never missed Mel as much as I did that weekend. I ached with regret at the decision to spend the weekend without him and longed somehow to bridge the distance between us instantly. I at least wanted to hear his voice on the phone, but he was camping. There was no way to reach him, no way to make the time go faster, and every minute seemed like an hour.

It took Jenny all that day and evening to recover from

Chapter Eight

her hangover. She was even too sick to go see the ocean. Early Sunday morning I strongly suggested we head for home.

In the meantime, Mel was having the time of his life. It had been cold and cloudy on the coast, but east of the mountains it was clear and hot. Lake Chelan was a hangout for young people, and the state park was packed with boats and water-skiers.

While Mel and Jenny's husband were skiing, they met a couple from Seattle, Tom and Lana. When I got back to Mel, Lana was the only one he seemed to talk about. She turned out to be the best water-skier he had ever seen. I didn't think too much of it, until the day I met her and Tom.

They lived near us and invited us to Lake Washington to go water-skiing. Lana was mouthy and aggressive, and her boyfriend was an unattractive wimp with limp hair, white legs, and a skinny chest. Lana treated him like a pesky insect, brushing him off and swatting him away with no regard for his feelings. He, in turn, put up with her behavior, which I thought was almost worse.

We were introduced, and then prepared to load the boat to go skiing. Their ski boat was tied to a dock at the lakeshore.

Lana was my opposite in many ways. Physically, she was petite instead of tall; her body was compact, her skin fair, and she had voluptuous breasts that she kept generously exposed by unzipping her wetsuit jacket. Her hair was white (bleached, I found out later) and she wore little makeup except for lipstick: a perfect, glossy red paint.

From the very first, I felt completely out of control of the situation. She literally dominated everyone and everything. After I stepped into the ski boat, she pretended to have a cramp in her leg and jumped into Mel's arms. She rubbed her breasts on his bare chest as her boyfriend looked the other way, pretending not to notice. She was an amazing water-skier, with unlimited stamina, and she skied with the confidence of one who had skied all her life. I, of course, had only been on water skis once before and fell constantly. She encouraged me and attempted to teach me, but I didn't like or trust her.

She talked constantly. Mel seemed captivated by her incessant chatter, and seemed to forget he was married whenever she was present. One evening we planned to ride our bikes downtown to see a movie. It was Lana's idea. She and Mel had the fastest bikes and raced far ahead, leaving her seemingly helpless boyfriend and me lagging far behind. She thought it was very funny and enjoyed having Mel to herself. By the time we caught up with them at the theater I was pouring sweat, and furious. I was out of breath, and sweating too hard to be out in public, especially downtown at a nice theater. It had been a very hot afternoon and I was unaccustomed to such strenuous exercise. Unspeakably angry, embarrassed, and hurt, I excused myself and said I was going home. She just continued to flirt away with my husband, looking sunny and gorgeous. He was having the time of his life.

After Mel met Lana, a damp chill settled into our marriage, and bit by bit we lost our ability to get along. I tried every strategy I could think of to renew his interest in me, but nothing seemed to help. He began to stay at work, or with friends, instead of coming home for dinner. He made excuses to stay out late, and I was forced to go to bed alone. I read self-help books to control my jealousy. I tried to be open-minded and not suspicious, but the more I practiced trust, the less often Mel came home. It finally got so bad that by the time we finally did see each other, I was in tears. He would say he didn't like coming home because I was never happy. Angrily, desperately, I pointed out to him that we had been unable to get along ever since he'd met Lana. To this there was no reply, only silence.

Then, as if things weren't bad enough, he announced that we were going to Lake Chelan for the weekend with friends, among them Tom and Lana. As a matter of fact, we were even to ride in the same car with them.

I was at a total loss for solutions. I knew that he would go, whether I went or not, so I decided to go, planning to keep myself between them if at all possible.

In the car on the way over, she sat turned toward the backseat, batting her eyelashes at Mel and jabbering constantly. I hated her fluffy white hair and her glossy red lips,

Chapter Eight

hated her bubbly cheerfulness as she gleefully attempted to steal my husband, right before my eyes.

We had brought along sleeping bags and were camping by the lake. At the bonfire, she hovered close to Mel, never running out of senseless conversation. It was nearly impossible to get a word in edgewise.

"Are you talking to Mel, or just at him?" I finally managed to squeeze in. She glanced at me briefly and continued. Just listening to her talk was exhausting. I was becoming very, very angry at Mel and the way he was treating me. However, we were in the company of several other people, and I was reluctant to cause a scene. Finally, I left them at the campfire, and went to bed alone.

The next morning I prepared to go water-skiing, determined not to let her show me up. I got up on one ski and skied around the lake, making sharp turns, crossing the wake and not falling. Lana jumped up and down, squealed congratulations and hugged me. Mel didn't even seem to notice.

Later that afternoon Mel and Lana, in the ski boat, failed to return to camp. Nobody seemed worried. But as time wore on, suspicions surfaced. I realized I was not the only person at the camp who knew something was going on. Some speculated they had run out of gas. Then someone blurted out loudly, "Oh, they're out there screwing, anybody could figure that out." I felt sick and numb all over. They were talking about my husband.

About three hours later, they returned to the camp, claiming that, indeed, they had run out of gas.

If I had had one of our cars that weekend, I would have been gone by the time the boat returned. Instead, I was forced to stay for the ride home. It was similar to the ride over, but worse. Mel continued to deny any wrongdoing, and I was treated as though I had a jealousy problem. Mel and I were not speaking by the time we got home.

The day after, I was furiously scrubbing the bathroom, something I always did when when I was extremely upset. Mel had left earlier, saying he was going to the shop. Lana's boyfriend called and sounded as upset as I had been. He seemed frantic. He had finally confronted Lana and was calling to inform me that my suspicions were correct. Mel and Lana had been sleeping together all summer, every time they got the chance. I was shocked and nauseated to hear it confirmed by him, but not really surprised. I already knew Mel hadn't been sleeping with me. It made sense.

Then, while I was standing there with the phone dangling from my hand, in walked Mel. We had a fight unlike any fight we had ever had. He was guilty and had nothing to say for himself. I kicked him out of the house and told him never to come back, then realized he was going to drive off in our only truck, which I needed for work the next morning. I was hysterically angry and deeply hurt. There was a heavy antique machete hanging above the fireplace. In a frenzy I grabbed it and was going to puncture the tires so he couldn't take the truck.

"Ah, Janet, you could never hurt these tires with that thing," he scoffed as I approached the truck.

"Just get out of here!" I screamed wildly, and he drove off. Months later he confessed, "God, I was sure glad you didn't pop those tires."

I returned to the house in an uncontrollable rage. My husband was gone, and my marriage had been ruined right before my eyes, willfully and deliberately, by some bitch who had popped out of nowhere while I had my back turned. I had helplessly watched the destruction, powerless and unable to stop it. The person I loved and trusted most in the world had been an eager participant in the ruination of our promise to each other. To him, it had meant nothing.

I began to throw the machete repeatedly at the closet door with all my strength, hoping to make it stick in the wall. Instead, it kept flipping around and deflecting, adding to my frustration. After knocking a large hole in the plaster, I gave up and lay down on the bed to cry.

NINE

My world was shattered. I thought about all the times Mel had come home late and I had trusted him. I wondered what she did for him that I didn't. The painful images of the two of them in bed, in the car, even at the grocery store, caused my eyes to flood with bitter tears. There was nowhere to direct my anger; it seethed. I felt I would explode if I didn't find a way to release it.

We didn't live together again for two or three months. I told Mel that I didn't want to see him, and I'm not even sure where he stayed while we were apart. Angry and in tears I called my mom and sisters and explained that we had split up, that Mel had been seeing a girlfriend all summer. Mel and I attempted to talk to each other over the phone one or two times, but just briefly. My feelings toward him had changed, perhaps forever.

I knew that I was facing an important decision, one that would probably affect me for the rest of my life. At the beginning I had been positive that Mel loved me. Now I was not so sure. My disillusionment and anger blinded me toward my own feelings for him, and I was caught, suspended, driven to inaction by my own confused emotions.

Desperately, painfully, I searched my mind for a reason for his infidelity. Had I driven him away by acting unhappy, or had his behavior caused me to be unhappy? Something told me that it was not my fault.

Who had made the first step? Lana. But why had Mel been so willing to stray, and why had it continued for so long? There were so many questions that I couldn't find any answers. I decided to bury my intolerable doubts with work.

About two months had gone by when I received a phone call from my father-in-law. He told me that Mel was at his house and that he wanted to come home. I answered that I wasn't sure I wanted him; then I fell silent, an ache in my throat making it difficult to speak. He pleaded with me to forgive Mel, and told me that Mel was crying. Mel didn't cry very often.

Slowly, and reluctantly, I sighed and agreed to let him come home. We were going to have to start over and it was not going to be easy.

I could barely stand to look at him as he walked in the door. The anger returned, and so did the hurt. He looked guilty as hell.

"I'm sorry, Gretch," was all he managed to say.

We slept together uncomfortably, without touching each other or making love. There was a palpable silence and distance between us.

After a week of miserable silence we decided to go on a trip in our old van together, down the coast of Oregon. Mel thought it would help for us to get away. We strapped two bicycles to the front bumper and brought along a mattress. We planned to camp near the ocean and ride our bikes through the state parks.

It was still summer, but the weather along the coast was terrible for camping. As soon as we neared the ocean, the temperature dropped and a heavy fog settled in. People who lived in the area told us that the fog had been socked in by higher temperatures inland and probably would remain so all summer. In spite of the lousy weather, we camped on the beach, lighting smoky fires with the abundant driftwood scattered everywhere. We tried riding our bikes, but most of the terrain was too sandy for the narrow tires, and after being dumped a few times we gave up.

It was very difficult to begin touching again. I knew that we would have to eventually, if we wanted to stay married, but it didn't feel right. We attempted to make love, but it was awkward and unnatural, with no spontaneity. I sensed that he was no longer used to the shape of my body; we tried positions that felt unfamiliar to me. Angrily I wondered if he'd come back because he'd wanted to, or just be-

Chapter Nine

cause he'd gotten caught. A wall of doubt continued to separate us. Without trust there is little joy in marriage.

After three or four days of driving and camping, the fuel pump on the old truck broke on a remote country road. We unstrapped the bikes from the front bumper and rode back to the nearest town, where we obtained a used fuel pump from a wrecking yard. Mel thought he could make it work; it was our best option.

It turned out to be tricky. The hours passed slowly, and, as nightfall came, four-letter words streamed in a torrent from underneath the truck. Right when I was beginning to think he wasn't going to be able to complete the job, the old Chevy engine—wired together with scraps and pieces of junk—leaped, coughed, and roared to life. "At least he is a good mechanic," I thought.

The next morning, we discovered a cozy cliffside restaurant with a magnificent view of the ocean. Fishing boats hauled in their catch at a small pier below us as we drank hot coffee and talked. Something about the tiny restaurant reminded me of Harrison, and a little of the happiness we once felt together returned. We ordered smoked-salmon-and-cream-cheese omelets, the restaurant's specialty. They were so delicious that we stayed nearby that night and returned the next morning for a repeat of the menu. Slightly, imperceptibly, my anger began to subside.

We traveled for two or three more days before returning home, and toward the end of the trip the bruises to my ego faded and our life together returned to normal. The events of that summer could never be completely erased from memory, and in the back of my mind the unresolved doubts gave birth to a silent phrase which repeated itself whenever Mel was unexpectedly late or absent: "I hope he's not with someone else."

Back in Seattle, my mother had gone forward with some real estate courses and was enjoying moderate success selling homes. It was her hope to support herself in this manner if her marriage failed. She'd shown talent in the field from the start and it looked as though she could be successful on her own if necessary.

Mel and I did not bother to concern ourselves with the

details of my parents' relationship. Including my last year of high school, I had already been away from home for four years, and we had our own lives now.

While growing up I had developed strong maternal feelings toward my youngest sister, Lisa; Mel was very fond of her also. She and my brother, who were both still in their early teens, loved to come to our house, and Lisa spent more time with us than at home. We carried on the family tradition of getting together each night for dinner, and sometimes invited their friends over to eat. Inadvertantly we became parent figures, even though we were barely beyond being teenagers ourselves. We didn't think much at the time about what values we might be instilling. We just provided them a warm, loving environment, a happy place where they could spend time. They were always welcome and loved.

It came as no surprise to me that they liked Mel. He was charismatic, outgoing, and fun-loving, the type of person others are drawn to. Wherever he went he was surrounded by friends; either love was very blind, or there weren't many people who truly disliked my husband.

Shortly after we were married, my grandmother Hafer became ill and was soon diagnosed with ovarian cancer. When I first heard the news, I was not overly concerned or upset because I assumed it could be cured. She appeared healthy and was still up and around and able to perform her usual activities.

After a series of minor surgeries, however, the cancer continued to spread and became inoperable. She was given a few more years to live, then was plagued with bouts of severe pain, loss of appetite, and digestive problems. She underwent chemotherapy and became miserably ill from it. The atmosphere in my grandparents' home grew dark and somber. It was very difficult to see Grandma weak and in pain, and after accompanying my mother on one of her nursing visits, I opted not to return. Fortunately, the cancer finally went into remission after the agonizing treatments, and everyone's life returned to normal for awhile.

In late spring Mom called to let us know that she had access to a "fixer upper" home in a nice area of Magnolia.

Chapter Nine

The home had not been lived in for three years and had fallen into a horrible state of disrepair; otherwise it was solid and well-built, with a fenced backyard, two bedrooms, a full basement, and even a garage. She wanted to buy it, and proposed that we rent it from her, offering to give us a break on the rent if we helped fix it up. We were ready for a change and, after looking at it, eagerly agreed to move in.

The first few months were spent ripping up dead brush from what had once been a yard. Weeds had grown three or four feet high each summer and died each winter, creating a thick, spider-filled tangle of impenetrable dead brush. After much hard work and countless trips to the dump, something that resembled a yard began to take shape.

From beneath the ground cover in the backyard emerged remains of a patio and a quaint old barbecue constructed of round gray stones. Along the fence near the barbecue was an herb garden full of thyme, basil, and mint. We had a pear tree, a fig tree, and in the center of the yard a tall tangled grape arbor, resplendent with bunches of large, firm grapes the color of green sea-mist.

After rescuing so many delightful things from the choking dead weeds, I became very attached to my treasures. I spent most of my spare time there, mowing and trimming the lawn and tending the gardens.

Mel and I had worked very hard at rebuilding our relationship after the traumatic split and had regained most of what we'd lost. I was convinced that Mel still loved me and wanted to stay married, and I knew that I loved him very much, but the disturbing fact remained that he was obviously attractive to other women and was vulnerable to temptation. The affair had cast a shadow of doubt over what would have otherwise been a deep, passionate, total commitment, and I found myself watching for telltale signs of his straying again. Mel seemed to sense my insecurity and made a special effort to keep in touch and come home at night when expected. I was not at all willing to give up my marriage, and I promised myself that if another woman ever attempted to infringe upon my territory, I would give her a vicious fight.

Soon after we moved, Mel sold the MG he'd rebuilt for

me, promising to replace it with something even better: a Porsche. The Porsche he bought was a miserable wreck, filthy and covered with mud. The front end was crumpled like an accordion. He planned to buy a new nose for it and weld it on, then repaint it its original shade of fire-engine red. The interior was perfect and just needed cleaning up.

I missed my convertible sports car terribly. As it was going to be awhile before the Porsche was finished, Mel found another old MG for me to drive. It didn't have any paint on it, just primer, so he warned me to keep it out of the rain. I drove it on sunny days as I anxiously awaited the rebirth of the 1962 1600 Super Porsche.

For many weeks, the house smelled like grinding metal and strong chemical substances. Mel called different friends to help with each part of the restoration. I became accustomed to the odors and the noise, and automatically expected extra company for dinner.

I loved to cook and thrived on the resulting compliments. Everyone's favorite part of dinner was my homemade French bread, which I twisted into a thick braid and baked with sesame seeds on top. One of Mel's favorite dinners was pot roast which I used, with the bread, for gigantic French Dip sandwiches. I always considered it worth the effort to cook for company because they appreciated it so much.

The new neighborhood was serene and quiet. I explored it on my bike and loved to go to the uncrowded Discovery Park and its sandy bluff overlooking the Sound. The grass in the park was allowed to grow long and was scattered with wildflowers. I rode through Fishermen's Terminal regularly, where the salmon and crab fleets moored after trips to Alaska. It was a magnificently beautiful place to live, and I was grateful to my mother for finding it.

I didn't work outside the home after we moved to the new house. We didn't need the money, and there was plenty of work to do at home. I had become a fanatical housekeeper and wasn't satisfied unless the house and yard looked perfect every day.

With all the new things to take care of, the idea of having children diminished in importance. Gradually we gave

Chapter Nine

it less and less thought, until it was forgotten altogether. I no longer used any form of birth control, but two years passed without the arrival of any children.

My love of sports cars and fast driving was nurtured by Mel. To us driving was a sport and a skill that had to be learned and developed. He taught me everything he knew, and coached and nagged me about listening to the engine. He warned me not to ride the clutch, showed me how to downshift instead of brake, and instructed me tirelessly on the exact moment to shift out of each gear, until he was finally comfortable letting me drive while he rode next to me.

By the time we moved to Magnolia, I had earned the dubious title of "the best woman driver" his friends had ever seen. I showed off by tearing up the street and onto the lawn whenever I knew they were watching.

Surprisingly, I had received only two tickets since I was sixteen: one for making an illegal left turn at a stoplight, and one for driving without carrying my license. My self-assuredness was only brought down a notch by an incident that occurred shortly after we moved.

It was a sunny weekend afternoon. People were coming and going, working on cars, and I had been hanging around with them, drinking beer and working in the yard. As usual, the sunshine made me want to race my car with the top down. I jumped into the old MG with no paint and headed for Fort Lawton, an old military fort that had been incorporated into Discovery Park.

The speed limit inside the gates was twenty miles per hour, but it wasn't patrolled, so I ignored it. I loved driving MGs because they were so maneuverable and well-balanced. Their engines had enough power to "chirp" the gears when shifting, and an MG could turn on a dime.

As I rounded the last corner of the dead end road at the far end of the park, I discovered a spacious, newly blacktopped parking lot, long and rectangular and divided into two sections. There were no lines painted for the parking spaces yet, so it lay there before me, totally deserted, an open invitation to test my new car.

I sped into the untouched parking lot and raced for the

other end, then cranked the wheel sharply until all four wheels broke loose from the blacktop and slid sideways along the smooth surface. Now facing the opposite direction, I repeated the maneuver, adding a little speed, delighted in the feeling of skidding at high speed, which was like being swung at the end of a rope.

I made several figure eights before I was joined by a car full of teenagers. They thought what I was doing looked like fun and decided to join me. It was definitely not safe with them in the same parking lot, coming the other way at me. I exited quickly, a little embarrassed at setting such a poor example, and drove out of the park.

As I pulled away from the stop sign at the gate, I heard a strange noise above me and sensed a flash of light that differed somehow from sunlight. Looking up, I realized I was being followed by a police helicopter. The flash had been a spotlight. They were shining it at the back of my car in an attempt to read my license plate.

My heart leaped to my throat as I envisioned the ticket I was about to be written: reckless driving, speeding, driving while under the influence. My panic doubled as I remembered that there was a half-finished six-pack of beer behind the front seat.

I was only about fifteen blocks from home. There wasn't time to think. With the helicopter following me, I took a jagged course up one street, around a corner, down another, traveling away from the wide open main avenue I would have normally taken. About halfway home I felt that I had lost them, but I didn't stop to look back. I tore around the last corner and down the block, into the driveway, and locked the car in the garage. I entered the house through the basement and ran to the front window to see if they were gone. I had lost them.

I hid the MG in the garage for the next few weeks, and drove much more sedately from then on. It had been too close a call; I had absolutely no desire to go to jail.

When the Porsche was finished, it was a masterpiece beyond anything I could ever have imagined. It was so expertly finished that it looked as new as a model on the showroom floor. The vibrant red paint was as smooth as glass,

Chapter Nine

and all the original trim was perfectly intact and free of signs of wear. The dash was constructed of padded leather. It housed a Blaupunkt radio that worked perfectly, and gauges encircled with shining chrome. There were two bucket seats in front, and a jump seat in the rear large enough for a child or large dog. Mel immediately cautioned me against parking in grocery store parking lots where there was a chance the paint might be gouged or scratched.

The car became our pride and joy, and we lavished attention on it the way that most people do their children. A short while after it was finished, we bought a one-ton black Chevrolet van to use for a second car. Mel finished the interior with wood paneling and carpets, and built a bed in back for camping. The van was also fun to drive, and we switched cars frequently, until I noticed a pattern beginning to emerge. When one car was dirty, Mel would leave it home, knowing I would wash it. Then he drove the clean car until it was dirty, and switched again. After washing the huge van a few times, I caught on, and made him share the car-cleaning duties.

We had a lot of friends, some of whom were very good people, and some who were not very nice. Many of them were single, and occasionally one would become so jealous of our relationship that they tried to cause trouble. The issue of trust had been difficult for me after Mel's affair with Lana, and perhaps others could see that I still struggled with it. This left me open, and very vulnerable to suggestion, until I was finally forced—by a friend—to resolve it for good.

Mel and I had both known the person involved since high school. He had been consistently unlucky in his romantic experiences, was very unhappy, and quite lonely. I was at his house visiting when it happened. We had been talking about his love life, or the absence of it, when the subject turned to my marriage. His approach was not subtle; it was more like an avalanche.

"I probably shouldn't tell you this," he began confidentially, "but I've heard rumors that Mel's been sleeping with that new blond secretary down at the shop."

He made the story quite convincing by saying their encounters had occurred when Mel was supposed to be away from home. I was completely devastated by the news. The concept of repeated infidelity was particularly painful in light of our apparent happiness. If cheating was still going on when things seemed so good, then I couldn't even trust my own perception or judgment. Perhaps I just wanted him to love me so badly that I was completely blind to the type of person I'd chosen as a husband.

Convinced that my marriage was over, I decided not to return home that evening. I just stayed at our friend's house until I could decide what to do. This time I didn't feel like telling anyone in my family. I was sick with shock and disillusionment. We sat up drinking and talking until quite late at night, mostly about his brief marriage, which had been a miserable failure. At bedtime he gave me my own room to sleep in, but in the middle of the night tried to crawl into bed with me. At that point I began to doubt his motives and wondered if I'd made a serious mistake.

The next morning I received a call from Mel, who had been looking everywhere for me. No one in my family had been able to tell him where I was, and he had finally resorted to calling all his friends to find me. He was extremely worried about my unexplained absence, and greatly relieved to find me.

When I told him why I had left, he denied any wrongdoing. The story the friend had given me had some holes in it, and Mel had proof to back up his whereabouts for the times in question. Although he didn't have concrete proof that he'd been alone, I chose to believe him, mostly because of his reaction to my absence. Unlike the other time, he was simply not acting guilty.

I returned home, sobbing and exhausted, and lay down on the living-room carpet to cry. The so-called friend who had started the whole mess was stricken from our list of acquaintances, and we did not see him again for several years

From that time on I vowed to pay more attention to the source of any accusations leveled against Mel. I was in love with him, and I knew this was my only choice if I wanted to remain his wife. He was to be considered innocent until proven guilty beyond a shadow of a doubt.

Chapter Nine

It was a weekday, and Mel had to work. He got out of bed to take a shower, and I followed him into the bathroom.

He was six-one, with smooth skin, broad shoulders, and powerful arms. He wore a mustache, which had become full and thick in beautiful contrast to his teenage years when Marie and I had filled it in for him with mascara. His chest was covered with fine, light brown hair, and it rippled with muscles. He had inherited his mother's high cheekbones, as well as her vibrant blue eyes. He still wore a full set of braces on his teeth, but even they did not do much to detract from his appearance.

We stepped into the shower together and washed. He stood directly between me and the spray, hogging all the water.

"Move over, I'm freezing," I protested, and tried to shove him out of the way.

His head was tipped back in the spray and what was left of the water ran down behind his back; his ears still stuck out when his hair was wet. I bent over to get the soap from the corner and he wrapped his arms around me from behind. One hand closed around my breast and he pulled me over to him. I put one foot up on the edge of the bathtub and leaned back against his leg as he pulled me even closer. I dug my fingers into his forearms and breathed in gasps as waves of pleasure passed through my body; I could barely remain standing as he released me from his grasp.

Sometimes the nature of our love was almost frightening. The power he had over me was complete and overwhelming, and I wanted nothing else in the world except to be with him. Many times, when we made love in the morning, it led to more lovemaking a few hours later. After four years of marriage, I was still head-over-heels, crazily in love.

We stayed in the shower until the hot water was gone, but I never did get much of a wash. He left me standing on the bathroom rug, feeling dazed, staring at my face in the mirror.

"Hey, Gretch, where're my shorts?" he yelled from the bedroom.

My legs were still shaking as I walked barefoot to the kitchen to make some tea. We always drank tea in the morning, the British way, very strong and with plenty of warm milk and sugar.

"Hey, Buddy, wanna play catch?" I heard him holler from the living room. I held the carton of milk firmly as he and the dog barreled past me through the narrow kitchen and out into the backyard. They were always so rowdy in the morning. I sighed, waiting for the water to boil; I always had a hard time waking up.

Mel was running around in the backyard in his boxer shorts, oblivious of our neighbors. "Who cares?" I thought to myself, smiling. "The neighbors think we're nuts already."

I put extra sugar in Mel's tea and hoped he wouldn't want pancakes. I just would never be able to make them like his mom. Luckily, we had already wasted too much time that morning for him to wait for breakfast. He kissed me goodbye and leaped down the front steps toward the driveway. "Bring me lunch," he yelled back, and I heard a low rumble as the Chevy van started up.

"Oh, good, he's leaving me the Porsche!" I thought excitedly, and ran back to the kitchen to shut off the stove. I watched the van disappear down the street, and then I cranked up the stereo and devised a strange combination of exercise and dance. Whenever I did this, it caused the dog to get excited and jump around, too. I had taught him how to stand up on his hind legs while I held his front paws, so we danced together. We jumped and kicked until I was out of breath, and then I vacuumed, threw in a load of laundry, and made the bed.

It was still pretty early, about nine. I pulled off my cotton nightgown and inspected my body in the mirror. I was tall and slender, with not much of a bust, and I had very long legs. Men often complimented me on my legs, and I considered them to be my best physical feature, but I saw one major flaw: ugly ripples of fat where my underpants ended. I had read once in a fashion magazine that ballet-

Chapter Nine

kicks help reduce cellulite, so I did them each day faithfully, watching myself in front of the mirror to be sure I was keeping proper form. When wearing a skirt that barely covered my underpants, it was important not to display bulges. At age twenty-three, my appearance was very important to me. I had to stay sexy if I wanted to keep the spark in our marriage.

I fixed some generous, open-faced tuna sandwiches for Mel, with no onions, of course, and melted cheese over the top. I would have to figure a way to get them to the shop before they got cold. The shop was about ten minutes from the new house, but I could make it in five driving the Porsche.

I drove like Mario Andretti, with the foil-wrapped sandwiches balanced precariously on the car seat, and arrived with them still warm. We closed the door to Mel's office and he started to eat.

Uncle Bob stopped in from the back office a minute later. "How's my Janni today?" he asked as he patted my shoulder and smiled. He had blue, kindhearted eyes filled with affection and warmth.

"I'm fine," I replied, returning the smile. He was one of my favorite people.

"Mel, line one," the loudspeaker crackled, as he took a large bite of his lunch.

"Shit," he exclaimed with his mouth full. He put down the sandwich and left the office to answer the phone at the counter. He talked on the phone for quite awhile, and by the time he got back his lunch was cold. He looked a little distracted and seemed to have lost interest in eating.

"Who was that?," I asked, anxious to know what was going on.

"It was Wayne," he answered, a little carefully. Mel knew I didn't think much of Wayne.

"He wanted to know if I would go to Oregon with him this weekend," he explained. "He wants to go visit some friends who live in the mountains down there."

I could tell I wasn't invited, but I wouldn't have wanted to go anyway if Wayne was going. Of all the people we knew, he was the craziest.

"I don't care if you go," I replied, lying through my teeth. "As long as you don't take the Porsche," I added.

Mel and Wayne were to leave for Oregon on Friday and planned to stay for four days. While he was away, I spent most of my time working in the yard. I was proud of the transformation that had taken place since we'd moved in, but there was always more to do.

The afternoon Mel was due to come home, I received a long-distance call from Oregon. In a crackly, distant voice, a woman explained that she was calling from a hospital. She informed me that Mel had been injured in a car accident and that I should come to Oregon as soon as possible. She was vague about the extent of his injuries, but stated that he had suffered a broken leg, cuts and bruises, and was not at all comfortable.

Shaken, I thanked her for calling and hung up. I contacted Mel's parents, and then called the airport to find out when I could catch a flight to Oregon.

The news from the hospital had been a shock, but more than anything else I was afraid of the extent of his injuries. The plane ride seemed to take an eternity. I had no one to talk to, and no idea what to expect. Mel very rarely got sick and I had never seen him uncomfortable in any way, except for the time he got all his crooked teeth pulled for his braces. He had been miserable then, and I had felt completely helpless. There was nothing I could do to take away his pain.

On the plane ride my imagination went wild, conjuring up visions of him lying unconscious and unable to move or speak, and I tried to force the thoughts from my mind. I was making myself feel worse by the second because there were no distractions on the plane, nothing to help dispel my anxiety.

The accident had occurred on a remote country road near a small town on the Rogue River. The surrounding countryside was farmland, and the terrain was flat, with only gentle hills visible in the distance. The weather was extremely hot, comparable to Chewelah at its hottest.

The pavement sizzled with heat as I got off the plane, and I wished I could go swimming. After a brief taxi ride, I checked into a motel across from the hospital and walked

Chapter Nine

slowly across the street to the entrance. My mouth was dry, and my heart felt as if it would pound right out of my chest. I tried to convince myself that I was overreacting and that he would probably be just fine.

Unfortunately, when I saw him, it was worse than I ever could have imagined. He was lying behind a drawn curtain in a dark, silent room on the orthopedic floor. He was only semi-conscious and did not appear to notice me when I entered the room. His leg was encased in a full-length cast and was up in traction. His face was badly bruised, cut and stitched in several places, and his features were distorted by swelling: one eye was swollen completely shut.

I reached toward him, and, barely audibly, he murmured, "Don't touch me."

"Oh, my God," I remember thinking. "He looks half dead."

A young, pleasant-looking nurse entered the room and motioned for me to follow her. She led me out into the hall and began to explain the details of the accident.

Apparently Mel and Wayne had rented a Volkswagen station wagon and were exploring up in the hills on an unpaved back road. They were driving fast around a blind corner, and a pickup full of teenagers was coming the other way, also driving too fast. Both vehicles were in the center of the road and hit squarely, head-on. Mel went through the windshield, but was kept from being thrown clear off the vehicle because his leg was caught. Wayne received lacerations, a broken arm, and broken ribs, and all the occupants of the pickup were also seriously injured. They were in a remote area, and all too badly injured to seek help. It was extremely hot, and they were forced to lie in the searing heat for hours, until they were finally discovered by a passing car.

After seeing Mel, I felt lightheaded and dizzy. The nurse led me back out into the hall, and asked me if I was all right. She gave me a flimsy paper cup full of water that collapsed in my trembling hand. I had never seen someone I loved so badly injured. The situation was completely out of my control, and there was nothing I could do but wait. The nurse suggested that I go back to the motel room to rest, promising that she would call me if there was any change in his condition.

I slept uncomfortably on the rock-hard motel bed, exhausted and worried sick. The room was starched and sterile and smelled remarkably similar to the hospital. Bob and Norma arrived the next morning and provided a welcome distraction. Norma kept up a friendly chatter about inconsequential things, and I found their presence enormously comforting. They both seemed to possess the ability to remain optimistic in discouraging situations, a quality I greatly admired. They suggested we rent a larger room so that we could all stay together. I gladly agreed.

The following morning, Mel's parents rose and showered before me. They left to go see Mel, and I planned to meet them as soon as I was dressed. There had been no break in the heat since our arrival, so I chose my lightest-weight skirt and top, even though it was rather skimpy to wear inside the hospital. When I arrived on the orthopedic floor, Uncle Bob was waiting to meet me. He looked worried, and reached out to touch my arm. "Mel's worse," he informed me and began to lead me down a different hall than the one we'd gone down before. Ahead of us was a sign designating the intensive care unit. My head started to tingle and my legs were unsteady, causing the wooden soles on my sandals to tap on the bare floors. "If he's worse than he was before, then he must be..."

For the first time in my life, I felt as if I were going to faint. A concerned nurse took my arm, and asked me to sit down. Then, in a calm, reserved manner she proceeded to explain what had happened during the night. Because of the severity of the break in Mel's leg, particles of fat from the bone marrow had entered his bloodstream, causing what the doctors termed "fat emboli." His blood oxygen was very low, and it was a potentially fatal condition.

He was unconscious when we entered the room, and a respirator was breathing for him. We stood there briefly, just looked at him, then went back out in the hall. After I recovered from the initial shock of his worsened condition, I began to give serious thought to the fact that he might die in this antiseptic place away from home, without ever even

Chapter Nine

speaking to us again. The thought of losing him was too painful to pursue in detail, yet it loomed near. The thought of leaving there and going home without him, never to see him again, was inconceivable. The worst part was my sense of total helplessness. I couldn't just stand around and watch him get worse without doing something.

All I could think to do was call the best doctor in the world, my father. Maybe he knew something that these doctors didn't know, something that would tip the scales and help Mel survive.

Sobbing uncontrollably on the phone, I related what the doctors had told us, and told him there was a possibility Mel would die. He said that he wouldn't mind coming down and would be there as soon as possible.

That evening Mel's parents and I huddled together in the motel room and prayed. I begged God to understand that, deep down, I was not such a bad person. I pleaded for this one favor and promised I would never forget the kindness if Mel lived.

The next morning Mel started to improve. By the time my dad arrived, he was out of danger. This time when we entered the room, he was alert and talking, complaining of his itching leg, and acting very grumpy, which the nurses said was a sign of recovery. His face still looked beaten up and swollen, but at least he was going to live. He would be kept in the ICU for a few more days, and then transferred back to the orthopedic ward.

It would be a long time before he was able to travel, because of his compound fracture of the upper thigh. After staying with him until he was more comfortable, I returned home to wait out the rest of his recovery.

It took about six weeks before he was well enough to come home. He arrived on crutches, pale and thin, with a fading black eye and superficial scars on his face. As he struggled up the front walk, Buddy jumped all over him, nearly knocking him down. His leg was still in a full cast, but he was safe and alive. He had been very lucky.

After hearing the story of how the wreck happened, I realized that I had also been lucky to have stayed home. Mel told me he thought I probably would have been killed if I had been riding in the car with them. There had been a considerable amount of reckless driving going on before the crash, and he showed me a picture of the rented Volkswagen airborne as it flew over a bump with Wayne at the wheel. Both vehicles had rounded the corner traveling at high speeds in the center of the road, and it was impossible for either to slow down or turn before colliding.

I didn't attempt to lecture Mel, or reprimand him; it only would have made him mad at me. However, we both agreed that he and Wayne were a bad combination, and he promised to see less of him in the future.

TEN

It seems strange, but I honestly can't remember which one of us came up with the idea to buy a farm. I loved the house in Magnolia and would have been content staying there indefinitely, but I probably mentioned something to Mel about how much I missed riding horses. Mel loved the freedom of country life; he wanted a place all his own, with some property and a little farmhouse where he could chop wood, build fences, and raise lots of animals. I still wanted to have children, and he was essentially noncommittal on the subject, so I interpreted his silence as an okay and continued to hope for the child who, month after month, never arrived.

Because of the propeller business, Mel had both credit and connections at the neighborhood bank, so financing of a farm would be easy. All that remained was to choose a place and proceed to buy it.

While Mel looked for a house and property, I planned a trip to Chewelah. I wanted to buy my horse there, so that Grammie and Grandpa could help me pick one out. They knew a lot more about horses than I did, and we would get a better price there.

Mel said I could take the Porsche, a prospect that made the long drive seem a little more inviting. I painstakingly waxed and shined every inch of it, so that Eastern Washington's prolific insects and gritty dust would not ruin the paint. It finally became so shiny that the sun's reflection on it hurt my eyes.

I left on a Monday and planned to be back by the end of the week. It was late summer, and although the weather was hot the drive went quickly. I stopped in midafternoon at Vantage to take my traditional, solitary swim in the Columbia River. I covered the car with a blanket to help keep the heat off, and ran down the cement ramp into the river. The pavement burned my feet as I ran, and the icy water took away my breath momentarily as I dove in. I floated on my back and gazed into the cloudless sky, trying to comprehend the endlessness of space. "What, and where, is heaven?" I wondered, kicking my feet in the cool water. "And how will we know we are there if we are dead?" There was still so much about life I didn't understand.

I wanted to reach Chewelah before dark. It was still three or four hours away, so I reluctantly swam back to the boat launch and got out of the water. The intense afternoon heat rose from the concrete in shimmering waves, and the car had already become so hot it would barely start.

I reached Grammie's house at about five o'clock, the time when Grandpa would be sitting in his recliner with his feet up to watch the news.

I was overwhelmed by mixed emotions as I watched my cherished grandmother step out onto the porch to greet me. Most of the extraordinary pleasure I derived from visiting this place centered around her being there. Once she was gone, I knew it would never be the same. I loved Grandpa, too, but Grammie was particularly irreplaceable, and she had cancer.

By the time I reached the porch, I was crying as if she'd already died.

"What's wrong, Janni?" she asked, looking worried and a little alarmed.

I had trouble speaking, and was embarrassed by my inability to control my emotions, even though I knew she would understand. Before too long I managed to choke out an explanation.

"It's just that I know someday when I come here, you won't be here anymore," I answered, feeling like a genuine idiot.

She laughed and reached out her arms to give me a hug.

"Don't you worry about that now, Janni," she answered. "I'm not ready to up and die yet. Are you hungry?" she said, turning toward the house.

The fresh dill Grammie planted every summer spilled

Chapter Ten

wildly from the overgrown flower garden that bordered the house. There were dahlias, chrysanthemums, pansies, and roses cascading in chaotic bursts of color from the fertile soil. Grammie's homemade dill pickles were one of her specialties and one of my favorites. The fresh dill was tough and stringy, but tangy and fun to chew on. I broke a piece off and chewed on it while we caught up on news about the family.

As usual, I anxiously inquired about Sundown and Scooter, both past the age of twenty. They were kept at my uncle's and were still ridden once in awhile, but only for exercise. Sundown still loved to run, but he tired easily and was only allowed to gallop for about a mile. I planned to drive over and see them after we'd had a chance to look at a few horses.

Grandpa was exactly where I thought he would be, reclining in his armchair watching the news. He had retired to that chair every evening for as long as I could remember. It was a predictable routine; one could have set a clock by its regularity. It was also a routine that seemed to annoy Grammie. While fixing dinner she hollered at him from the kitchen, and he appeared to be too engrossed in the television to hear. Actually, Grandpa himself seemed to annoy Grammie, but I was never exactly sure why. I had a feeling it was just that they had grown too accustomed to one another and had begun to take each other for granted.

Grandpa was wrinkled from the sun, and stooped from years spent driving a tractor. One of his arms was gouged and misshapen from having been caught in a hay baler. It was a very serious accident; they had barely been able to save the arm, and it had required many surgeries before he could use it again. Grandpa had looked like an old man when I was little, but he never seemed to get any older. He was quiet and intelligent, a diligent worker and wise businessman. He was also deeply religious, and I avoided entering serious conversations with him because of his tendency to preach. My grandparents were devout Jehovah's Witnesses, and Grandpa was convinced that, at a certain date, the world would come to an end. He had been moving the date forward each year for years, but the story itself remained the same. He claimed that wars, disease, and pestilence were foreseen in the bible, and were proof that we were moving rapidly toward The End. He believed that only Witnesses would be saved, and that heaven was a beautiful place where everyone got along with each other and the crops had no weeds.

Grammie had been expecting me, and the table was set. We had hamburgers from the beef Grandpa raised, mashed potatoes, gravy, and fresh beets with greens. Grammie set out the homemade pickles and jam. She had also baked a rhubarb pie for dessert. I loved to drink the fresh milk from the dairy. There was always plenty, arriving in gallon jars encrusted with several inches of thick, heavy cream. The cream was scraped off to make butter, but some stuck to the jar and remained in a ring around the top. High fat content in the milk was considered highly desirable; the cows that produced the most cream were considered superior dairy cattle.

Grammie had located some available horses, but she didn't know much about them. She did know that one was a gelding and one was a mare. I decided to try the gelding first, because I loved riding Sundown so much.

The first horse's name was Honey, a stunning looking animal. He was a light palomino of medium height, and appeared well-mannered. When I tried to ride him, however, he turned out to be the spookiest, most unpredictable horse I'd ever encountered. Small, common objects like the garden hose would cause him to rear up on his hind legs; he achieved such a vertical position that I felt he was going to fall over backwards. He could walk on his hind legs and maintain this position. After dangling from his neck for awhile, I jumped off, indicating my defeat. A horse is always able to sense when it has won, and usually continues its errant behavior triumphantly until disciplined. Someone suggested that I hit him between the ears with a switch when he reared, to bring him back down onto all fours. I wasn't a good enough rider to manage it, as I needed both hands to hang on. After a few attempts to master him, he made me so nervous that I could barely get him bridled. I should have quit at this point and admitted he was not the

Chapter Ten

horse for me. Instead, I did something so idiotic that it still amazes me to think about it.

There was a potato field down below Grammie's house, where black plastic tarps are anchored down with sandbags to maintain proper soil moisture. When the wind blew, the tarps flapped noisily, something I knew would alarm the high-strung, skittish horse. I thought that, if I rode him long enough near the flapping tarps, I could "ride the spook out of him."

As we left the lane and entered the field, he became alert and tense, occasionally jumping sideways, but keeping all four feet on the ground. We made a ninety-degree turn and started across the back perimeter of the field, where the black tarps lay in place. Suddenly, a gust of wind ruffled the plastic, and the horse shot into the air as though he had been launched from a rocket pad. He literally jumped out from under me, and when I landed, I was straddling his neck. Both my feet had come out of the stirrups, and I was seated just in front of the saddle, with the saddle horn poking me in the tailbone. He was now just standing still, and the reins were still in my hands, so I tightened up on the reins and prepared to get off.

For some reason, I was wearing tennis shoes that day instead of boots. I had, of course, been warned about this in the past. As I attempted to dismount, my tennis shoe wedged in a small space underneath the saddle horn and left me hanging in front of him with one foot barely touching the ground. I was in the ideal position to be dragged and trampled, and I couldn't seem to get my foot loose. "Whoa, Honey," I repeated, patting his neck and praying for him not to spook. Miraculously, he stood still until I got my foot free and was standing safely beside him. I didn't have the nerve to get back on, and by then I realized I didn't have the riding ability. Discouraged, frightened, and embarrassed, I led him home.

The following day one of my many cousins came to visit and we discussed the unpredictable gelding. He was being kept in the corral across from the kitchen, and as we spoke and gazed out at the horse a glimmer of recognition came into my cousin's eyes. "I know that horse," she exclaimed,

Return To Chewelah

after hearing descriptions of his behavior. "He's not a gelding, he just looks like one. I almost bought him myself. He's actually a stallion, and that's one of the reasons he's so crazy."

She explained that Honey had a very uncommon condition: his testicles had never descended properly from his abdomen. Therefore he could not be gelded, a procedure which calms the horse down considerably. Not only was he a stallion, he was a frustrated stallion. This particular horse had been passed from one unsuspecting person to another, and no one wanted to keep him.

The experience with Honey shook my confidence and left me with an unpleasant fear of horses that I had never before felt. Grammie remarked that I was a little out of practice handling horses, and we unanimously agreed that we should find a tame, trustworthy horse that didn't buck. She made a quick phone call and arranged for us to go see a mare.

The mare was sorrel, the same color as Sundown, but much smaller. She was bred from champion racing quarter horse stock, but didn't have papers and was being sold for a mere two hundred and fifty dollars. The people who owned her were poor, and she had been completely neglected. By the age of three she had already borne two foals, at least one too many for a horse that young. She had a round, protruding stomach because of this, and her chest and leg muscles weren't properly developed. The other quarter horses I had seen were stocky and muscular; in contrast, she looked petite and out of proportion. Her hooves hadn't been trimmed or taken care of for quite some time. They were much too long and had been allowed to split and crack. In spite of the poor care, she was still a fine, agile-looking horse with a delicate head and nice coat. With a lot of exercise and proper nourishment, she would develop into a strong, healthy animal of which I could be very proud.

As soon as I rode her, I decided I wanted her. She was docile and sweet, had smooth gaits, and was easy to ride. Her second colt hadn't yet been weaned, so it tagged along with us wherever we rode. We stuck to enclosed areas away from the road, where he would be safe. My mom had given me a brand-new saddle when she heard I would be getting a horse, but this horse had such narrow shoulders, the saddle didn't fit properly. I settled for riding bareback most of the time, which was fine because she was so well-behaved. Instead of wearing a bridle, she was trained to use a hackamore, a type of bridle with a nose strap instead of a bit. I had never used a hackamore before, but Grandpa helped me adjust it, and it seemed to work just fine.

Everyone who saw the mare remarked that she looked like she could run, but I didn't feel like testing her speed. The first horse had really scared me. Now all I wanted was a nice, quiet animal I could relax around and trust.

I couldn't believe I was finally going to have a horse of my own, to ride whenever I wanted. We tethered her in the yard, so I could look at her when I wasn't riding, and I named her Jesse, after Grammie.

Just as I was getting ready to call Mel and tell him about the horse, he called to tell me he had found a farm on Vashon Island, an island between Seattle and Tacoma accessible only by ferryboat. I had never been there before and was a little disturbed to learn he had been there several times himself. I wrote it off as insecurity and didn't press for details. He told me he'd found ten acres and a house for twenty thousand dollars, a little less than what a small house would have cost in Seattle. There would be plenty of room for horses, and we would probably be able to move in by fall.

I hung up the phone and excitedly told Grammie the news. She seemed delighted to see me so happy. She had always liked Mel, and I knew she was glad that I had married him. When we were first dating, she had been so impressed by the attention he showered on me that she warned me, in a confidential tone, "You better not let that one get away, Janni." He was the only boyfriend she had ever indicated approval of, and it made a big impression on me.

I wanted to do something special for Grammie to thank her for helping me find such a wonderful horse, so I decided to drive into town and buy her a gift. I wanted to surprise her, so when I left I told her I was going to visit friends. After a little searching, I found a tall, ornate pitcher made of genuine blue-and-white Delft china from Holland. I brought it home and sneaked it on to her kitchen table while she was outside. It looked uncommonly elegant on her red-and-white checked tablecloth, and was perfect for her large bouquets. When she came in and saw it she looked momentarily stunned.

"Oh, isn't that a beautiful thing," she exclaimed, and then turned to take her vegetables to the sink.

"It's for you, Grammie," I explained, walking over to the sink to hand it to her. Jehovah's Witnesses did not celebrate the holidays, and she was obviously not accustomed to receiving gifts. "I wanted to get you something really special, for doing so many nice things for me."

"Oh, Janni, you didn't have to do that for me," she replied, but I could tell she was deeply pleased.

Later we sat down together for a cup of coffee, and somehow the difficult subject of the future, when Grandma would be gone, came up again. With much effort and careful choice of words, I managed to express to her how much she had meant to me during my life, and how very much I would miss her when she was gone. I asked her if I could have a few things from the house to remember her by: the cream-colored butter churn with blue speckles, which had been retired to the basement; and our greatest childhood treasure, the palomino-horse clock with the removable plastic saddle. We packed them carefully for the trip home, and I went in to take a bath before dinner.

The following morning I rose at the crack of dawn with Grandpa, and went out to prepare Jesse for one last ride. I dressed her up in her new saddle and saddle blanket so we could take pictures. Grandma would keep her for me until we had moved, and they would wean the colt. Then Mel and I would bring a trailer over to get her. I paraded her proudly around in the yard, and Grandpa shot the pictures with his Polaroid. The sun had just begun to peek above the mountains to the east, casting slanted golden rays across the lawn. The air smelled clean and fragrant, as though it had rained during the night. I made Grammie come out of the house in her robe for a picture, which she didn't really want to do. Her hair was down, long and heavy around her face, and she smiled sheepishly at the camera because she was in her nightclothes.

Chapter Ten

Finally I jumped in the car to go, feeling torn as always between my two homes. It wasn't quite as hard to leave Grammie's since I had fallen in love with Mel, and I knew that soon we might have a farm of our own. The reassuring hum of the Porsche motor greeted me like an old friend. I waved goodbye to my grandparents one last time and pulled out onto the road without daring to look back.

I arrived home on Friday, and Saturday morning we went to look at the new place. It took us about twenty minutes to drive from Magnolia to the West Seattle ferry dock where cars waited in line for Vashon and a neighboring town called Southworth.

The ferry dock provided a beautiful, sweeping view of the Sound. To the north lay a large city park with a curving, narrow beach. A series of shallow concrete steps led from the beach to a grassy clearing with picnic tables. As we waited for the ferry, we watched small children cautiously test the freezing salt water with their toes. The grassy area was crowded with people throwing Frisbees for their dogs. Many of the ferry commuters got out of their cars and lined the docks, simply enjoying the view. It was a bright, clear day and the water glimmered invitingly, a spectacular shade of blue under the late-summer sun. Expensive beach homes lined the water to the south, and a large sailing yacht moored a few hundred yards from the terminal created a scene so picturesque that I regretted not bringing my camera. Even people with no particular destination came to ride this ferry; the trip across the water was an experience in itself.

It took several minutes for the incoming boat to unload, and after waiting for the foot passengers to walk on, the cars on the dock were loaded. The captain started the engines, a signal that people could leave their cars, and we climbed the stairs to the upper deck. I had ridden ferries many times before, and liked to stand outside on the upper deck with my face in the wind. The salt water had a very distinct smell, a pungent odor of barnacles and kelp, which I had learned to love. It welcomed me home whenever I had to leave Chewelah, and always reminded me that Seattle had one very unique quality that Chewelah lacked: salt-water beaches.

The suspense mounted as we returned to the car to unload at Vashon. This was a very important and exciting moment in my life. I couldn't believe we were actually going to buy a farm. I squirmed around in the car seat like a little kid, nearly unable to wait any longer. Luckily, the new place was only about five minutes from the ferry, and we were almost there.

After traveling up a steep, winding road, we reached the main highway. The atmosphere on the island was rural, a sharp contrast from Seattle. Occasional farmhouses lay scattered along the road, separated generously by wide-open fields. There were no businesses, no gas stations, and no fast-food restaurants, just a glorious countryside, uncluttered and unspoiled.

After a few minutes on the highway, we turned back toward the Sound. This part of the island was covered by a thick evergreen forest, and Mel told me we were on the road that would take us to our new place. The property was close to the beach, but we wouldn't be able to see the water from our house.

We knew that the house on the property was essentially worthless. It needed a new foundation and had been allowed to fall into a state of unlivable disrepair. Some real estate people had disparagingly remarked that the property would have been worth more without the house. Mel and I had discussed this, and we both felt that the land was such a good deal that we shouldn't pass it up. We could always work on the house, and it would be an excellent investment.

Our property was entered by a long driveway bordered by dense brush and forest on the left. To the right, there was a vast, overgrown field which belonged to the neighbors below us. The driveway led to a grassy clearing that had once been an orchard of apple and plum trees. The trees, about a dozen in all, were still standing, but were gnarly and untended. Broken branches lay everywhere, and the long grass was blanketed with a thick layer of overripe fruit. There were two sheds at the top of the clearing: one which was open in front, and one that had windows, two rooms, and a couple of old beds. We decided to use the open shed for a makeshift garage, and let people sleep in the other

Chapter Ten

building when they came to spend the night. After joking around about having a guesthouse, Mel named the shed the "Pest House," and the name stuck.

Ten acres sounds like a lot of land, but very little of it was cleared. Except for the area with the orchard and sheds, we had purchased a totally secluded forest. Even the road that led to the place seemed deserted. We had one neighbor to the right of us at the end of the driveway, and another home was somewhere in a field below us, invisible from our house.

I was delighted with the property, which we immediately began to call The Farm. I did not care what the house was like, as long as it was a roof over our heads.

At the time of our first visit, the house was still inhabited by the owner, a hostile old widow who was being forced to sell for financial reasons. She let us see the inside briefly, then made it clear she didn't want us there. Since I had been thoroughly warned about the condition of the home, I was fortunately not expecting much. The house was small and dark, all built on one level, with two bedrooms. It had a spacious, unremarkable kitchen, with horrid counters, floors, and sink. Not only was the house filthy; it was falling apart. There were broken windows in the small bedroom, and even the mirror on the bathroom medicine cabinet was shattered. There was a clawfoot bathtub standing on only three feet; one had rusted completely off. We would be limited to taking baths, as there was no showerhead. Neither was there a hookup for a washer and dryer, only a laundromat in town.

Eternal optimists that we were, we barely considered the drawbacks of living in the wretched home. A little paint and it would be as good as new. All I cared about was having a place to keep horses, and Mel's main priority was to get out of the city.

The deal closed in the fall, but the old lady who sold it to us refused to move out. Her husband had died a few years before and she was living there alone with her dog, a hideous little creature with thin, white skin and bulging round eyes clouded by cataracts. She kept him dressed in a little dog-sweater, but he still shivered uncontrollably as if he were cold. He snarled and snapped at visitors, then wheezed heavily.

It would have been hard to say who was in worse shape, the dog or his owner. The old woman spent her days drinking vodka and sitting wrapped in blankets on the damp, smelly couch. We felt sorry for her at first, but when the closing date passed and she still refused to move, our patience wore thin. We wrote a letter and received no reply. She refused to talk to us on the phone.

We were anxious to move before winter, and were faced with the prospect of having the sheriff go out and evict her. Finally, her relatives talked her into leaving, and she was moved to a more manageable apartment in town. To spite us, she left our welcome in the form of rotting garbage in every nook and cranny imaginable.

The house itself was rotting, especially its kitchen floors and cabinets. Situated downhill from the orchard and driveway, water streamed freely underneath the poorly fitted front door and created an indoor mud puddle on the kitchen floor. The downspouts were also broken.

It turned out to be the rainiest fall I can ever remember, even for Seattle. The floor was beyond hope of ever being clean, and when we started extricating the ancient cans and bottles from underneath the sink, we discovered that the plumbing leaked and apparently had been leaking for years. The wood had decayed and was crumbling in soft chunks. Mel's mom bravely helped me scrub, and we coated the pathetic cupboards with red and white paint.

Norma amazed me when she was out of her element. I had never seen her wear a pair of jeans, nor had I ever seen her get dirty. She could be up to her elbows in filth and grime, or paint an entire kitchen without ruining her clothes. She always wore a skirt, and she never even ran her nylons. I was immensely grateful for her help in making the new home livable; it was a messy, discouraging job, and I couldn't have done it by myself.

The bathroom was as depressing as the kitchen, with peeling paint, rusty fixtures, and broken glass. It was cold and drafty, and completely lacked storage space. However, the ancient toilet, sink, and bathtub were at least functioning and would get us by.

Chapter Ten

The old widow had applied stick-on pastel ducks to the bottom of the clawfoot bathtub so she wouldn't slip. They had shifted, exposing areas of glue that had turned black. I decided to remove them completely, but when I pulled them off the adhesive remained in the tub. It was impossible to get off, at least with paint remover, and seemed to get stickier in hot water. The first time Mel tried to take a bath, the glue stuck to the fine hair on his butt, and when he stood up he had ducks outlined on his cheeks. I laughed until I cried, but he didn't think it was funny.

The muddy stream of water running into the kitchen continued to be a problem, so Mel and his friends tacked up a makeshift porch to try to divert some of it. Since we didn't have a washer and dryer, it also gave us a covered place to hang muddy clothes and boots. After getting soaking wet in a dressy leather coat and slacks while riding my bike to town, I moved all of my city clothes to the back of the closet and bought the heaviest Levi's I could find. I also bought a lined denim jacket and a pair of copper-brown—sorrel—cowboy boots, top-of-the-line Tony Lamas for serious horse people. Grammie had already given me a cowboy hat made of soft brown felt, and for the first time I began to appreciate the hat for its true function. It kept me warm and dry.

Mel was also planning to buy a horse, so he and his friends built some stalls in the back of the open shed in which to keep them, and they also built a small corral out of green poles. Our space was limited by the thick forest behind the shed and by several other large trees that stood on the perimeter of the clearing, but at least we had an enclosure where we could put the horses away at night.

In spite of the rain, it was beautiful outside. I spent hours wandering through the drenched underbrush, waiting for glimpses of the exotic wild pheasants that inhabited our property. I fed them fresh corn in the same place every day, hoping to catch sight of them. But when they appeared it was always startling and unexpected, wary as they were because of hunting season and relentless hunters from Seattle who terrorized the island on drunken shooting sprees.

Occasionally a deer wandered through the yard, totally unaware of my presence. With Mel at work, I was, in fact, the only human being around for miles. It was lonely waiting for the birds to appear; then one day Mel brought home some chickens.

The chickens were of the most uncommon species: Bantams, brightly colored, petite, and very unusual in appearance. Some had bizarre topknots and wild speckles. One was very tiny, with long legs like a stork, and some were matched pairs. We built my chickens a roost up in the open shed and made a large cage to keep them in at night. Each evening, I climbed up on a sawhorse and lifted them down one by one, carefully holding their wings against their bodies, and tucked them into a bed filled with nice soft hay.

One evening as I bent down, putting a chicken in the pen, I heard a flapping sound behind me and felt something land on my back near my neck. I slowly straightened up, turned my head, and saw the skinny black chicken with the long legs perched on my shoulder. I extended my arm and he wobbled down the sleeve of my coat, looking at me sideways with beady black eyes. He appeared to like me, and he wasn't the slightest bit afraid. He walked back up my arm and started pecking at my hair as if he were looking for food. I think he confused my hair with hay.

After that evening he followed me everywhere, and I named him Skinny Jimmy after one of our friends. I spent many hours with him perched on my arm. He was a very tiny bird and couldn't fly much, but he could run very fast. When I needed to go to town, he chased me to the car and ran circles around it while I got in. He stood on the window sill and watched me while I did the dishes, and crowed outside the bedroom window every morning. If he found the front door open, he marched right into the kitchen and living room, and even into the bedroom to wake me up.

Our second favorite chicken was a hen we called Mrs. Natural because of her topknot. She was black-and-white speckled, with a thick bunch of feathers sticking straight up out of the front of her head. Mrs. Natural was so comical-looking that we allowed her into the living room during parties. Her appearance sent people into total hysterics, particularly if they'd been smoking pot.

At first the mortality rate of the chickens was high, due

Chapter Ten

mainly to our dog Buddy. Time after time, after a terrible commotion I would find him chasing the chickens around in circles. After he caught one he shook it viciously, sent feathers flying everywhere, then killed it. The rest of the chickens squawked in terror as they witnessed these attacks. Only rarely did one of the birds survive being caught by the dog, so I watched my prized collection of chickens diminish at an alarming rate. The only solution I could think of was to tie Buddy up for the entire day, something I didn't want to do. He was a very good dog, except for his weakness for chickens.

By the time he had killed four, I decided it had to stop. When all other forms of punishment had been exhausted, I resorted to an old trick I'd learned in Chewelah: I tied the dead chicken around his neck and tied him to the hitching post. When I came out later to let him loose, he had pulled the knot so tightly around his neck that he was nearly choking. I had almost killed Mel's only dog and favorite pet. Thankful that he was all right, I untied him and brought him indoors. He never killed another chicken.

ELEVEN

We were finally ready to move the horses. My horse Jesse was still waiting in Chewelah, and Mel and a friend made a quick trip over to pick her up. When she arrived, she looked healthier and appeared more alert than she had before, perhaps because she was no longer nursing her foal. She had taken on the appearance of an extremely well-bred animal, and I was excited and proud to own her. Her only outstanding flaw was the terrible condition of her hooves; they were chipped, dry, and deeply cracked, and needed immediate attention.

Mel had discovered a horse in Reno while visiting his brother who ran a propeller shop there. It was not uncommon for Mel to make a long trip, like the one to Nevada, in a few days, and he seemed to like this horse so well that he thought it worthwhile to bring it back. He rented a trailer and hauled him from Reno all the way to Vashon.

"Oh, my God!" I exclaimed under my breath as he unloaded him from the trailer. The horse had been purchased from a riding arena, looked like a swaybacked skeleton—bag of bones was the first term which entered my mind—and was in the worst condition I had ever witnessed for a horse. He was huge and awkward, with an enormous square head, and dull, nappy fur resembling burlap. Every bone in his body protruded, particularly his hips, knees, and ribs. His coat had a sweet, sickish odor unlike anything I had ever smelled, and his lungs wheezed when he breathed. In spite of his appearance, however, I had to admit he was quite enjoyable to ride. He had a couple of gaits that most horses don't have, one a very smooth, fast walk, and the other, a rhythmic, high-stepping trot usually taught to show horses.

Chapter Eleven

We decided the ratty old horse must be part Tennessee walker, a distinction that made him somewhat special, and after some deliberation, we named him George, after Grandpa.

We asked the vet to come out and look at him, in hopes of improving his health and appearance. The vet suggested he was malnourished and should be fed alfalfa hay and beet sugar over the winter to fatten him up. That sounded like a good idea to me, so I bought him plenty and fed *my* horse with it, too.

Keeping horses was a lot more work than I thought it would be. They were not always well-behaved and became experts at getting loose and running to the far corner of the neighbor's field. Once they were loose, it was very difficult to get near enough to catch them. After a few broken ropes and speedy escapes, I went to the feed store and bought the strongest nylon lead ropes and halters available. After this Mel's horse once tried to break loose while I was leading him in the yard and I quickly doubled the rope around a nearby pole and held on with all my strength. When he hit the end of his line, it nearly pulled him off his feet. It also nearly pulled the pole out of the ground. When I looked up I noticed that the pole was really a rather flimsy stake and that it was holding up the main power line to the house.

I didn't blame the horses for wanting out of their corral. They were both accustomed to wide-open spaces, and the corral was very small. After a few months of nonstop rain, they were ankle-deep in mud and horse manure. We hauled truckloads of sawdust to the stalls which helped keep their feet dry as they ate. I just couldn't seem to keep ahead of the accumulation of horse poop, however. When I tried to pick it up, my pitchfork got tangled in the wiry underbrush and I ended up just spreading it all around. During the day I sometimes tethered the horses in the orchard, but George wasn't used to ropes and would get his legs entangled and panic. Jesse knew how to step out of a rope. Having nearly strangled the dog, though, I didn't feel comfortable leaving her tied on long ropes.

Despite the high-calorie food, Mel's horse continued to look pathetic. We decided to have both the horses wormed, which the vet accomplished by shoving a long tube up the horse's nose and down into the stomach. It was nauseating and horrible to watch and gave poor George a nosebleed I thought was never going to stop. Afterwards, several species of live worms were expelled into the drenched corral where they continued to thrive in the weeds and manure. The worms were all it took to make the corral a real-life nightmare. I despise worms, and when I looked down and caught sight of them still flourishing days and weeks after the procedure, it made me want to throw up. I at least had to keep trying to keep the stalls clean. I faithfully hauled manure off the sawdust every day, and gradually it began to form a mountain in the far corner of the corral.

Jesse had become a different animal than the one I'd ridden in Eastern Washington. She developed a hyperactive gleam in her eye, and could no longer be described as a docile, gentle mare; a partially trained colt would have been a better description. It didn't occur to me that part of the problem might be what I was feeding her.

When her feet got better, I discovered she could run short stretches amazingly fast, and scramble around sharp corners like a rabbit. I had ridden some very spirited quarter horses in high school, and she was just like them; excitable, and a little hard to control.

Finding an open, safe place to ride was a bit of a problem. Although Vashon has beautiful horse trails, they are located on the opposite side of town. It would have been an all-day trip to reach them, ride on them, and then return home. Jesse was also afraid of the smell of the salt water, so the closer we got to the beach, the spookier she became. She was very talented at hopping sideways while tossing her head around, and I would have been better off riding her with a saddle. My saddle, though, just did not fit her. She was too narrow through the shoulders and wide in the back and I was afraid it would either fall off or rub her skin raw.

I was also concerned that her hackamore didn't fit properly. A hackamore is designed to put pressure on a sensitive part of the horse's nose, providing the rider with a greater degree of control. Hers seemed to hang ineffectively off the end of her nose, and I felt as though I were trying to ride

Chapter Eleven

with nothing but a halter. I tried to switch her to the gentlest type of bit, but she tossed her head and chewed the bit like it was driving her crazy. I didn't have enough experience with horses to know whether or not it was hurting her, so I went back to the hackamore. I might have been able to find the solution to some of these problems if we'd lived on Vashon longer. But we were so new on the island, I was short on resources.

So, I spent most of my time riding on the side of the road, and in the field next to our driveway. Jesse's feet were getting better, at least. They were soaking up all the moisture from the corral.

The real George and Jesse came to visit a little while after we got the horses. As usual, it was a cold, rainy day, so I cooked homemade bread and made thick, peppery split pea soup with ham to warm us up.

Grammie didn't seem too impressed with The Farm, after all she had heard about it. "I wish you wouldn't work so hard, Janni," she commented quietly as I handed her a bowl of soup.

"It's all right, Grammie, I like to work outside," I replied honestly. "I've got the horses, and my chickens. We'll get the house fixed up eventually."

After lunch we went out to the corral so I could show them George. As I led him from his stall, Grandpa began to laugh as though he was being let in on a private joke. "Are you sure they told you he was only ten years old?" he chuckled as he examined George's gums and teeth. "I'd say this horse is over twenty if he's a day."

"Just look though, Grandpa, look how neat he walks," I protested, leading the bony animal around in a circle. He laughed even harder.

"I think somebody sold you kids a bill of goods," he replied. I was beginning to wish we hadn't named him after Grandpa.

It was a bittersweet visit with sad goodbyes; as much as I had wanted to live in the country, I had to admit that it was lonely, and I knew Grammie sensed this. She was not feeling well again, a sure sign that her cancer had returned. She was facing more tests and hospitalizations. Tears ran down my cheeks as I watched them pull away from the house and disappear down the driveway, and I returned to the house to cry.

Mel arrived home, after dark as usual, and, as usual, he had company with him. It seemed we spent very little time together these days, less time visiting friends or parents, less time talking or making love; he wasn't even home for dinner most of the time because of the ferries. And in the morning, he was up before dawn to get back on the ferry for work. It was no mystery to me why I wasn't getting pregnant now; I hardly ever saw my husband.

TWELVE

If I had been riding alone the day I broke my neck, I surely would have died lying in the spot where I fell. The grass in the field was overgrown, and no one could have seen me from the road. The way it worked out, the aid car arrived within about twenty minutes.

"Get the clam scoop, Jim," the ambulance driver said quietly as he gazed down at me with concern on his face.

Their manner was professional, and I trusted them. A clam scoop is a big curved stretcher resembling a giant snow shoe. They gently slid me onto it and we started toward the ambulance. I asked Mack to put away the horses as the medical technicians covered me with a blanket and loaded me.

The medics explained that they were going to transport me by helicopter instead of waiting for a ferry. I had never been on a helicopter before and thought it might be fun, but it was rather disappointing. The engines were extremely loud and the ride was bumpy and uncomfortable. Instead of letting me rest, the medics asked questions the whole trip. When they ran out of questions, they repeated the ones they had already asked.

"Please spell your last name," they kept ordering.

"I've already spelled it," I replied wearily. I was feeling drowsy, and just wanted to close my eyes and go to sleep. "Spell it again, please, ma'am," they ordered. They talked like the cops in the Department of Motor Vehicles. I wished I had never changed my name. "May" had been so much easier to spell. When we got to Seattle I told the helicopter attendants that my father was a surgeon on the staff at Swedish Hospital and that I needed to go there, but they didn't seem to listen.

Instead, the helicopter landed at Harborview, the county's center for trauma victims. I was too sleepy to comprehend that this hospital was the only place set up for helicopter landings. I remember thinking they were just being uncooperative, but somehow the proper message got communicated and they loaded me into an ambulance headed for Swedish. The hospitals were only a few city blocks apart, and the downtown traffic was congested and slow. The ride seemed to take a long time. I was growing tired of staring up at people I didn't know, weary of their stiff, formal demeanors and military airs.

When we arrived at Swedish, my dad and several other people were waiting at the emergency entrance. "Hi Dad," I said as cheerfully as possible. "I think I broke my neck." The fact that I might have broken my neck didn't seem like a big deal to me. I could still think and see, and while I didn't feel good, I didn't really feel that bad. It hurt a little, but it was a strange kind of pain, unlike anything I'd ever experienced. I felt numb and tingly all over, and my body felt like it was floating.

Despite all the medical terminology and dictation I'd taken in business school, I knew absolutely nothing about spinal cord injuries. I was completely unaware that neck injuries can result in permanent paralysis, or that cervical fractures can cause loss of arm and hand function. Consequently, I just lay there, blissfully ignorant of the true extent of my injury, and determined to be a good sport no matter what the outcome.

Next, the emergency room attendants did what I thought was the craziest thing anyone had ever done; they started cutting up my clothes with scissors. "Don't chop up my favorite shirt," I protested, but they explained it was necessary. Then they started on my jeans and underwear. When they got to my underwear, one of the nurses asked, "Did you start your period today?"

"No," I replied wearily, "Those are my horseback riding underpants." I always wore my ugliest pair of underpants to ride in because they were made of stretchy, heavy fabric that didn't slip or climb and they were dingy and stained. "Just my luck to get sent to the hospital with them on," I thought to myself.

Chapter Twelve

The boots I was wearing had laces, so they didn't have to cut them off. I was silently grateful I didn't have on my Tony Lamas.

At about this point I realized I had become a helpless spectator of the events which would transpire, someone who had a voice but no actual control over the circumstances. It didn't frighten me that I couldn't move my arms or legs; the fact didn't even bother me. I was aware on some level that I had been seriously injured and that perhaps I might not even survive the injury, but I felt very strongly that, above all else, I wanted to continue living.

The nurses took me in to do some x-rays, and I can't remember anything that directly followed. My Mom said that later I began screaming and she pleaded with the medical staff to give me pain medication. They denied the request because it would have been too dangerous at the time. Apparently the body has a way of protecting itself from severe pain because I don't remember experiencing it at all. I must have lost consciousness during or after the x-rays, and only remember waking up afterwards.

When I awakened, the first thing I saw was Mel and my Dad sitting together, both crying very hard. It took me a second to assimilate the situation, to remember where I was and what had happened.

"It's really bad, baby," Mel choked. I had never seen him look this way, and it worried me.

"Jesus Christ, Janet, it's the worst broken neck I've ever seen," my dad added, and he, too, looked quite devastated. I still had a feeling things would be all right, that no matter what happened, I could get through it, so I just answered "Don't worry, I am going to be okay." What really hurt most was seeing them cry.

During the first few days in the hospital, I received over a hundred bouquets of flowers and equally as many visitors. I don't remember who came to see me, or any of the conversations, but I do remember seeing the flowers. They were stacked in colorful rows all around the room, a silent testimony that more people loved and cared for me than I ever could have imagined. Finally, the visitors had to be limited so I could rest. It made me very tired to try to talk.

When my father remarked that I had the worst broken neck he'd ever seen, he wasn't exaggerating. The fracture was at the C-6 level, and the C-6 vertebra was completely shattered. In the x-ray, the vertebrae above the fracture were clearly visible, but little or nothing appeared in the film below the break, indicating a severe dislocation along with the fracture. In order for the doctors to treat such an injury, I would have to be put in traction until the swelling went down enough for surgery.

The doctors drilled two holes in my skull, one on each side at about eyebrow level, for traction. They were very considerate of my feelings and tried not to traumatize me any more than necessary; they apologized for having to do it at all and promised not to shave off all my hair. Tongs were inserted into the holes and large weights were hung from them. Then I was sandwiched into a canvas Stryker frame so that they could turn me at regular intervals. The purpose of the frame is to immobilize a patient completely, while preventing skin ulcerations or pressure sores.

The only place I could really feel pressure was on my forehead, but by this time I was beginning to feel stiff and uncomfortable everywhere. I didn't like being on my back because I choked whenever I tried to drink, and I hated being on my stomach because the straps hurt my forehead and my chin. For the hours I was face down, nothing but the floor was visible. The nurses placed magazines underneath me to read, but I didn't really feel well enough to be interested. When someone wanted to visit with me, they lay underneath the frame on the floor so I could see them.

My breathing muscles had become very weak because of the level of my injury. I couldn't cough at all, and after choking on water a few times and having to be flipped so I wouldn't choke to death, my mom started using a baby bottle to give me liquids. The nurses made her stop doing this after awhile because they were afraid I would "regress psychologically."

They kept me in the Stryker frame for what seemed like an eternity, sustaining me with promises that after my spinal cord was fused I would be able to sleep in a normal bed. That's the way it was during all the months following

Chapter Twelve

my injury; small increments of progress gained monumental importance, and things which had always been taken for granted, such as eating and breathing, became daily obstacles to overcome.

As time went on, I lost weight and became very weak, and there was fear that I would catch pneumonia. As far as the doctors could tell, the accident had left me completely paralyzed, because at first I was unable to move even my arms. My family tried to remain optimistic, but I could tell they were feeling the strain as we waited out the tedious, uncomfortable days before surgery.

When Mel returned home he nearly shot my horse, and was talked out of it by friends. I have always been glad I didn't have to witness firsthand the way Mel felt about my injury. To share his grief at that time would have been too much for me to stand. I needed to focus all my energy on surviving, and getting well.

A few days before surgery, exhausted by the struggle of remaining positive, I finally broke down and began to cry while talking to my dad. "She's not having a good day today," he explained to the other doctors as they made their rounds.

"I guess that's not too hard to understand," one of them responded. I was finally obliged to stop crying before I really wanted to, because there was absolutely no way I could breathe lying on my back with a plugged-up nose.

The day of the surgery everyone seemed nervous, as though they weren't exactly sure what was going to happen. I guess I was a little scared myself, but it was exciting in a way. It seemed like things might begin to get better after the operation. I couldn't imagine them being any worse.

I was wheeled down to main surgery on a cart, with my father alongside, wearing a scrubsuit. He would be present during the surgery, which was being performed by a neurologist who was his former office partner. We waited for awhile in an outer operating room as they prepared for the operation. My father talked to me and held my hand.

The operating room was cavernous and surrealistic. Shiny-blue domes inverted in the ceiling held dim lights, reminding me of the inside of a spaceship. Everything was made of steel, and the room was hushed and quiet. The doctors and nurses were covered from head to toe in blue fabric, paper hats and shoes. Finally, my dad kissed me on the cheek and told me it was time to go.

Once inside the inner room, they gave me some ether and told me to take deep breaths. I remember feeling a strange heaviness inside my head, and after only a few breaths I was out like a light.

During the surgery, the doctors carefully removed the pieces of shattered vertebrae and then shaped a new vertebra from a piece of bone they had removed from my hip. The spinal column was then fused together by wrapping wire around the C-5, C-6, and C-7 vertebrae. They determined that the spinal cord had been completely severed due to the nature of the break and degree of dislocation.

When I woke up, Mel and my dad were sitting near my bed watching me anxiously. Mel was trying to tell me I was all right, but all I could sense was excruciating pain. I could do nothing but cry and say how much it hurt. After a few minutes Dad asked if anyone had given me any pain medicine. They had forgotten, so after they medicated me for pain I fell asleep again and don't remember anything that happened for quite awhile afterwards.

For the sake of the story, I asked Dad if he could remember any of the details of the next few days; but he, too, had blocked them from his memory. "Well gee," was his reply, "I really don't remember much. That was such an unpleasant time for you and everyone else. There just isn't much I can think of to tell you."

Although the surgery had gone well, it was extremely painful. Graduating to the normal bed wasn't quite the relief it should have been. I asked Mom to look around the house for the old foam pillow I used when I was little, hoping that it wouldn't hurt my neck as much as the hospital pillows. She managed to find it, but when I tried to use it, it was even worse. There didn't seem any position I could sleep in that didn't hurt my neck.

On the day I was supposed to be transferred from the ICU to a regular floor, the nurses discovered that I had de-

Chapter Twelve

veloped a raging case of pneumonia. After they listened to my lungs, I had to be rushed back down the hall to the ICU to be intubated. This was accomplished somehow while I was still conscious, although it felt like they were going to break every bone in my face before they got the tube down. The doctors complained that I had a little nose, but actually it was a big tube. I think the reason I was able to tolerate the procedure was that they were all acting like I was going to die any second, and I sort of believed them.

My parents left that night with specific instructions to the nursing staff to call them if necessary, particularly if I was scared. The tube resting in the back of my throat made me feel like I was choking; it was breathing for me, though not at the rate I'd have preferred. My arms still wouldn't move; they were strapped down so that the only thing I could move was my eyes. When I tried to speak, I discovered this was impossible; also, the tube was resting on my vocal cords. It was frightening and horrible and I desperately wanted my parents. I tried to mouth out, "Call my mom!" to the night nurse, but he just kept saying, "You are fine. Everything is going well. There is no reason to call your parents. Just try to go to sleep."

I was in pain and felt like I was going to strangle. I was scared half to death and didn't trust any of the people around me. By about four in the morning I was convinced that the night shift nurse was the most sadistic, selfish person on the face of the earth. He didn't want to call my parents, even though they had requested he do just that if I was frightened. He was afraid it would make him look bad. He was oblivious to my anxiety, which was turning to sheer panic as I realized that any request I made was going to be ignored. I knew the nurse was fully aware of my request to have him call my parents or sedate me so I could sleep. At about five in the morning he finally gave in and gave me something for sleep. I was intubated for three or four more days before my lungs started to clear. It was one of the most frightening and uncomfortable experiences of the first part of my hospital stay.

The new room was a nice private room with spacious windows and a television, but my condition after surgery wasn't improving as much as we had hoped. The doctors determined immediately that I would never walk again, and now there was even some question as to how much arm and hand movement I would regain. The doctors carefully explained that fractures of the cervical spine can often result in quadriplegia: paralysis of all four limbs. I was able to move my arms slightly, but not well enough to touch my face or feed myself. I had no movement in my hands or fingers, so I couldn't pick anything up. One afternoon, one of the orthopedic doctors who helped perform my surgery gave me a small stuffed animal, and I discovered that it would stay in my hand if I positioned it between my thumb and forefinger. I was very excited because it was the first object I was able to pick up. I practiced holding it and tried as hard as I could to lift my arms, but they were extremely weak.

Although I had to be fed and completely cared for by others, the reality of my newly acquired condition and the details of how it would affect my life still had not sunk in. I asked the doctors if I would still be able to have a baby, and they smiled and said yes. It didn't occur to me to wonder how I would manage to take care of a baby. It didn't seem to me that being in a wheelchair could be too bad. One of the physical therapists told me that wheelchairs came in neat colors like orange and yellow and I visualized myself sailing gracefully through downtown Vashon in a yellow wheelchair, dressed in a long billowy skirt. I had seen people in wheelchairs on TV, and they seemed to get around just fine. If I could still go outside, travel around in cars, and be with the people I loved, then it seemed like life would still be worth living.

With spinal cord injuries as severe as mine, the brain can no longer send a message to the body to pump blood from the lower extremities back to the head. Therefore, if I had tried to sit up I would have passed out. This problem would be dealt with later in rehabilitation, but for the time being I had to remain completely flat at all times. I caught pneumonia twice before I was considered for rehab, and the doctors feared that my lungs would never regain their former health and strength.

Chapter Twelve

We were given a special dish, like a large bedpan, so that Mom could wash my hair in bed. She also brought in a couple of her silky nightgowns and helped me apply eyeshadow and lipstick so that I could look nice when Mel came to visit. The procedure was very time-consuming, and usually the day I washed my hair would end up being a day Mel didn't show up. This was very disappointing. Mom sensed my disappointment, and felt bad along with me.

Mel didn't seem to be taking my accident well. He was grief-stricken and depressed, and it became very difficult for us to communicate our feelings. I really needed him to be there for me, and it hurt a lot when he wasn't. At the same time, I didn't understand what he was going through; basically, we were not viewing my situation in the same way. To Mel it was a terrible tragedy, an immediate and devastating loss.

I could not afford to be as concerned with loss because I needed to focus all my energy on what could be regained. My optimistic attitude lasted until I was transferred, lying flat on my back on a stretcher, to the rehabilitation center. There, during the course of my stay, bitter pieces of reality slowly began to drift together.

THIRTEEN

The rehabilitation center belonged to the same university my father had attended as a resident. It was the largest rehab facility in the area, and nearly the only one. I had fond memories of the halls and laboratories Marie and I had invaded as children, and thought it would be fun, in a way, to return to the place of my childhood adventures, even though it would be as a patient.

The process of being transferred in the ambulance was exciting because it was the first time I had been outside since my accident. Mom went along with me and helped transfer my few belongings. When I arrived we were greeted by a young, conservative-looking woman who would be my primary care nurse. After introductions—which were somewhat difficult as I was lying flat on my back—I was admitted to the hospital and we were shown my new room.

The woman I was supposed to share a room with was about fifty years old and nearly comatose after her stroke. All she could do was writhe in the bed and scream. Her loud cries and moans were upsetting, and my mother suggested to the staff that she probably was not the best choice as my first roommate.

My second roommate's name was Donna. She looked about my age and was sleeping when we came in. Her eyes were swollen and bruised and her entire head was bandaged with white gauze. After I settled into bed, my nurse told me Donna's story.

She had been homesteading in Alaska with her fiancé and his parents in an area so remote that the only access was by air. Donna and her boyfriend had approached the property in their plane to signal for a landing. After tipping

Chapter Thirteen

their wings over the house, they turned to land. A load of ice dumped into the carburetor and the plane's engine failed. The plane crash-landed on one wing with the passenger side downward buried in snow.

    Both passengers had to be cut out of the wreckage because the plane was so badly damaged. Partway through getting Donna out, the cutting torches sparked and threatened to ignite the airplane fuel which had soaked both her and the inside of the plane. The rescuers, one of whom was Donna's future father-in-law, just ripped the wing off the plane by hand and got her out. She suffered a broken back and neck, fractured ribs, and her skull was shattered like an eggshell. Her fiancé was killed in the crash. They speculated that Donna was able to survive her injuries because of a lowered body temperature that slowed her blood circulation and reduced internal bleeding.

    Despite the bandages, bruises, and swelling, it was apparent that she was a very pretty girl. She had large eyes, high cheekbones, and a delicate, ivory complexion. After everyone left, I started to cry about her and accidentally woke her up. "Why are you crying?" she blurted out, thinking I was in pain.

    "Because I feel sorry for you," I answered. "They told me your boyfriend got killed in the plane wreck. I don't know what I would do if my husband died." I wouldn't even want to live, I thought to myself.

    She explained that it had been a tremendous shock at first, but that she had been hospitalized for quite some time and was grateful to have survived. We got along well right from the beginning and it was a pleasure to discover that Donna's sense of humor remained undisturbed. She entertained me with stories of wild bar fistfights she had gotten into with tough Alaskan women. She was an obvious fighter or she wouldn't have been alive. She'd lived through two cardiac arrests in the hospital, and sported a large, deep purple pressure sore on her forehead, sustained during the emergency procedures necessary to save her life. Her head had been shaved, and she now wore a choppy, uneven crewcut. She told me regretfully that she once had long, thick red hair. It's going to take forever to grow it out again,

I thought again to myself. As badly injured as we both were, we were not so miserable that we stopped worrying about our hair.

The rehab center was a teaching institute, which meant that resident doctors and students of the university were assigned to part of our care. My resident's name was Henk, a Dutch doctor who had been born in the British West Indies. He spoke softly, with the most fascinating accent I've ever heard. Right from the start, he was optimistic about my recovery, and he had a way of saying things which instilled confidence in me.

"I theenk you will be able to do very well," he would say, "But it's going to take some time. First we have to get you sitting up and then we will see what we can do from there. It will not be easy, but you must not give up. And I will be with you every step of the way in case there are any problems."

He meant every word he said, too. Recovering was difficult, but he was with me every step of the way. People with cervical spinal cord lesions have to retrain every system in their body before they can resume normal life.

The medical staff had already explained to me that my brain no longer knew how to pump the blood from my lower body to my head, and that if I sat up I would pass out. The remedy for this is an instrument called a tilt table onto which a supine patient is strapped and gradually tipped upward until they feel dizzy. Then they are let back down. This is repeated until, finally, the patient is able to tolerate a standing position. At first I felt dizzy and nauseated when the table was tipped even slightly. If it wasn't let down right away, all the color would go out of the room and I would start seeing stars. I had good days and bad. All told, I believe it took a month or six weeks before I was able to tolerate the board all the way up. Dangling from Velcro supports on an upright board was an eerie sensation; ninety degrees felt greater than ninety degrees, and I remember feeling like the straps were going to slip and I would dive head first through the plate glass window in front of me.

After graduating from the tilt table, I was outfitted with an amazingly uncomfortable neck brace, long elastic stock-

Chapter Thirteen

ings, and an elastic corset which wrapped around my ribs and abdomen. I was now ready to get up in a reclining wheelchair.

I was excited about my progress, and it surprised me to discover that other people found my condition so upsetting that they would burst into tears when they saw me. My best friend from junior high was the first one to react with shock when he saw me. He seemed to be afraid to look at me, so I tried to reassure myself with the thought that he just wasn't used to hospitals. When I pointed out that I was actually much improved, he replied, "Damn, Janet, I'm sure glad you feel that way, but I feel terrible about it," and there was nothing more I could say to cheer him up.

After Grammie crumpled into tears as she walked into my room, I truly began to wonder what was going on. Obviously, people were seeing something horrible in this situation that I was not. In retrospect, I probably did look pathetic with my body encased in white elastic like a mummy, and my head and shoulders clamped in a bizarre metal brace with a chin rest.

It was also obvious that Mel was having difficulty accepting the severity and permanence of my injury. He didn't come to visit as often as I would have liked, and although he attempted to be encouraging, he often seemed focused on the things I could no longer do.

The day my hand function was tested was very disappointing for Mel. I had recovered partial movement in my arms, but no independent movement in my fingers. Whenever he visited, he would stretch my hands and want me to try to open them. "C'mon Janet," he would plead, "You can't let them curl up. Just try to move them." No matter how hard I tried, I could not move my fingers. We had both seen quadriplegics in the rehab center with their hands atrophied and their fingers curled, and it scared us.

In order to test my hand function, I was taken to a room where electrodes were strapped to my arms to determine whether any brain impulses were still getting through to the fingers. The prognosis was that it was unlikely I would ever regain use of my hands. A doctor explained to us that tendon surgery might be an option in the future, but that it was doubtful whether it would help; it could also be disfiguring. It was just too much for Mel. He swore angrily at the doctors and left the hospital in tears.

    I don't know what was going through his head after I broke my neck; it was too painful for me to think about how he or the other members of my family felt. I assume that he felt shocked, abandoned, and lonely. He was faced with the fact that his wife's life had changed permanently and irreversibly, and that the person he had loved for years and promised his entire life to would never walk again, ride again, or feel again the way she had. Even my physical appearance would gradually be altered in ways beyond my control. Because I chose to live, I would eventually have to accept these changes.

    Mel was faced with a very difficult decision, one that would haunt him for the rest of his life. He had to determine whether he could change enough to remain with me.

    My days were total drudgery, and looking back I can barely stand to think about them. Every morning an occupational therapist came in and helped me learn to feed myself. I was outfitted with special elastic cuffs which attached the silverware to my hands. I needed to drink from a straw because my arms were still too weak to lift the glass to my mouth without spilling it. My lack of coordination kept reminding me of a heartless joke we used to tell when we were in grade school about a child with cerebral palsy who accidentally crammed his ice cream cone into his forehead instead of his mouth. Now, I was on the other side of the fence, and I knew what it felt like. The only thing that was worse than spilling food was having someone else feed me, which made me feel like a helpless infant. I was finding out the difference between a paraplegic and a quadriplegic, the hard way.

    A large part of my rehabilitation was to determine the extent of my strength and balance. The other most critical focus was the tedious process of bladder and bowel retraining. Theory had it that each individual possessed an ability to retrain the bladder, a belief which piqued researchers' imaginations and gave birth to much experimentation.

    I was placed on an intermittent catheterization program

Chapter Thirteen

with carefully restricted fluids. Even the fluid content of the food I received was painstakingly measured. Then I was shown how to hit myself repeatedly in the bladder to cause the bladder to spasm and empty. This was difficult and sometimes painful. Due to the risk of infection, the procedure was not considered successful if any urine remained in the bladder. It never worked for me, and the cath team always had to come and insert a straight-in-and-out catheter afterwards.

The catheterization was set on a schedule of every six hours: six a.m. and noon, six p.m. and midnight. A special team of nurses traveled around the rehab department doing nothing but catheterizing patients, so that we wouldn't have to return to our rooms each time. I very rarely made it to the allotted time, and would end up soaked with pee, lying on a stretcher in a deserted hallway waiting for the cath team to finish emptying my bladder. I was then changed to a dry gown and sent back to continue physical and occupational therapy.

I remember my fascination with graphic wall posters showing the different positions an indwelling catheter assumed once inside the bladder. The tubes resembled coiled worms, which I found disturbing. The posters didn't make sense to me. Wouldn't the possibilities be infinite, given that every person is shaped differently? I pondered this question at length while I waited for the grisly nurses in rubber gloves to come and clean me up.

Bowel training was also an essential part of the rehab program. I took routine bowel care by nurses for granted, not sure if I were ready to explore how to deal with this highly personal, delicate matter. Independence was the primary objective.

In order to accomplish an independent bowel program, the patient is seated on a commode in the middle of their room. Rather than a standard bedpan-like device under the commode, the nurses drape the floor with a plastic tarp so that nothing can obstruct the view. Then the patient is instructed to locate their rectum in the mirror.

A long rubber poker with a disposable cover on it was fitted to my hand with a strap. I couldn't help but notice that the device was exactly like the ones we used to hold our silverware. The nurses called the device a "fickle finger" and it was to be slipped into the rectum and moved around in a circular motion—"digital stimulation"—which is intended to cause the bowel muscle to contract and create a bowel movement.

On observing my anatomy in the mirror, I became immediately, acutely aware of the reason people wear clothes. At the same moment, I made a firm mental determination not to cooperate with the experiment.

I was dismayed to learn that the "fickle finger of fate," the subject of many hilarious skits from the *Laugh-In* television show in the 1960s, had a basis in reality. I wondered whether one of the writers for the show had had personal experiences with the finger, or if my nurses just had a tasteless and bizarre sense of humor.

The policy in rehab was that patients should try everything at least once, so I pretended to try, acting as uncoordinated as possible. They finally determined that I was having too much difficulty getting the right angle on the instrument and the experiment was abandoned almost immediately.

Next they announced that family members, including the husband, should actively participate in the nursing care so that I could visit home. At the hospital's request, Mel came in to learn bowel programs.

It was awkward to discuss or even explain in medical terms. My primary care nurse was apologetic and visibly embarrassed during the instruction, explaining that it was just part of her job.

Again I was positioned on a commode chair in the middle of my hospital room with a piece of plastic draped underneath the chair. The nurse inserted a suppository and gave Mel a pair of examination gloves to put on. He was shown the technique of digital stimulation and asked to perform it on me. It produced an odorous bowel movement which landed, steaming, on the plastic. The procedure was to be repeated until the bowels were empty, a lengthy, time-consuming process. I perched uncomfortably on the plastic commode chair and passively observed the scene. My hus-

Chapter Thirteen

band squinted and held his breath as he peeled a poopy glove off his hand, turning it inside out. The nurse's face flushed with humiliation as she talked him through the ordeal.

Inwardly I attempted to detach myself from the situation. I was not the subject of this gruesome situation; I was somewhere else, a different person. The episode was unreal. We were both having a bad dream and would wake up soon at home together, in a soft, warm bed, shaken but relieved.

They could have been a little more discreet, or perhaps allowed us to discuss our options beforehand. They could have thought, just a little, about our marriage. But to do this would have interfered with the hospital's goals. While striving to maintain a facade of training people to do things for themselves, they glibly overlooked the fact that a full twenty-four-hour nursing staff was right at the end of the call light. They transferred the nursing care to the family as though it were nothing but a mechanical action.

The dictionary defines patient as "a person who is under medical treatment" and as "bearing annoyance and pain without complaint or anger." Some synonyms for the word are "accepting," "forbearing," or "tolerant." This is a fairly accurate description of the way I thought I was supposed to act as a patient.

I realized immediately when I broke my neck that I was going to need to depend on others. Faced with a total inability to do things for myself, it wasn't difficult to accept help. By the time I had been in the hospital for about three months, the patient mentality had firmly taken root. I was living from day to day, relying on others for all my needs, without any hope of being released any time soon. I told myself it didn't do any good to wonder why I was going through these experiences. I felt I didn't have any choice.

There was something important I missed when I developed this passive attitude about accepting help. I didn't distinguish between physical and emotional independence, and, because I was physically dependent, I felt obliged in some cases to let others make decisions for me. Part of the reason for this was that I didn't feel I had the knowledge to direct my own care. But I did have the ability to make informed choices, if they were offered.

When I was signed into rehab, my family was told that the rehab goal was to teach patients to become independent. "Independent enough to live all by yourself, if you want to," they repeated, when speaking of this lofty goal.

The term independence implies freedom, autonomy, and a license to choose. This is not the way the hospital treated us as patients; we were told exactly what to do, and when to do it. Objections to the program were simply not allowed; Mel's participation in my personal care was considered mandatory. Simultaneously the staff quoted us statistics, indicating that the success rate for marriages in our age group in similar situations was close to zero.

They should have explained to Mel that he would be committing himself essentially to full-time nursing care, and that not all people have the patience and care-giving qualities necessary for this type of work. It was his right as an adult to choose whether he wanted to become involved, and, if so, to what degree. Instead, he was made to feel that participating was his duty as a husband. The end result was that he felt unbearably guilty when he realized he could not clean up poop and change wet beds in the middle of the night, and take it all in stride. It was pointed out by staff that his "inability to cope" was due to his age, that is, his immaturity. No one attempted to help him resolve his feelings. They were left silently unacknowledged, and we both suffered a great deal from the consequences.

The next nursing procedure Mel was required to learn was that of performing intermittent catheterization, a challenging procedure which even professionals sometimes find difficult.

The person performing the catheterization must observe sterile technique, taking great care not to contaminate gloves by touching nonsterile surfaces. The vaginal area of the patient is first cleansed with iodine, then a sterile, lubricated catheter is inserted into the urethra. The urine is drained into a plastic tray, and the catheter is removed. The opening of the urethra is tiny, and lies encased in folds of tissue. If the urethra is missed, the catheter usually finds its

Chapter Thirteen

way up the vagina instead. This violates the catheter's sterility and the whole operation has to be repeated.

Despite the fact that Mel had always hated hospitals, he became very adept at the demanding tasks assigned to him. He made every effort to cooperate with the staff and do what they told him he should do. He deserved much more credit than he got from anyone.

Since I had broken my neck at the C-6 level, I was left without feeling from midchest down. This meant that I could not come to a sitting position from flat on my back without pulling myself up. My hospital bed was a hideous stainless steel contraption with large bolts protruding from all the joints, somewhat resembling a medieval torture rack. The head and the foot of the bed could be raised, and its height was adjustable. It was outfitted with a series of khaki green canvas loops, and I was taught how to travel up them by using one arm and then another until I was at a sitting position. Mel expressed pride the first time he saw me do it. Whenever he encouraged me, I took it as an indication that he was handling things okay, and that we were going to be all right. I wanted to work as hard as I could so I could get out of the hospital and go back to my home, husband, and animals, and resume my former life.

We decided emphatically that we did not want the ugly steel bed in our farmhouse. Against the hospital's heated objections, Mel built me a beautiful bed frame from cedar four-by-fours. The only difference between the hospital bed and the one he built was that its height was not adjustable. It was therefore less versatile for transfers. However, we tied one of Jesse's reins in a knot for a loop, and the bed suited our purposes just fine.

FOURTEEN

Once I was up in a wheelchair, the staff determined I should be allowed to go home "on pass" for the first time. It would give Mel and me a chance to be together again, and he could take care of me, because he had been shown how to do it. I was still on an intermittent cath program, with carefully restricted fluids. Mel was instructed to perform the catheterizations at the regular six-hour intervals.

The house was pretty much the same as when I had left: broken windows, clawfoot bathtub, and all. The horses hadn't been ridden at all since my accident and were wild and unruly. There were only a few of the bantam chickens left. Most of them had fallen prey to raccoons or wild dogs, since I was no longer there to tuck them in at night. My favorite, Skinny Jimmy, was still alive and seemed happy to see me.

Adjusting to home life with my new injury was, in simple terms, not easy. The intermittent cath program didn't work any better at home than it did in the hospital, and, with Mel alone as a twenty-four-hour nurse, it was totally unworkable. I peed all over the double bed at midnight, so Mel had to get up and change it before he could even catheterize me. It was very difficult for him; he was unaccustomed to making beds, and nursing seemed to try his patience. It was frustrating for me to cause him so much work, and then be unable to help him with it. All I could do was watch helplessly as he tried to hold back his frustration.

At six in the morning, the alarm clock sounded, alerting him that it was time to drain my bladder again. Later in the morning, he carried me into the musty old bathroom to give me a much-needed bath. While he was attempting to

Chapter Fourteen

bathe me, I pooped in the bathtub, just like in my childhood. I felt like the ashamed small child who had once angered her father by soiling the bath water. I remained silent, hearing the child's voice in the back of my mind saying, "I'm sorry; I didn't mean to do it." He had to chase the poop around in the tub while holding on to me so I wouldn't fall over and drown. He finally managed to drag me out of the murky water, cleaned me up to the best of his ability, and took me back into the bedroom.

We both felt confused and discouraged by the outcome of the first home visit. There certainly wasn't anything fun about it. The house didn't even seem comfortable any more, and my personal care consumed so much of Mel's energy that we barely talked. He didn't hold me at night the way I had hoped he would. Instead, he curled up with his back to me, falling into a deep, exhausted sleep. I was glad to return to the hospital, where it was a normal job to take care of me. The humiliation of no longer being in control of my body was made a hundred times worse when it consumed someone else's life.

There was no one on the regular hospital staff who could help us sort out the many painful and difficult issues we were facing in our lives and marriage. When the patients were visited by a psychologist, it was for routine examinations to determine whether or not we were crazy.

Without emotional support, Mel and I began to deny our situation and withdraw from one another. My resident, Henk, tried to talk to Mel, but Mel didn't open up as much as I hoped he would. We needed counseling as a couple. We were never offered it, nor did we comprehend at the time how much we needed it. For fear of saying the wrong things, we said nothing to each other about our feelings.

Looking back, it seems to me that many of the rehab hospital's commonly accepted practices were not in the best interest of the patients. One misleading and potentially damaging piece of information we received was that paralyzed people needed Valium; tons of Valium. It was routinely prescribed to each spinal cord-injured patient for muscle spasms, which, we were warned, "could be strong enough to make your knee fly up and hit you in the chin." Since none of us wanted this to happen, we dutifully took all that was prescribed; ten milligrams at breakfast, lunch, dinner, and bedtime. This was an astounding amount of a drug that was linked to depression, sleep disorders, and memory loss. Now, large doses of Valium are only administered to patients to render them unconscious. I've often wondered if the use of such heavy medication was the reason my emotional response to our situation was conspicuously void.

As recreational drugs, especially marijuana, were a part of many people's lives during that time, additional hospital-prescribed substances were probably less noticed, and therefore possibly all that much more dangerous. Soon Valium was being passed around at parties just like beer and pot, and I became everyone's best friend.

A few days after the first disastrous trip home, I was visited by a stuffy team of doctors, who pompously announced that they had determined the intermittent cath program to be a failure and were going to allow me to wear an indwelling catheter. They explained that catheters greatly increased the risk of bladder infections and that it might be necessary for me to take extra medications in order to prevent this. Now, rather than restrict my fluid intake, it would be important for me to drink plenty of fluids. I listened to the announcement with relief. It seemed the best solution to what had been a very upsetting, time-consuming problem, and I was glad the experimentation was finally over.

Physical therapy was becoming more frustrating, as the difficulty of the tasks increased. I was initially taught to transfer myself, with or without a sliding board, onto a mat. I was good at straight-on transfers, but the sliding board, which was necessary to transfer sideways, tended to slide out from under me, and I didn't trust it.

Once on the mat, I was supposed to try to come to a sitting position from lying down, and roll from my back onto my stomach without the aid of loops. When we were little, Marie and I had spent a great deal of time rescuing beetles which had flipped upside down on the sidewalk, and I thought of them as I struggled helplessly, unable to turn over or sit up.

They also worked at teaching me to empty my legbag,

Chapter Fourteen

a seemingly impossible task that frustrated me to tears before an hour passed. The reason it was so difficult was that I was required to bend over frontwards and grasp a plug located by my ankle. Since I had to keep one arm around the back of the chair to avoid falling, this left only one hand for the plug. With no finger grip, it was impossible. They tried a plug which twisted shut, but it leaked. Bending over so far also caused me to lose my balance when I resumed a sitting position. Had the therapists understood simple body mechanics, they would have realized that leaning forward and reaching down were causing my weight to shift in the chair, and either the position of my leg or the location of the bag needed to be changed. I learned these things gradually, year by year, after my release from the hospital.

My confidence in the staff eroded quickly when I realized many of them were just students. More than once, my therapist for the day actually walked into the room with an open textbook and said, "Well, I think we'll try the transfer on page 26 today." Methods for car transfers changed daily, with each separate therapist, who often substituted the car owned by the university with a car owned by an employee. Some of the cars were so tiny and low to the ground that the transfer would have been hard for even an able-bodied person to master. Often I found myself twisted like a pretzel, with the sliding board jammed crookedly between me and the door. At such times I had to be extricated by two physical therapists. On one such occasion, one of them remarked, "I always like to see a patient really botch up a transfer. Then we can see if they can get themselves out of it."

We were allowed to slip and bump our heads, and my arms became covered with bruises from the brutal physical therapy sessions. I was never able to manage a car transfer safely or independently, but they kept trying to teach me until I left the hospital. We were also supposed to pull a forty-pound wheelchair into the seat beside us without falling out of the car. I couldn't even pick up the footrests. I did well pulling weights, and the strength in my arms was coming back, but the lack of trunk balance and limited use of my hands made things very difficult.

Occupational therapy, however, wasn't quite as bad. I was fitted with a brace for my arm—a "hinge splint"—which helped bring my thumb and forefinger together so I could write. The handwriting was shaky and illegible at first, but improved with practice.

As soon as I got the splint, I started to paint again. The first painting I did was one of my cherished pet chicken, Skinny Jimmy. Later, I started on a large watercolor of some high, black cliffs with a river running down through them. The scene reminded me of the cliffs Mel and I had climbed at Lake Harrison. I carefully wrote "To Mel, Love Janet" at the bottom and had it framed for him.

In occupational therapy we were encouraged to try cooking, although the therapist did all of the actual work. She showed us some easy recipes, and cautiously allowed us to use an electric frying pan. We were warned repeatedly against burning our arms in places where we had limited feeling. She tried to show us how to crack an egg without crushing it into a million pieces, but none of us could do it. The only exercise I really hated was being seated at a table and told to try to pick up little tiny beans with our stiff, motionless fingers. It seemed nearly impossible, and was very trying to one's patience.

After awhile it became apparent to me that certain patients were being used by the institution as models of success. People who excelled at a particular task were asked to demonstrate it in a little film made for the benefit of the university. Failures were dealt with by fatalistic threats of total dependence on others.

A good example of this was learning to open and pass through the hospital's heavy fire doors. We were taken to a deserted hallway and instructed to position the wheelchair next to the door and pull it open. I couldn't do it then, and it is still impossible for me to do to this day. It tips a manual wheelchair up on two wheels to pull against that much weight. If one manages to work a wheelchair partway through a heavy door with a spring, it closes on the wheelchair and one is really stuck. I have never had to wait in a public place for very long for someone to come along and help with a door. The weakest old ladies and the most dis-

Chapter Fourteen

reputable-looking people around can usually manage a smile and provide assistance for a person in a wheelchair who needs to get through a door.

A great deal of emphasis was put on learning transfers which were considered a key to true independence. While learning, we were instructed to wear polyester pants, because they slid easily onto other surfaces. These unattractive garments were then outfitted with loops sewn into the waistband and we were taught to pull them up by turning from side to side in bed. With great effort, I was able to pull up my pants, but I couldn't put on my own underwear because it would just rip. I also couldn't pull up the pant zipper, so it was outfitted with a large metal ring. Day after day, I practiced pulling up my pants, after having the nurse help me with my underwear. Someone also had to help me fasten buttons, and put on my shoes.

I still thought of myself as a cowgirl, and considered it a supreme insult to wear polyester pants. By the time I'd been outfitted with the neck brace, hand splints, and shiny pants with loops and rings, I felt like a freak from outer space, and vowed to throw away the pants the second I left the hospital.

I was able to manage a transfer fairly well wearing slippery pants and sliding onto a hard mat, and so was deemed successful with the technique. However, the first time I tried it at home, my wheelchair—with brakes fully locked—slid out from under me and I landed on the floor. The floor was not the *right kind* and the friction of regular clothes on blankets was too great to allow a successful sliding transfer.

The rehab program did not allow conceptualization of our life as a human. For example, what would have happened if I had gone home after successfully learning to drain my bladder by "tapping," or hitting it with my hand? Each time I had to go to the bathroom, it would have been necessary for me to transfer onto a bed, undress completely, transfer onto a commode or toilet, complete the tapping, get back to the bed to dress again, and finally transfer back to the chair. The process of simple urination would have been so time- and energy-consuming it would have been impossible for me to do anything else.

These oversights became stumbling blocks to my adjustment during the years following my initial injury. When a learned technique failed at home, I tended to abandon it, rather than experiment until I got it right. The changes we were facing in our lives were so overwhelming that we had no energy left for the experimentation necessary to make progress. It took me years of difficult emotional adjustment before I was really prepared to face some of the important physical challenges which would increase my independence. Each new accomplishment required a long period of trial and error, considerable adjustments to the home environment, and a dogged determination not to give up.

By this time it was late spring. I had been in rehab for five months and was ready to try another home visit. We expected things to be much easier now that I had the new catheter, and Mel even wanted to take me on a trip. "Finally," I thought, "things are going to return to normal. We both just need to get out of town together like we used to."

Mel's brother lived in Reno where he operated his propeller shop. We planned to visit him and his wife. We had been very close in the past, and wanted to go camping at Lake Tahoe for a few days.

We desired to go alone as a couple, so Mel had agreed to tend to my personal needs during the trip. He borrowed his parents' mobile home. It was fairly roomy and had a small bathroom in the back that I could use. There would be enough room to store the wheelchair and the supplies we planned to take. Mel was looking forward to the expedition, and neither of us anticipated any problems.

It was very hot on the way down, and we stopped often to pick up necessary items like sunglasses and ice. At one point, Mel stopped at a department store and bought me new clothes to wear. All my jeans from the farm were so worn that they looked terrible, and he wanted me to look and feel pretty. He went into the store without me, guessed my size by just looking at the clothes, and came back out carrying two outfits that fit perfectly.

Although the weather was uncomfortably warm, we really enjoyed the long drive to Nevada. I was ecstatic to be with Mel once again, and the first few days we traveled to-

Chapter Fourteen

gether seemed almost like old times.

We spent the first evening in Reno, catching Mel's brother up on family news. We slept in a comfortable spare room, sharing the same bed, but not making love. It was much too soon after my injury to begin thinking about sex. I blithely assumed that our marital relations would return to normal naturally, when I had recovered a little more.

In the morning, Mel rigged up a makeshift shower seat and helped me take a shower. While bathing me, he noticed that the elastic abdominal binder I thought I needed to help maintain my blood pressure was hanging loosely around my ribs in a manner that was not doing any good at all. "Look at this, Janet, you don't even need this thing," he said as he pulled it off. I waited a few minutes, expecting to feel dizzy, and then acknowledged that I no longer needed it. We threw it away and were minus one reminder that I was still a patient in a hospital.

After breakfast we all loaded into the mobile home and headed for Lake Tahoe to swim and picnic. It was extremely hot and dry in Nevada, and I couldn't wait to get a tan.

After a spinal cord injury, a person's body loses its ability to regulate temperature. Therefore one must take great care to dress properly for the weather. We had been amply warned about this, but I had only experienced what it was like to be too cold. "The hotter the better" I thought to myself. "For once I'll finally get warm enough."

The searing heat felt wonderful and we sunbathed at the edge of the lake all afternoon. I wore the top to my swimming suit, but didn't want to take off my pants because there was no way to hide the catheter and legbag. After a few hours of baking myself in the direct sun, I finally admitted to being overheated and Mel carried me out into the water, holding me by beltloops so I could practice floating. It was great fun. The water was so icy it took my breath away at first, and we shrieked and hollered like little kids. Once in awhile, Mel pretended to let go of me until I started to sink. We found that I could still float on my back pretty well, but when I was on my stomach, I sunk like a rock. Mel's brother watched from the shore, amazed that we still had the ability to act crazy in spite of what we'd been through so recently. I had to go swimming several times that afternoon, but wouldn't consider getting out of the sun.

By evening, the temperature only dropped a few points, and the four of us retired to the stifling mobile home to sleep. During the middle of the night I woke up suddenly, feeling extremely short of breath. My nose was stuffed and my eyes watered as I struggled for breath. "Mel, I'm sick," I called. He was sleeping in a nearby bunk.

My sister-in-law sat bolt upright in bed. "What's wrong?" she yelled, with panic in her voice.

By this time, everyone was awake. "I just feel like I can't get enough air," I gasped, scaring everyone in the trailer.

Mel gave me a drink of water and opened the door of the mobile home. "You're probably just way too hot," he said, fanning me with fresh air. "You really got sunburned today."

After about twenty minutes, I recovered enough to go back to sleep. I was embarrassed that I had caused such a commotion, and had trouble going back to sleep. After my sister-in-law's reaction, it was obvious that some people still thought of me as someone who could die any second. We monitored my exposure to the sun for the rest of the trip.

By the following morning, it was time for me to have a bowel program, which Mel helped with in the mobile home's tiny bathroom. The air was stagnant, the quarters were cramped, and the septic tank gave off a sickening chemical odor all its own. While necessary, the procedure was very unpleasant due to the heat and lack of space. Mel appeared to have lost his tolerance for nursing well before it was over, and I was beginning to regret ever having come on the trip. My physical needs seemed endless and were made infinitely more difficult by the confines of the mobile home. Getting me cleaned up and dressed on the narrow bunk was another ordeal, and Mel was aggravated and sweating by the time he finished.

Even though Mel was physically strong, he soon grew weary of lifting me and carrying me through small, nearly inaccessible spaces. I was as dependent as a baby, but much taller and heavier. For the first time, I regretted having such long legs. They were useless to me now, and served only to get in the way.

Chapter Fourteen

On the fourth day of the trip, we decided it was time to go home. By this time, Mel was so tired of taking care of me that he laid me down on a bunk behind the driver's seat and made me stay there until we got home. He drove straight through from Nevada to Seattle without even stopping to sleep. It was boring lying on the backseat alone, and I felt rejected. At the time, I didn't understand his frustration. I understand it now.

The hospital had an annoying "we told you so" attitude when they heard about how the trip had ended. After all, it had been our idea. "Now are you beginning to see that your husband isn't going to be able to take care of you in the way you had hoped?" one doctor asked maliciously.

"My husband and I will be just fine," I responded defensively. They didn't seem able to resist any opportunity to blame our difficulties on Mel. I was a little hurt by Mel's lack of patience, but I wasn't mad at him.

"He's been through enough without everybody criticizing him," I continued. "I know he loves me, and that's all that matters to me." The doctor gazed back scornfully for a second, turned on his heel, and left the room.

Afterwards I cried bitterly, overwhelmed by discouragement and loneliness. In spite of the recent difficulties between Mel and me, I was not yet ready to acknowledge that our life together would never be the same.

A short time later, I awoke in the morning to discover that I felt like making love; not just emotionally, but physically. I didn't think this was possible due to the paralysis, and hoped it was an indication that I was getting feeling back, in spite of the doctor's predictions. When Henk came to visit, I told him about it. He explained that it was, indeed, possible for quadriplegic women to enjoy sex, and that the reason I was beginning to have these sensations was because I was coming out of "spinal shock."

It was time for the hospital's sex education routine. Mel was called in so we could experience it as a couple, and we were shown some very explicit films demonstrating ways disabled people can have sex, different positions, what to do with catheter tubing, etc. They were graphic and unappealing and certainly not the type of thing that would make you want to run out and try it. As with everything else, I viewed the films with a sense of detachment, as though the spinal cord injury hadn't happened. I thought confidently: I will never look as miserably disgusting as the people in this film; we don't need movies to show us how to make love. Little did I realize how connected this physical act was to the fragile, underlying emotions which were fraying under the stress of care.

My accident had occurred in mid-February, and it was now early summer. The weather was warm, and I was permitted to go outside in my wheelchair. The horrible layers of acne I had developed from so many months of wearing a neck brace had finally begun to disappear. I was allowed to go without the brace except during physical therapy, and had no discomfort in my neck at all. I looked a little more like my old self, although my body had begun to change shape considerably. My legs, which had once been muscled and shapely, were now thin and atrophied and reminded me of table legs. My stomach had become quite round because I no longer had the abdominal muscles to keep it flat. I felt like a stick person with a big ball for a stomach and became self-conscious about my body. The polyester slacks we were required to wear exaggerated the bulge, so my Mom began to look for feminine, loose fitting blouses that would help disguise it.

Mel's Mom came to visit faithfully, almost every single day, and brought homemade lunch to give me a break from hospital food. Often I came back from physical therapy frustrated, angry, and in tears, to a roomful of visitors. They were kind and sympathetic, but not always successful in their efforts to cheer me up.

One of the problems with physical therapy seemed to be determining the point at which I should be allowed to give up. My roommate, Donna, had almost successfully learned car transfers, and my level of function was similar to hers. She could sit up without loops, roll herself over, and move the fingers on one hand. The staff's comparing us brought back my childhood insecurities over being unfairly labeled an underachiever.

As an alternative to car transfers, they suggested that

Chapter Fourteen

we purchase a van with a lift. The specially modified vans, however, were prohibitively expensive and our finances were already near the disaster point. By the time I left the hospital, we had exhausted a half-million dollars of medical insurance, and were stuck paying twenty percent of that. Needless to say, Mel didn't have that kind of money at the age of twenty-seven.

The university constantly stressed the importance of learning physical tasks, always with the firmly stated message, "You will become totally independent if you learn to do these things; independent enough to live all by yourself if necessary."

The statement was unrealistic, misleading, and neglectful of the truth. I interpreted it to mean that when I went home life would be the same as it was. For nine months I lifted weights, cracked eggs, and slid on mats, when I should have been in counseling with my husband, preparing mentally for the upheaval we were about to experience in our relationship and lives.

There is an important distinction between hope and denial, which was not dealt with during the hospital stay. Hope should only be nurtured when it is realistic. Hope turns into denial when a person is not facing the truth.

I wanted to believe that we would stay together. I wanted to think that our lives hadn't changed. I desperately wanted to believe that I had not been changed, that the injury was only physical, and deep down inside I had remained the same. I hoped that those who knew me well would understand this and that life would resume its normal course. Reluctant to discourage my progress during rehab, the professionals allowed me to play out my futile fantasy.

The emotional traumas resulting from the accident were seldom mentioned. Our immediate and total separation, the physical losses, the shock and regret, were all brushed aside as inconsequential. I had lived through it. All that remained now was to learn to live with the spinal cord injury.

It would have been better had I begun to accept my limitations before going home. I would rather have faced part of the grief in the hospital, where I was sheltered from the harsh realities of financial and emotional survival. Even a

Return To Chewelah

small statement like, "You may need to hire a little outside help," or "it might be better if you let someone other than your husband tend to your personal care," would have made a great deal of difference to us later. But these ideas interfered with the rehab department's pipe dream that all C-6 quadriplegics can achieve total independence if they learn to do their transfers.

FIFTEEN

Mel only visited me at the hospital every few weeks, and it worried me. He wasn't even keeping in touch by phone, which was very unlike him. I was beginning to feel abandoned, and in the back of my mind I wondered if he still loved me. The thought of losing him was too painful to pursue, so I told myself that he was just busy and tried to let it go at that. When a certain song was played on the radio or I was reminded of an event we had shared, it brought back happy memories, yet bitter waves of regret flooded my eyes with tears. The closeness we had shared was conspicuously absent; our marriage was suspended, in limbo, awaiting the next turn of fate, and I was very afraid of what the future would bring.

During this impasse in our relationship I came to the disheartening realization that I might never have Mel's children. It happened one morning when Mel walked in unexpectedly with our best friend's two little girls. He was wearing his sunglasses and his flannel shirt was unbuttoned, with the long tails flapping as he walked. He looked healthy, confident, and happy; the way he had looked before my accident. One little girl was riding on his shoulders and the other held his hand, as if he were their father.

I felt just like I was seeing him with another woman. The children should have been our children, the ones we intended to have. From my hospital bed I sensed a gulf of time between us that was growing deeper and wider every day.

The head of the rehab department was a crusty old German doctor with a personality similar to a goat's. His voice was loud and unpleasant, and he shouted orders at nurses and patients alike, frequently cutting us off in mid-sentence to do so. I despised him and he seemed to reciprocate my feelings. He appeared to think that I wasn't trying hard enough during physical therapy, and insisted that I must stay at the hospital until I had learned to do car transfers. I rebelled against his authoritarianism and developed an attitude like a prisoner plotting to escape. I was caught repeatedly while drinking beer with my visitors, and once the staff found some joints of marijuana on the floor in my room. The marijuana caused a major uproar and I was warned that, if I didn't reform, I would be expelled from the illustrious program.

The distance growing between Mel and me made me desperate. I knew I had reached the limit of my physical capabilities and had learned all I could in rehab. It was time for me to bite the bullet and try to resume my life. The only trouble was that the hospital wouldn't let me go.

They had a myriad of excuses for keeping me; among them the repeated protest that our house wasn't ready. Eventually I realized that the hospital wasn't a jail, and that they couldn't force me to stay against my wishes. I asked my mom to come help me pack, and I announced that I was leaving, with or without permission. A large group of hospital staff gathered in our way as we attempted to exit the room, among them the German doctor, and a nasty argument ensued.

I explained that I was getting nowhere in physical therapy, that it had been too difficult to learn car transfers with musical-chair therapists, alternative methods, and cars. I used the term disorganized to describe the program and the doctor threw it right back at me. "Well, we think you are the one who is disorganized," he hollered as we pushed past him through the door.

Mel was waiting outside in a truck to take me home. It had been nine months since my accident. He seemed uncomfortable as he lifted me into the truck, but I was too preoccupied with the details of getting away to notice his mood until we started driving.

As we pulled onto the freeway we realized we'd forgotten our dog, Buddy, at the hospital. Mel was worried we

Chapter Fifteen

weren't going to be able to find him, and as we looked for a place to turn around I realized he was crying.

"Oh, my God," I thought to myself, "He must have felt like the dog was all he had left." I had never before seen him cry so hard. He seemed unstable and very frightened. I told myself that we would find Buddy right where we left him, and things would be all right. I didn't try to make him talk, hoping that he would recover and become his cocky, self-assured old self. We found the dog near the hospital and drove home in uneasy silence.

Mel had taken a second mortgage out on the farm, and he and his friends had remodeled the interior of the home according to the hospital's specifications. We were greeted at the door by several of the helpers, and Mel seemed to cheer up when we got around the others.

I couldn't believe what I saw inside the house. The once-muddy, rotten kitchen had been transformed into a room awash with light and color. Skylights above the counters lifted the darkness, allowing shafts of light to illuminate the warm wood and colorful wallpaper.

The dirty, cracked kitchen linoleum was replaced with a bright new floor. Teak counters were designed at wheelchair height, and the low cupboards contained lazy Susans for storage. The kitchen was complete, with a sparkling new stove, sink, and dishwasher.

A spare bedroom and the existing bathroom were combined to make room for a luxurious roll-in shower with dual shower heads. The walls and shower floor were decorated with two different patterns of tile and accented with one of my favorite colors, Delft blue. The sink and toilet were a trendy sandstone shade and set into cedar cabinets. One wall was pieced together with small pieces of wood in a delicate pattern like a patchwork quilt.

Each time the shower was turned on, steam brought out the fragrance of the cedar. I recalled the cold, damp room with the cracked, moldy windows and the clawfoot bathtub and wondered how this could possibly be the same place. There was new carpeting in the living room, a new bedspread and drapes, and Mel had even bought some large and exotic house plants, among them a palm and a fig tree.

As we were gathered around in the kitchen, someone made a comment which didn't sound quite right, something to the effect of "Mel thought he better make it a nice place for Janet because she's going to be spending so much time here." It was a disturbing reminder that much of my independence was lost, but Mel's remained.

Mel had made a large number of new friends during my absence, and he seemed to need them around, perhaps for emotional support or to help him avoid facing the changes in our relationship. They stayed in the outbuildings at night and were around the house during the day, like roommates in a college dorm. The company literally never went home; at times they seemed to feel more at home than I did.

That first night, after I was tucked safely into bed, Mel and his friends went to see a rock band in Seattle. A few people stayed with me in case I woke up and needed anything. I soon got to know these people well.

At the time I left the hospital, my mother was still living in Seattle with my dad. Since Mel had to leave the island early in the morning for work, we knew I would need some outside help. With this in mind, Mom had hired and trained a lady from Vashon to assist with my showers and personal care.

Unfortunately the woman turned out to be a hopeless drunk who wrecked her car repeatedly while coming down our driveway. She was totally unreliable. We finally let her go after finding a week's worth of laundry balled up in a muddy pile on the front porch.

Shortly afterwards, my best friend Liz agreed to come and help. She was actually the only friend I'd managed to make on Vashon before my accident, but I felt quite close to her. The mornings became a happy time while she was there. We cranked up the stereo and sang country music, and she helped me dress and fix my hair the way I would have on my own. She was positive and optimistic, but also realistic. She was sympathetic, but avoided treating me like a baby. She replaced the counselor I badly needed and I relied on her tremendously.

After being home awhile, I began to realize how much

Chapter Fifteen

time had actually been wasted in rehab. At home, the whole routine which supposedly would have made me "independent" was ridiculously impractical.

The hospital plan had been for me to transfer myself in the morning to a shower chair, placed there at the bedside by someone the previous night. Transferring to and from the shower chair wasn't covered during rehab; it was overlooked in the training and, in the end, was an impossiblility in my case anyway.

Then I was to wheel to the shower, shower, then go back to the bedroom, transfer onto the bed and finish drying, and dress myself using straps after retrieving clothes out of the closet, including underpants, bra, and socks. The dressing was to be done with the help of an incredibly frustrating little instrument with a handle and small wire loop designed to help fasten buttons.

The wheelchair would then be waiting for me to transfer onto, even though the shower chair would still be in the way. I was finally to change the nightbag to a legbag and tie the legbag on safely and securely. All of this was to be accomplished even though I had virtually no finger grip or trunk balance.

By then, about four hours would have passed, assuming nothing in the transfers or dressing routine went wrong. I would then be ready to go into the kitchen and cook breakfast.

Needless to say, we abandoned the whole plan and had someone help me. Getting me up and ready for the day was time-consuming enough with someone else doing the work. Nobody wanted to sit around and watch me struggle with "buttonholers." It made people extremely nervous to watch me try to transfer myself. It was simply easier, faster, and safer for someone else to do it.

Resuming some of my normal duties as a housewife brought some surprises. There were many things I could no longer do, even though the home had been visited and certified by the occupational therapist. I could not load plates into the lower shelf of the new dishwasher, because they were too heavy; they simply fell from my hand and landed on the floor. I had to hang on to the wheelchair with one arm while I leaned over because of my lack of balance, which left me one arm with which to hold the dishes. I could turn my wrist, but I couldn't grasp with any strength. I tried my big claw-type brace, a hinge splint, that was designed to improve my thumb-forefinger grasp. The dishes still slipped from my hand. Also, once the splint was on, I had to stay in one place because I couldn't wear it and wheel the chair at the same time.

Despite my first discouraging attempts at housework, I realized I was still expected to be the one who cleans up other people's messes in the kitchen. It didn't take me long to get angry about this once I realized what was happening, and I had some very uncharacteristic tantrums over it. "You guys just can't throw things all over like you used to!" I screamed. "It just took me half an hour to clean this up!"

I had always hated women who acted like I was, and so had Mel. My emotional outburst was met with embarrassed silence, as if everyone thought I had gone completely nuts.

Our horses had been neglected during my absence, though Jesse had been overeating and was quite fat. She had, in fact, stored up so much energy that no one could ride her without getting bucked off. I no longer tried to do anything with the horses, because I felt unsafe around them while I was in the wheelchair. They didn't seem to realize there was a person in it, which made me feel in danger of being pushed over like an empty wheelbarrow. For the first time in my life I saw the horses as dangerous, and even began to dislike them.

It wasn't even much fun being outside anymore. It was virtually impossible to get around on the uneven terrain without help, and I always had trouble staying warm enough. Once I got cold, I started to shiver uncontrollably and had to bury myself with blankets to warm up. I was often plagued with sweats. Perspiration poured off my head, face, and shoulders and made me soaking wet, though not from being too hot. In fact, I felt miserably chilled. It was my body's way of reacting to a stimulus of which my brain was unaware. Ultimately we were unable to pinpoint the exact reason. Sometimes it lasted for hours until I was so exhausted from shivering that I had to go to bed. When it

Chapter Fifteen

happened at night, perspiration drenched the sheets all the way to the mattress. There wasn't anything we could do to make the problem go away. Usually I took extra Valium and attempted to escape the discomfort by falling asleep.

The first time we tried to resume having sex after my accident was the last time I ever made love with my husband. It was strange to be unable to move anything but my arms and not feel his skin touching mine. I could sense motion and pressure, still feel my shoulders, arms, and breasts, but most of the rest had to be left to the imagination. While it could have been enjoyable, it was over much too quickly for pleasure.

We held each other for awhile, but Mel was very quiet. When I asked him how it felt to him, he said, "It feels the same, except you're really still." For me it had not been unpleasant, just vaguely disappointing. I liked being close to him again, but we weren't close long enough. Soon afterwards he got out of bed and complained that I had "medicine breath." He went to sleep somewhere else.

After that night he avoided intimacy by not coming to bed. If he eventually crawled in next to me, it was well beyond midnight when he was positive I would be sound asleep.

Our house continued to be filled with company, friends who had helped Mel remodel, and the new people he had met during my absence. My favorites were two brothers, Ron and Steve. Ron was five or six years younger than his brother, who was almost my age. They were sweet, attentive, and creative, and I enjoyed their company very much. They seemed genuinely interested in taking part in my care, and became just like brothers. My sister Lisa stayed with us most of the time too, but she had taken my accident very hard and seemed to spend most of her time with Mel.

During the remodeling, a room was built in the attic and it became the gathering place for parties that sometimes lasted all night. The entrance to the attic was a narrow crack only half the width of a normal doorway, so it was impossible for me to enter. Once everyone was up there, I could no longer even hear them from my bedroom; it was just like being in the house alone.

Return To Chewelah

There was no telephone in my bedroom or even a television, because we had not anticipated any confinement in bed. Either of these things would have greatly relieved the sense of alienation I felt while lying in bed alone.

One night I couldn't sleep and began to call to the people upstairs. Nobody responded, because they couldn't hear me. It wasn't until that moment that I realized what being paralyzed really was, or what it might mean to me. It might mean needing help when there was no one to help. It might mean being separated, physically and emotionally, from some of the people I loved.

I wanted to get out of bed but felt trapped and claustrophobic, as if locked in an elevator. I felt like screaming at the top of my lungs. Angrily, I began to grab pillows and whatever else I could reach and throw them off the bed. After running out of things to throw, I just gave up and lay there in silence to wait.

Lisa and Mel came downstairs a few hours later and saw the things I had thrown around the room. They looked discouraged and disappointed, as though they had done their best to make me comfortable and could not understand why I was upset.

"I don't want to be left in here by myself," I tried to explain. I wanted them to understand the way I felt, but they looked very uncomfortable, and I was afraid it would alienate them further if I said more.

What I wanted more than anything else was for Mel to send the company home and come to bed with me, talk to me and hold me. I wanted to be his wife again. And it was becoming very clear that this just wasn't going to happen.

Often I heard people comment about my relationship with Mel, as if I were a mere outsider. Typical was, "Mel is just not the type of person who can give Janet what she needs now," or "Mel just doesn't have what it takes to live with someone like Janet." I ignored these dire predictions because they were coming from people who had only known Mel briefly, and they didn't know me at all. I stubbornly wrote them all off and continued to deny the possibility that what they said might contain some truth.

The first few months home at the farm slipped by in a

Chapter Fifteen

blur, with the details involved in my care consuming most, or all, of my time. There was so much to adjust to that I couldn't adjust at all. It was like being a visitor in a strange place, surrounded by people I knew only slightly, and inside a body I no longer even knew.

    I had been taught to drive with hand controls while in the hospital, and had obtained a disabled person driver's license. Mel installed hand controls in our El Camino pickup in hopes that I could use it for transportation. Someone would have to lift me in and out, but it would at least be better than not driving at all.

    After being home about a month we decided to go for a ride together to test my driving ability. When Mel lifted me onto the seat, it seemed very different from the hospital's car in which I had learned. The seat was wider and there weren't as many places to grip. He fastened the shoulder strap securely so that I wouldn't fall forward, then climbed in beside me, slightly apprehensive. I had always been confident in my driving skills and didn't share his uneasiness. We started off down the driveway and I felt okay. Mel, on the other hand, was jumpy and kept yelling things like, "Don't cut the corner that way!" and "You're on the wrong side!" He punctuated the panicky remarks by leaning over and grabbing the steering wheel as though we were going to crash any second. We were on a completely isolated road and not in danger of hitting anything, and I found his protests disturbing and unnecessary.

    It is very difficult to relearn balance when driving again, especially when turning corners. Every car is different, and it takes practice to gain familiarity with different vehicles. Mel was so traumatized by the first car ride that he never let me try again. I didn't do anything drastically wrong; I just couldn't handle the car the same way I drove the Porsche. Soon afterwards, we loaned Liz the car so she could get back and forth to our house to help me in the mornings.

    Among the throngs of young people who congregated at our farm was a teenage girl named Linda. She was wild and rebellious and had broken her neck jumping out of a car during a fight with her boyfriend. The resulting quadriplegia had settled her down considerably, almost to the point that she was withdrawn. She seemed to look to me for support. Her best friend Carey had taken a special interest in helping her adjust. She learned how to transfer and dress her, and got her out of the house on weekend excursions to entertaining places like our farm.

Carey was a large sixteen-year-old with stringy bleached blonde hair, huge boobs, and a full set of braces on her teeth. Mel said he admired her because of the way she was able to "get her little friend around," that is, in and out of the car, etc.

I resented so many uninvited guests at the farm; extra carloads of people were always showing up. It began to feel like a permanent Woodstock. Those who helped us remodel sometimes stayed on, then just moved in with us. People slept in the outbuildings on the property or stayed up all night partying in the attic. It seemed, too, that the gang was getting younger and rowdier all the time.

I was too unhealthy to partake of any of the illicit substances that were passed around, and went to bed early each evening. But reports of all that was happening at the farm eventually filtered in to me through my bedside visitors.

One evening, when Mel had been outside a particularly long time, a rumor started that Mel was "screwing Carey up in the barn." Those spreading the rumor seemed to think it was terribly funny, and none of them seemed to realize he still had a wife.

I was hurt, angry, and disgusted. The immaturity and insensitivity of these so-called friends of Mel's amazed me. They didn't seem to have any real loyalty toward Mel, and they were definitely not friends of mine.

I didn't attempt to discuss it with him. We barely ever saw each other, and whatever ability we once had to communicate was completely gone. He kept his distance from me, and it was impossible to have a serious talk.

Lisa and I had been extremely close all her life, and I think, of all the members of my family, my accident was the hardest on her. After the accident, she and Mel clung to each other and struggled to accept the unacceptable. Mel and I had provided her with a family life during the difficult years of my parent's divorce, and she has remarked that

Chapter Fifteen

when I broke my neck, it was as if it had happened to her mother.

I felt I would never be able to resume my previous role as wife, mother, and guardian. Now someone had to take care of me.

Though reality was staring me right in the face, I couldn't see it. Finally, it was Lisa who told me what she thought was the truth. I will never forget the look on her face, or the way I felt when I heard what she said.

I had asked her what was wrong with Mel, and why he was avoiding me. She answered, carefully but directly, "Janet, Mel just doesn't love you any more. You're different now." She continued to try to explain, but none of it made much sense. Finally she gave up and put her arms around me. She said simply, "I'm really sorry, Janet. I sure love you a lot. I'll always be your sister." We both cried as she hugged me and I held her. I felt dazed and numb with shock.

Liz and Jim lived on a cliff above the Sound; they had moved to the Northwest because Jim loved to sail. They had a large two-story house with an extra bedroom on the main floor and invited Mel and me over to stay for a few days.

When I was away from home, I was more helpless than ever. We had to manage all my personal care, including bathing, in the bedroom. Liz took it all in stride, even though I was as dependent as an infant. At the time, this was all right with me, as I considered it the trade-off for being able to spend time with friends. They did everything they could to make me feel accepted and normal. There were lots of people in the house; my sister Lisa; all of Jim and Liz's kids; and our best friends, a married couple named Steve and Laurie.

One afternoon Liz transferred me to the couch, and everyone sat down for pictures. It was hard for me to keep my balance on the couch and they had to sit on both sides to prop me up. I looked like a rag doll in the pictures. My clothes hung off me crookedly and my arms and legs were awkward as I tried to hold myself up. My skin was oily and unhealthy-looking, and my hair was dark and limp from months of being indoors. There was hardly a trace of the strong, energetic farm girl I once had been.

I continued just to exist among the people around me, totally dependent on them for my care. Mel was somewhere around during this time, but he was not with me. I rarely saw him. At this point, although we shared the same home, we had become completely separated and lived our lives apart.

One day about three months after I returned home, I awoke to discover that it was late and Liz had not shown up. After awhile, I heard Mel's heavy footsteps returning home from work. He said Liz had been in a terrible car accident and the El Camino, which was very light in back, had flipped on some black ice near Liz and Jim's home. The car left the highway and tumbled headfirst down an embankment. Liz suffered a broken jaw and nose, and had a severely crushed elbow. They saved the arm, but told her it would require many surgeries before she could use it again. Her husband and children rushed to the hospital where she was in serious condition.

Without Liz's exuberant presence in the morning, my spirits began to sink. My mother commuted from Seattle to help, but I knew it was extremely draining on her, and she was having enough problems of her own. We looked for another helper and finally found a replacement, but no one could really fill the void of Liz's absence. She was hospitalized for two or three weeks, and returned home pale and weak.

One Saturday after her accident I was again awakened from sleep, this time by a commotion in the upper orchard. Something was chasing the chickens again. In a short while, Mel came down to the house and told me Skinny Jimmy was dead. The big rooster, John Wayne, had killed him in a fight. Mel wouldn't let me see him, saying he was "too torn up."

I cried for awhile, and then the tears gave way to anger. Chickens die, I told myself. At least he died nobly, instead of getting eaten by the dog.

The fact was that I really loved that chicken. Except for the Siamese cat Mel had given me before we were married, he had been my only real pet.

Chapter Fifteen

The following Monday Mel also hit a patch of black ice on the way to the ferry and totaled the Porsche. He walked away unhurt, so we were grateful. He brought the twisted mass of metal home on a trailer, saying he hoped to reconstruct it. He had to borrow a pickup from the shop until we found another car to drive.

The mood at the farm turned from bad to worse, and most of the company left. The downward spiral of bad luck caused Mel to grow even more distant, and life was unjustifiably painful. I hated our farm; it had a curse on it. I had felt it the day we moved there, something evil, maybe the ghost of the old lady's husband, lurking in the drainpipes, intent on ruining our lives.

SIXTEEN

The endless series of accidents and bad luck were discouraging, but they had little to do with the actual reason I decided to leave the farm. It had more to do with the feeling that during my hospitalization I was replaced by someone more physically capable of assuming my role as wife.

I had two good reasons to believe this was true. The first, most obvious reason was that my husband avoided me night and day. The second was that I was told by the person involved.

From my bedroom I had observed a carload of women who came to visit Mel. They dressed as hippies, Vashon-style, in long skirts and earth shoes. I was introduced to them one day when I was outside, but in general they did their socializing at the far edges of the cleared property or stayed in their car.

The woman in question was thin and plain-looking, with long, straight brown hair. Not the type of woman to evoke jealousy, but beneath her nondescript exterior lay a personality with an aggressive approach to people in general, especially men. She was aware that Mel and I were no longer intimate, and perhaps thought it was by choice; at any rate, she didn't believe in wasting time while other people made up their minds.

She approached me with her proposition by telephone, identifying herself as a close friend of Mel's. She said that she had been through a lot with Mel during my long absence and that she felt he needed help. She said that, since she was in love with him, she would be the best person to take care of him.

I listened to her announcement with a sense of disbelief

Chapter Sixteen

and outrage. Obviously my marriage had been pronounced over before it ever had a chance to resume. Some had judged me to be an unfit wife even before I had left the hospital.

Under different circumstances, I would have laughed at the woman's behavior, told her to stay out of our lives, and confronted my husband for the truth. However, there had already been so many indications that our marriage was in serious trouble that her declaration just served to confirm my worst fears.

I thought about the many lonely weeks I'd spent without seeing Mel at the hospital, about the day he brought me home, and about the time we tried to make love. Everything suddenly seemed to make sense. They all knew, but no one until now had possessed the nerve to tell me. With this realization, my spirits dropped to a point so low I had no strength or desire to stand my ground or fight back.

When my parents finally divorced, my mother decided to buy a home on Vashon. It was around Christmastime when she moved, and it was becomingly too painful for me to continue living at the farm. I felt powerless to change what was going on around me, and out of place in what was supposed to have been our home. Desperate to escape my miserable situation before the holidays, I decided to go stay at my mother's. Someone had to go find Mel so that I could tell him I was leaving.

As I tried to speak, the undeniable reality of what was happening was like a hard, stinging slap in the face. I still loved him very much, but now, as he stood before me, he seemed like a total stranger.

"I can't stay here anymore," was all I was able to say. He looked miserable, guilty, and relieved, all at the same time. I explained that it would just be for awhile, until things got better. I didn't realize, at the time, that it would be forever.

My impulsive move was somewhat of a surprise to my mother. Although she had moved to Vashon so that she would be close by in case I needed her, she also planned on getting her own life back in order. When I moved in with her, she hadn't even had time to buy any furniture.

I brought my bad luck with me, and shortly after my

Return To Chewelah

arrival, I developed a deep and serious pressure sore on my tailbone as a result of sleeping in an unfamiliar bed. It was at least two months before I was able to sit up again.

Each day, after giving me a bedbath, Mom tried to position me on a portable lounge in the living room where we could visit, and I could watch TV. The pressure area was so sensitive that we didn't want to risk my getting up for a shower, so she washed my hair while I was lying on my stomach. It was very difficult for her to get me settled on the narrow lounge. I felt twisted like a pretzel, and it caused my back and neck to ache. There wasn't a comfortable position I could lie in without putting pressure on the sore.

Mom's patience wore thin as she struggled to adjust my position and prop me up with pillows. They inevitably slipped and I just rolled back onto the injured tissue. Even drinking water from a straw was a major challenge and my mother never had a break from the stress. I was with her and needed her twenty-four hours a day. I even had to be turned frequently during the night because I was without my own bed. The constant threat of developing another, larger sore was always present, and we watched for signs of healing.

The strain she was under caused my mother to become irritable, and at times the tension between us was palpable. I shared my Valium with her, and each evening we saluted the end of the day with a glass of McNaughton's. After a few long, miserable months, the reddened area began to fade enough so that I could get up for short, cautious periods of time. The weather was warmer, and I spent most of my time just sitting outside, enjoying the sun.

Mel came to visit me once while I was there. We didn't talk about our marriage, our separation, or our future. Relieved of his responsibility as a caretaker, it was as though he'd become a teenager again and was paying a visit to his girlfriend. The visit was short; he was on his way to join some friends.

One of the most painful things about a marriage breakup is the way a former couple's friends take sides. A few of our acquaintances tried to remain in touch with us both, but a great many others were polarized and became

Chapter Sixteen

either Mel's friends or mine. People often made what I considered tactless remarks like, "It's about time you finally decided to leave him. You should have done it before you broke your neck." In other words, we'd had a crappy marriage right from the start, in their opinion.

When the dust settled, most of the couples we'd known gravitated toward Mel, and some of our single friends stayed in touch with me. I heard through the grapevine that Mel was dating someone he'd met on Vashon, and that she had begun staying with him at the farm soon after my departure. I, of course, knew who she was because of the conversation she and I had had.

Steve, one of the resident carpenters at the farm, began to stop by Mom's to visit me. He was the older of the two brothers who had become my friends. Unlike Mel, Steve was very interested in taking part in my personal care. He wanted to become a doctor and seemed to approach the entire matter as a learning experience. He seemed to have absorbed most of the details just by being at the farm, gaining part of his knowledge by asking questions of those who helped me. We became closer friends that spring, and he began to visit often.

Steve and Mel were as different as night and day, both in looks and temperament. Steve was polite, sensitive, and a little shy; he was about my height, and just slightly younger. He showed up at a time when I greatly needed a friend, and when he began to act affectionately toward me, I didn't mind at all.

It probably was a great relief to my mother when we decided to go to the ocean for awhile. We planned on taking Steve's old Dodge Dart, and invited Lisa to come with us. I had yet to become intimate with Steve, and wanted to have Lisa around to help me get up in the morning.

After driving up the coast, we rented a small, two-bedroom cabin on the beach. Liberated from the confines of my mother's home, and feeling a little more like my old self, I went completely wild. I slept with Steve that night and woke up in the morning feeling refreshed and pleased.

I had not appreciated being rejected sexually at the age of twenty-four, particularly when I was still capable of such strong feelings in a normal way. At first, it took a little experimentation to get comfortable, but once we found the right position, there was little difference in the way my body felt physically.

Whatever was lacking in physical sensation was made up for by the overall experience: being touched, held, and loved. It was gratifying to know someone able to accept me as a whole woman again, and the fulfillment of this need was probably the greatest reason that I ended up with Steve.

Springtime was making me feel like starting a new life. "What do I have to lose?" I remember thinking to myself. "It's sink or swim."

And so it was, with this thought in mind, that I decided to move back to Chewelah, where I had always been happy. I had reached the conclusion that Steve was a person who would do anything for me, so I decided to take him along with me.

Steve had big plans for our future. He was going to go to school to become a doctor, buy a farm, and convert all the tractors and other machinery into things with hand controls so I could drive them and become a farmer. I had not bothered to think that far ahead. Getting away from Seattle, my broken marriage, and my painful memories, was my top priority.

No one in my family tried to discourage me from going, and even if they had, I wouldn't have listened. My father gave Steve and me the beautiful old British Rover sedan that I had driven in high school, along with a fair warning that it probably wouldn't continue to run much longer. It had a four-speed transmission, so I would never be able to drive it myself, but it would get us across the mountains for sure. It was a sports model with bucket seats. We packed as many clothes and dishes as we could in the back seat, but were unable to take any furniture. The wheelchair took up the whole trunk, but at least it fit. We planned to return later for the large things, once we got settled.

As soon as we crossed the mountains, the euphoric sense of freedom I always experienced when leaving the city returned with great intensity, and I felt certain I was doing the right thing. The words to an Emmylou Harris song kept

Chapter Sixteen

going through my head, a song Liz and I used to sing while she was getting me dressed . . ."One of these days, it will soon be all over, cut and dried/And I won't have this urge to go all bottled up inside/One of these days I'll look back, and I'll say I left in time/Cause somewhere, for me, I know, there's peace of mind."

Spokane was the last big city before the real farming country began. We stopped at a Ramada Inn to spend the night, because we hadn't yet arranged for a place to stay in Chewelah. Steve left me alone at a table in the bar, and went to look at rooms. I sat in the dark, deserted lounge, staring at my hands, contemplating the complex turns my life had taken. Why had this happened to me? Was it true God had a plan for each person's life and a reason for the plan? If so, the reason still remained a mystery to me. I was not in love with Steve, of that I was certain. He was my friend and he was helping me; I guess that was as good a reason as any to be with him. I would always be in love with Mel, but knew without a doubt that we would never again live together.

I slipped off my white-gold wedding band and set it in the clean ashtray on the table. Someone else could have it. I kept the engagement ring with its small, brilliant diamond; it was much too beautiful to throw away.

Steve returned and wheeled me off to a bleak hotel room with a rock-hard bed and orange plastic furniture. We put an eggshell mattress on the bed to prevent me from getting a pressure sore, and prepared to go to bed.

It was hot and dry when we got to Chewelah, one of those ninety-five degree days that had sent us into the house when we were small to beg Grammie to take us swimming. My mind drifted back to my childhood as we passed the familiar sights of the valley I loved.

On the hottest days of the summer, Grammie was busy in the kitchen, baking pies, canning fruit, or making pickles with the rangy bunches of dill she grew in the frontyard. After begging her to take us swimming she usually replied, "Maybe later, if I have time." We then whined and tormented her until she told us to take a nap in the cool back bedroom, which we liked because it was where she kept the honeycomb. With our small, grimy fingers, we broke off a piece of the semi-brittle waxy chambers and chewed until all the flavor was gone; it tasted like the clover that grew wild in the horse corral, and the darkened room was safe from hornets. The only sound in the room was the ticking and buzzing of the unlucky insects which were caught between window and screen. Very rarely did we sleep during our naps, but Grammie didn't seem to mind.

Now, some twenty-odd years later, I was returning, as an adult, to the place of my birth. It was comforting to see that nothing about the countryside had changed much. There were no fast food restaurants or shopping malls cluttering up the landscape; the valley remained untouched by the unappealing signs of modern progress. The air was still fragrant with ripening oats, wheat, and chamomile. I leaned my head out the car window, and breathed in the sweet country air. Now I was really home.

Since I was related to huge families on both sides of my family, it didn't take long to locate a place to live. There was a basement apartment in my Great-Aunt Betty Jean's house, and it was only a hundred dollars a month. It had a living room, kitchen area, and bathroom. It was furnished with a folding table, chairs, and a hide-a-bed. We gladly took it and hurriedly unpacked, desperate to get out of the searing heat.

Grammie and Grandpa were still living in the same place, but they had added a windmill to the corralled area near the house, which Grandpa year after year kept vowing to paint red. Grammie was very ill and had to spend most of her time in bed, but she was still at home.

Steve and I went to visit them a few times, but it always made Grammie sad to see me in my wheelchair. She kept saying that she wished there was something she could do to help me, and I only wished that I could help her. She was thin and weak, and suffering a great deal of pain.

The cattle horses were still alive, but very old. They had been retired to the giant meadow at the top of the mountain. I asked Steve to take me up to see them soon after we got there. The horses were bonier than in their younger days; and I was surprised to see they had white hair around the face, and silver streaks in their overgrown manes. I pre-

Chapter Sixteen

ferred to believe that Sundown recognized and remembered me from year to year, but he really didn't give much indication of it. He was so tall that I had to sit more or less underneath him to pet him, and could only reach his shoulder and the base of his neck. He stood quietly while I stroked awkwardly and inhaled the familiar scent of his coat. Steve asked me if I would like to sit on him, so I decided to try, but as he lifted me up I realized there was nothing to support my back. I just had to lie on him on my stomach with my arms around his neck. I couldn't keep my balance at all and it was very uncomfortable. I got off right away, feeling wistful and discouraged.

Afterwards we discovered that during the struggle to get my leg up over his back we pulled out my catheter. My jeans were becoming wet. We were faced with a very uncomfortable forty-five-minute drive back to town before we could put it back in.

My best friends Jack and Cheryl owned a large, spacious tavern on Main Street, and they had live music on Friday nights. The bands were notoriously bad, but there were several pool tables and a few game machines. The atmosphere in a small-town tavern where everyone knows one another is very party-like and fun. Chewelah was full of people my age, and it was a wonderful feeling suddenly to have so many friends.

Many of the people I'd known in high school had stayed in Chewelah, working, farming, and having kids. Nearly everyone had two or three children, and those of us from the city suspected it was the direct result of a lack of other forms of entertainment. One of the couples Mel and I had liked best, Bill and Sue, had three children and were divorced. They still lived so close to each other that the kids rode their bikes back and forth between their parents' houses. I always expected them to get back together, but they never did.

I wondered why all of my friends were able to have children, but I was not. I probably wouldn't have waited so long to seek medical advice if I had known something was wrong. Anyway, it was too late now, and if I had been able to have children I would have wanted Mel's.

There weren't many options in the way of birth control after I broke my neck. The doctors said that, because of my decreased circulation, I was at risk of developing clotting if I took birth control pills. A diaphragm was also ill-advised. It was quite apparent I would not be in any position to take care of children in the near future. After all, I couldn't even take care of myself.

Still, the unconscious, now seemingly inappropriate desire to become a parent lurked dangerously close to the surface and threatened to become a reality. I still wanted children so much that I was afraid I'd allow myself to get pregnant with someone I didn't really love.

Gradually I abandoned the idea of motherhood. I eventually went into the hospital and had a simple tubal ligation, so as not to give myself the opportunity for further complication.

This decision, along with the fact that I was now single, created an unspoken, intangible form of separation between myself and many of my former friends. They seemed to accept my disability more than the fact that I was no longer part of a married couple. I felt out of place during conversations, as though everyone avoided talking about the things that concerned them most. They didn't want to make me unhappy. The subject of my broken marriage remained set aside and unmentionable, a closely guarded secret.

It was good to be back in Chewelah, despite all the changes. Living there, I thought I had found a way to remain a cowgirl, at least in heart. On rare cloudy days I put on my old Tony Lamas and bandanna and they helped me feel like my former self.

Steve became noticeably excited when I was happy, and I failed to see the reason: he was in love with me. I cared for him as a friend, but the rest of the relationship, including the sex, was more like an experiment. It may not have been completely fair of me, but he entered the relationship more than willingly, even if somewhat naively. At times I did say "I love you" to him, which was probably a mistake. Perhaps it was his mistake to believe it. I had unwittingly entered the realm of casual single relationships.

Things between us were complicated, more so than I

Chapter Sixteen

realized. I was, by nature, fairly independent, yet in a physically dependent situation with an entire life to rebuild. I needed to relearn basic things like how to cook and handle a pen without using a complicated splint. I needed a new profession and new interests. I needed to learn how to balance a checkbook, how to pay my own bills, and how to stick up for myself in business situations. Now, when someone treated me like a brainless idiot in a tire store because I was a female, there was no one to defend me. Steve wasn't aggressive at all; he was soft-spoken, mild, and sensitive.

Steve was well aware of the circumstances which had contributed to the breakup of my marriage. He thought it was unfair of Mel to be turned off by nursing duties, and now it seemed his goal in life to prove that my personal care could be shared by others without embarrassment, regardless of sex. He steadfastly maintained that the things I had to do were just a natural, necessary part of life, and certainly nothing of which to be ashamed. Although these were noble beliefs, I wasn't prepared for the effects they might have on our friendship.

To save on packing space, we had brought along a raised toilet seat as a temporary substitute for the cumbersome shower chair. Steve began to use it too while I was washing my face or brushing my teeth. I hated it when he pooped while I was in the bathroom. You could see the poop fall from his body into the toilet through the space underneath the raised seat, a sight which I did not find entertaining. The smell was bad too.

"Why can't he just wait until I'm out of here?" I would fume silently. "Do I have to smell his poop because he has to smell mine, to be fair?" It was very hard to express these thoughts. I felt guilty for not being able to reciprocate his unconditional acceptance of me, and I couldn't deny that I needed his help. I definitely needed him to help take care of my physical needs.

I began to hate our situation. I felt like he was always waiting on me. How could he spend every second of his day just doing things for me?

A few weeks after our arrival in Chewelah, I completely lost interest in him sexually. There no longer seemed to be a difference between our sexes. It was as if we were both "its." Steve wasn't an easy person to cut off in this way, and one day, in order to impress the extent of his misery upon me, he lay down on the couch and began to masturbate in front of me. He claimed that I was torturing him and that, when he thought about how we used to make love, he just couldn't stand it.

The drama of the scene he was staging made me want to throw up. I found myself wishing his pecker would just fall off. That would cure his problem. Seeking escape, I wheeled myself out the front door into the searing heat.

Maybe we've been seeing too much of each other, I thought. I'll talk him into getting a part-time job, and I'll get one too. We were going to need some money anyway.

The problem of money had never really been addressed when Mel and I had separated. We had never discussed money during our marriage. We both had a checkbook, he put money in the bank, I went to the grocery store, he bought me presents; it was simple. At any rate, after I moved, I talked Mel into giving me a few hundred dollars a month, and that's what we were living on.

Living in Chewelah was inexpensive because there weren't many jobs. Steve ran around for days looking for one, but no one wanted to hire him. He had long, curly hair and long eyelashes, and the farmers clearly thought that he was a city boy, and a sissy.

I didn't know where to begin looking for work, but word traveled fast in Chewelah, and before long I was offered a job as a transcriptionist in the town's tiny hospital. The hospital was run by Catholic nuns who remembered me when I was little. When my Grandfather May had been the town doctor, I had spent a lot of time visiting with the nuns, eating their homemade cookies. My favorite nun was Sister Erwina; she was still alive and looked exactly the same as I remembered her. She told me that they could use someone with my skills because there was only one other girl in town who could type and knew medical terminology. Of course, I could no longer type sixty words a minute because I had to type with two pegs strapped around my hands. But this didn't seem to matter to them.

Chapter Sixteen

Steve was very inventive, and he made me a little box with hand switches so that I could use a dictaphone. With the hand-controlled box, I was all set to transcribe records for the hospital. I had my own desk in the cool, quiet basement of the hospital, and, though it was rather tedious, I enjoyed it. It was good to get my mind off things and concentrate on work for a change.

Soon after I started my job, a man who worked in the hospital told me he had a house to rent at a very low price. We went to see it, and I loved it, an ancient, two-story house with three little porches and a garage built of the driest boards imaginable. The wood was so worn and parched that it no longer held nails. It appeared that weeds, dust, and spider webs were all that held the porch up. The home had once been painted white with turquoise trim, but most of the paint had peeled and crumbled in the sun.

It was a real house, though, and I was happy to have found it. Now we had a comfortable bed, and I could get some of my belongings back. I didn't care, however, for the idea of going back to Vashon to get them. I couldn't bear the thought of going back to the farm, back to the rain and weeds, into that place where I never belonged. I hated Vashon Island, especially the ten acres where we had lived, and the untended field where I had fallen and broken my neck.

My brother Karl and my baby sister Lisa joined us soon after we found the house. I was so glad to see them that I immediately suggested they move in for the summer. The house had a large upstairs, and there was plenty of room.

Steve and Karl volunteered to return to Vashon for my bed, and Lisa helped me during their absence. Lisa and I had some good long talks over beer, avoiding the most painful things. She said she hadn't seen much of Mel since I left, which was what I wanted to hear. I told her of a few of the difficulties I was having with Steve, leaving out the embarrassing parts. She and I both knew why I was here. Now it was time to forget about it and have a little summer vacation.

We lived like very uncivilized people that summer. Our house was a hub of activity, the front door always wide open and cars coming and going all day long. We had no furniture, not even a wastepaper basket, and beer bottles frequently got loose from their respective sacks and rolled across the floor. There was no place to take a shower, so we packed our soap and shampoo with us, and bathed at the lake. Lisa and I found an old refrigerator at a nearby junk store and brought it home in back of the pickup she and Karl had borrowed from Dad. The refrigerator's door was broken, but with a little manipulation we managed to keep it fairly well shut with a coat hanger. We also spent five dollars on a cooking device which had been some kind of an antique steamer. We plugged it in on the floor and tried to cook a pot roast. It worked, so we considered ourselves to be all set up. In the end, it was too hot to cook much anyway.

I continued with my job at the hospital, but for some reason always broke into a sweat and got shaky when I sat down and started to type. At first I thought it might just be stress from concentration, but each time I ignored it, it got worse. By the time a few hours passed my teeth were chattering and I started feeling nauseous. I would go upstairs to the main part of the hospital and admit myself as a patient. The illness always turned out to be a raging bladder infection which required IV antibiotics to clear up. After a few days, I felt better and was sent home, only to have it recur.

I just saw the regular family doctors during that time, and they seemed to accept the frequency of these infections as normal for someone who had an indwelling catheter. I was never questioned about my personal hygiene or home situation, nor did they have any helpful suggestions about how to avoid future hospitalizations. Finally, word got around town that I was spending a lot of time in the hospital and one of my uncles, whom I barely knew, came to my house and built me a roll-in shower. Unfortunately, it didn't cure the problem, but it was a very nice gesture, and one I've never forgotten.

The relationship with Steve ended badly, culminating in a hysterical fight which occurred in the middle of the night. I had avoided him for quite awhile, which made him frustrated. And he just kept wanting to talk, while I didn't

Chapter Sixteen

feel there was much to say except that I didn't want to be with him any more.

Finally one afternoon, in a fit of rage, he got in the old British car and drove it up the highway at about a hundred miles an hour until he blew the engine. Then, with the motor clanking and banging, he brought it home to the driveway, put on his steel mountain climbing boots and jumped up on top of the car. He kicked and jumped up and down until the car was completely destroyed.

I was already in bed when this occurred, but the racket was incredible. Then I heard the back door slam so hard that the window broke. He ended up sitting on the floor of the bedroom, sobbing and begging me to talk to him. He kept repeating that he wanted to have "final words" before the whole thing ended.

I cruelly stated that my final words to him were "Get screwed!" and told him I wanted him to leave. No matter how mean I was, I couldn't get him out of the house. The fight went on for about an hour before he finally left. I don't know how he left, but presume he left on foot, and hitchhiked back to Seattle.

The next morning I called the local police. After viewing the wrecked car and the broken door, they put a restraining order on Steve and warned me to call them immediately if he returned. He didn't come back, and I never saw him again.

Looking back, I am not at all proud of the way I treated Steve. I could have tried a little harder to communicate; but who knows, maybe he wouldn't have listened. Anyway, I feel sorry for him now when I think of what happened, because he tried so hard to help me. It just didn't work out.

SEVENTEEN

It was by chance that George and I became involved with one another. His ex-wife had been our neighbor in Wright's Valley during high school. She was calling around town looking for someone to go to a Carol King concert with George because she'd suddenly decided she didn't feel like going. Since I was one of the only single women around, someone suggested me. I had never met George, and although I was very skeptical about the success of blind dates, I agreed to go rather than have them waste a good ticket.

When George's car pulled up, he was in a comical state of near-hysteria; out of breath, very sweaty, and very wet. He was wearing jeans and a tank top. I could tell right away he wasn't the type of guy who was going to make me nervous.

"Gee, I'm glad you didn't get all dressed up, because I didn't either," I said after introducing myself. "Um, you look sort of wet," I observed, trying not to laugh.

With wild gestures and flailing arms, he explained how he had driven through an automatic car wash with the back window down. He had tried to reach around from the front seat and pull up the window but couldn't get ahold of it. He ended up going through the whole wash cycle with the window down and soapy water spraying all over his head and shoulders, and filling the back of the car. Luckily it was one of the hottest days of the summer, so he was drying out quickly. The car stood a chance of getting dry too.

The car was parked on the scorched grass in front of the house. Waves of heat shimmered up from the ground and streams of perspiration ran off George's head and chest, despite his prewash. It was seven at night, and the tempera-

Chapter Seventeen

ture remained stubbornly at ninety degrees. He opened his trunk and got a couple of beers out of his cooler and we drank them in the front yard. When it was time to go, he lifted me out of the chair and popped me in the car as if he had done it a million times. I suspected he'd already seen me around town or at the lake, because I didn't even have to explain what to do with the wheelchair. He was very easygoing. We played tapes and talked like old friends all the way to Spokane.

When we got inside at the concert, he picked me up and put me in one of the folding seats so we could sit together. Nothing about my disability seemed to make him uncomfortable; it was just like we had been around each other for years. The music was excellent, and seemed to get better as the night progressed. Afterwards, we went to a crowded, snobby restaurant for a Margarita, and attempted to talk in the noisy bar. All in all, it was a very enjoyable evening.

He stayed with me that night, and every night which followed. Once in awhile we went to his little house to sleep, but it was not as comfortable for me there. The atmosphere of the place disturbed me, like a family home which had been deserted with all of the furnishings still intact. We slept in a room which had been decorated for a child; the tiny bed had Snoopy sheets on it, and the cartoons gave me a headache if I looked at them too long.

George had a small son who was now living in Spokane with his wife. His only companion was his female German shepherd, whom he left at home to protect his belongings. His divorce was in the process, but I got the feeling that things were far from settled between George and his wife.

Anyway, all of a sudden, there I was involved in another relationship. My life had become totally directionless, unplanned, and without any goal except day-to-day existence. I felt like a rock being kicked down the street by a child, from one side of the curb to the other, rolling and stopping, then another kick, all the way down the street. I wasn't really thinking about it too much; that's the way I lived that summer.

Not long after I met George, I received news that Mel had quit his job. He was so discouraged by the financial chaos my accident had caused that he had simply decided to give up. He bought himself a Harley-Davidson motorcycle, took off across the country, and was not heard from again for weeks.

Consequently my medical insurance would only be in effect for three more months. The small support checks he had sent me also stopped, and the money I was making at the hospital was barely enough to pay my rent. With high hopes I headed for the Social Security office to collect what public assistance I naively thought was available to all citizens who had worked and paid taxes.

Once inside, I met an extraordinarily unpleasant woman who appeared to hate her job and everyone in sight. I explained that I was a quadriplegic from a horseback riding accident and wanted to collect Social Security Disability. She told me first I needed to prove that I was truly disabled, and not just pretending in order to get money. This could be accomplished, I was icily informed, by submitting written proof from a doctor.

I then made the mistake of telling her that I had a part-time job and only hoped to supplement my income with Social Security. Her eyes flickered with contempt as she replied, "Then you are not eligible for Social Security Disability. Under state laws, you're not considered disabled unless you are completely unable to work."

"What about your husband?" she continued, "Does he work?" By this time, I was fighting off angry tears of humiliation. She was too hateful to cry in front of, so I told her a little more about our situation, how my accident had ruined us financially, that we were permanently separated, and that Mel was no longer working. This seemed to make her like me even less, if this was possible.

At this point, I asked, "What do they expect me to do? Go home and turn into some kind of vegetable?"

"Yes," she replied in a tone that was nothing less than vicious, "You should go home and vegetate." I gave up and left the office, so insulted that I could barely think straight.

I sat in the sweltering pickup truck and related the con-

Chapter Seventeen

versation to my brother, who also became offended and angry. We talked about driving the truck into the side of the building for awhile, but then decided not to because we didn't want to damage the truck. We considered some other options, like blowing the building up, but it was getting way too hot. Without wasting any more time, we went to the store for some beer, and headed for the lake to swim and lie in the sun.

My brother was so sweet and attentive that people thought we were married when they saw us together at the lake. I had to be very careful because the one-hundred-degree sun had the potential to make me faint if I didn't stay wet. Every half hour or so, Karlos faithfully carried me out into the water, and held onto me while I cooled off. Although I still loved the water I didn't feel entirely safe unless I knew someone was nearby. This was very hard to get used to after spending most of my former summers swimming like a seal.

As with the rest of the town, things didn't change much from year to year, so each trip back was like a nostalgic trip into childhood. Chewelah had two popular lakes, each very different from the other.

Waitts Lake was a large, crowded lake with several resorts that sold tackle and rented rowboats. There were jukeboxes with original records from the 1950's, and old-fashioned pop machines that sold icy-cold glass bottles of Coca-Cola, Green River, and strawberry soda. The ancient metal water slide we had used as children was still mounted in the same place. The slide became so hot in the sun that it burned the tender skin on the back of your legs if you didn't pour water on it before going down. The air sang with the shrieks of excited children as they hurdled from the high dives, and the pleasant aroma of motorboat fuel wafting across the lake completed the atmosphere of euphoria and the freedom we associated with summer.

Browns Lake was a smaller, privately owned lake. It was very deep and cool, and the water was crystal-clear. We went there when we wanted to bathe, and on the days when it was too hot to do anything but swim.

Chewelah is a long, winding valley with endless back

roads through fields and hills. Oats grow as high as a person's shoulders in the fertile valleys, fragrant and uninterrupted except for an occasional fenceline. The fences are of no concern to the deer, who just curl up in the fields to sleep, hidden from sight by the tall, silky strands of oats.

We often drove the back roads in the evening just to enjoy the scenery, after the sun had left the valley. One such evening, black, rolling clouds appeared, quickly filled the sky, and created a terrific thunderstorm. We parked the car and went out into the oats to watch the clouds blow past in the semi-darkness. Large drops of warm rain splattered onto our faces as we sat in the field, viewing the magnificent show of nature. The thunderstorms always seemed to come in the evening, blessing the ground with a little welcome rain, and they left as quickly as they came. Chewelah was a magical place to spend the summer, and I loved it as much when I was an adult as I did when I was a child.

Our house became much more livable after George started staying with me. The first week he was there, he and his friends built a ramp off the front porch so I could get in and out safely. They could barely believe I had tried to live without one. We moved some of his furniture and dishes, and I brought an old stove over from Seattle which had been in our kitchen before Mel remodeled. The stove was fire engine red, and had sentimental value for two reasons: Norma had given it to me when we first moved onto the farm, and it was exactly the same color as the old Porsche. I hung the sheer, white curtains I had brought from the farm, and my older sister Marie, when she visited, helped me sew drapes for the kitchen. We made them out of bright yellow cotton with little red flowers to match the stove. The kitchen looked quaint and country-like in spite of all the cracked glass and peeling paint, and the old house began to feel like home.

In spite of my carefree attitude, there were still a few responsibilities which could not be overlooked, such as going to the bathroom and getting dressed. With Steve gone, most of the work involving my personal care had fallen on Lisa, a fact that she didn't particularly appreciate. Lisa was only sixteen at the time, and possessed neither the tempera-

Chapter Seventeen

ment nor the caregiving qualities necessary to enjoy nursing. She was temporarily relieved from the duties by Marie's visit, but it was apparent that I needed to make some permanent arrangements before much longer.

My hospital bills were stacking up all over the counters, and I would have been happy enough to ignore them, but my older sister was a little more grounded in reality, and she wouldn't let me. Marie had become a veteran of "the system" during and after an unhappy marriage, and she strongly suggested that I go to the Welfare Office to apply for benefits. I balked at the idea after my experience with Social Security, but she insisted that I go, and offered to take me there herself.

To my great surprise, the people at the Welfare Office were friendly and helpful. As I listened to them talk, I became aware of a very puzzling fact: the laws supposedly intended to help people didn't make any practical sense. For example, a woman who had never worked and borne children was eligible for housing, support payments, Medicare, and food stamps. If she had more than one child, her payments increased proportionately. I would have been much better off being less responsible about birth control.

The welfare officers explained that on my application my husband's assets would also have to be taken into account, that I might be better off if I got a divorce. One of the women explained that even happily married couples sometimes choose to divorce legally to qualify for benefits if one of the couple is disabled. I would then be eligible for Medicaid, and in addition, be put on the Chore Services Program which would pay for my helper.

Next, they advised me to go back to the Social Security office and re-apply, but this time to apply for Supplemental Security Income, or SSI. They felt that, from the information I had given them, I was surely eligible for SSI payments. "But, if I qualified for SSI, why didn't they tell me that last time I was in there?" I asked.

"Probably because you asked to be considered for Social Security Disability," they replied. "You need to be specific in your request. The Social Security Department is not legally required to inform you of the laws. It is their goal to keep as many people as possible off the system."

"But I thought that if you worked, and then became disabled, you could automatically collect disability," I continued, still feeling confused.

"Only if you worked enough hours in enough quarters to qualify," they explained. "Simply having a disability does not qualify you for anything. You must have paid a certain amount into the system before anything will be returned."

"Well, what about the job I have now?" I asked. "I don't make enough money to live on, but I'm not too disabled to work. Will I be able to collect SSI in order to supplement my income?"

The reply was incredibly discouraging. For every dollar I earned, my payments would be decreased proportionately. When the mathematics were completed, I would disqualify myself for SSI by earning only $160.00 per month. Without working, I could receive a little over two hundred, still not enough to live on, but slightly more than I was presently earning. In other words, the term "Supplemental Security Income" was a hoax. In reality, it did not supplement anything.

The next day, I went in and applied for SSI. The counselor was more receptive this time, but warned that if I qualified at all, it would be a very close decision. My earnings during the time I was married barely satisfied the law's requirements, mostly because of the fact that my work as a Kelly Girl had been sporadic and part-time.

Eventually I was granted Supplemental Security Income, which made it pointless for me to continue my job at the hospital. In dollar amounts, I would come out ahead letting the system support me. I apologetically explained this to the nuns, and abandoned the idea of working to support myself.

George had a full-time job working at a mine in the nearby town of Addy. He was trained as a land surveyor, but had not yet passed the State Boards. Most of his work involved explosives, for which he had to have a blasting license. Often he returned home from work coated with blasting powder, and looking a little singed around his mustache and eyelashes. Apparently, the blasts were not a hundred

Chapter Seventeen

percent predictable, and sometimes he accidentally gave himself quite a scare.

Even in the middle of an emergency, George seemed funny to me. One day while he was at work, a friend gave him a sample of some smoked fish to try and he got a fishbone stuck sideways in his throat. He couldn't reach it without gagging himself, and finally had to be put in an ambulance and taken to the hospital to have it removed. His description of the incident made me laugh until I had tears rolling down my face, even though at the time it was rather serious. The thought of him panicking, gagging, and sticking his fingers down his throat just cracked me up.

Everyone else thought he was funny too. In a house full of people you could always trace George's location by listening for the laughter. His friends were also entertaining, and they stopped by often to watch football in the afternoons. Awhile after I met George, his friends gave him the nickname "sick animal" in honor of our relationship. "You sick animal, you finally found one that couldn't run away," they teased. I suppose I could have taken this as an insult, but they acted like they liked me, so I chose to consider it, instead, as a perverse sign of acceptance.

I hired my first real helper in late summer and trained her myself, careful not to pass on any of the terminology from the rehab hospital. I showed her how to clean the nightbags and legbags, how to transfer me in and out of bed, and how to help me get dressed.

Her name was Terry, and she was from New York. She and her husband were hippies who had fled the Big Apple to seek a simpler life. They had built a tiny cabin high in the hills outside Chewelah and were trying to live off the land, with minimal success. Terry's husband had been a jewelry maker, and their only real source of income was the small amount of money he made by selling jewelry at the hippie fairs in neighboring areas. Their cabin didn't even have running water, so they had to haul water for cooking. They had planted a vegetable garden, but most of the emphasis was on marijuana and they remained happily stoned every hour of the day.

I got along well with Terry, but not her husband, who

was pushy, aggressive, and extremely tactless. It seemed that Terry went home and shared most of the details of my personal care with him, and he was discussing it freely with whomever would listen. The thought of this made me extremely uncomfortable, and I developed an intense dislike for him.

All the company went home at the end of the summer, and George and I were on our own. There wasn't much to keep me busy, but I was comfortable just sitting in the house drawing pictures and daydreaming, still grateful to have escaped the chaos of my ruined marriage and my former life.

EIGHTEEN

In late fall we drove to Dad's cabin where the autumn scenery was breathtaking. The trees had turned vibrant gold and scarlet, and the crisp fall air was fragrant with smoke from outdoor fires. The steep, winding roads were as peaceful as they were scenic, and the fields were full of wild deer grazing, undisturbed by passing cars. I felt elated and free, and fortunate to have found a person like George. Without his unconditional acceptance and willingness to overlook the inconveniences presented by my paralysis, the life I was living wouldn't have been possible.

He took me on picnics in the mountains, out to dinner at night, and to the city to shop for clothes. We had good friends, an entertaining social life, and a great sex life. I was by no means ready to venture into the world alone, and although I knew I needed him, we had so far managed to avoid developing the unhealthy type of dependency I had experienced with Steve. The only thing I failed to realize, or managed to forget, was the fact that I was still in love with Mel.

It was my first trip back to the cabin since my accident, and I was overwhelmed by mixed emotions as we drove the last few bumpy, dusty miles to the top of the hill. Intrusive memories cropped up at each familiar landmark along the way. Unwelcome visions of Mel's exuberance at being there, away from the cement and the traffic, pulled at me, threatening to spoil the day. I forced them out of my mind and tried to forget the past.

Managing the wheelchair on the rutted ground between the car and the cabin was difficult, and Dad and George finally had to lift it up on to the porch. Once inside, they sat me on the broken down old couch near the fire while they unpacked. I watched the activity, wishing I could get up and help, and unwelcome tears began to sting my eyes. I held them back in the semi-darkness, grateful for the dim lights. Dad was cheerful, almost falsely cheerful, it seemed to me. I felt I should try to appear happy; I was glad to be there, in a way. It was just very different from the way it had been.

In the morning, George, Dad, and Kathy got up to light the fire and start breakfast while I waited in bed. It was extremely cold on the sleeping porch and I had the sleeping bag pulled up over my head. I lay there quietly, listening to the thumps of boots on wooden plank floors, the creaking hinges of the wood stove, and water running in the metal sink. Finally, the fire started crackling and the kettles began to hiss on the stove.

"Anybody want some coffee in there?" a voice called from the other room.

"Sure Dad, that would be great," I answered, attempting to sound enthusiastic.

During the night, a feeling of sadness had settled over me like a choking fog, but I couldn't allow myself the luxury of exploring the reasons. There were just too many losses to face at once, all equally painful and competing with one another. The tears remained trapped inside and caused a dull pain in my chest. I was afraid that if I started to cry I wouldn't be able to stop. I was also afraid I wouldn't be understood, or that my sadness would be interpreted as self-pity. I longed to stay underneath the covers and escape from the world, from reality, and even from my family. From my place in bed, as I observed the sights and sounds of the outdoor life I loved so much, I felt overwhelmed by the true extent of my disability.

My old self rose from the bed, pulled on jeans and boots, and went out into the cold without a coat to haul water and bring in wood for the fire. She stood by the hot stove, watched the bacon sizzle in the black wrought-iron pan. Next she made pancakes, which always seemed to turn out perfect at the cabin, and fried a strong-smelling trout caught during an early morning trip to the algae-filled lake. Mel was in the cabin with her, taking long strides across the floor,

Chapter Eighteen

his flannel shirt unbuttoned, sleeves rolled partway up. He was wearing the survivor boots she gave him, especially for the cold weather.

I blinked hard a few times and forced the memories away. I tried to rationalize my feelings; I was still alive, still here. I was still the same person, wasn't I? I should be able to relax and have fun.

While breakfast cooked, Dad and Kathy came in to dress me, arguing good-naturedly over how to do it most efficiently. Finally one of them took the top and one the bottom. It wasn't easy for them to pull up my jeans with me lying on the sagging, broken down old bed, but they managed. George lifted me into the wheelchair, and I rolled over to the mirror, the one with the foggy glass that usually made you look better than you actually did. I'd been sweating during the night and my skin was dull and oily, my hair matted and pushed into a funny shape from sleeping under the covers. I hoped someone would help me haul a tub of water to the kitchen table and wash my hair.

The morning and the rest of the day passed slowly. I spent most of the time sitting and watching as everyone else went about their activities. It seemed that when I tried to help I just got in the way. I read a little, and in the afternoon George and I decided to go for a ride in the car.

We got out at the lake, but the ground was so rough it was uncomfortable being pushed around in the tippy, lightweight wheelchair. Unexpected ruts in the ground tossed me sideways and I had to hang on very tightly to keep from being thrown out. There was also a piercing wind which howled through the valley and across the lake. I couldn't seem to stay warm in spite of being fairly well-dressed for the cold. On returning to the car, we turned the heaters and fan all the way up, and I sat there and shivered while George sweated.

After the trip to the lake, I was more than content to sit by the wood stove and read. We spent one more night and then prepared to return home. I was looking forward to a hot shower and our warm, cozy bed.

I had started to cough a little while we were at the cabin, and in the car going over the pass I began to feel exhausted.

Return To Chewelah

I lay down on the car seat and rested my head on George's leg. Suddenly there was tightness in my chest, and I couldn't seem to stop coughing. By the time we got home, I was almost too sick to sit up.

After one night at home, George took me up to the little Chewelah hospital and checked me in; they said I had pneumonia. The small-town hospital didn't have much experience treating people with spinal cord injuries, so after a few days of lying flat on my back I grew much worse and had to be transferred to a larger hospital in Spokane. There, supposedly, they would take care of everything, and I would get well.

I trusted all those involved in the medical profession because my father was a doctor. I had not yet learned that bad care was a possibility. My situation was also different this time because I was in a place where nobody knew me. I was no longer the daughter of someone's friend, a prominent surgeon and colleague; in Spokane I was just a sick young woman with a history of frequent hospitalizations, a history which probably indicated I had not been doing a very good job taking care of myself.

My lungs were full of fluid which I was unable to clear by coughing because of a weakened diaphragm. The respiratory therapists were supposed to suction out the fluid by passing a tube up through my nose and down into the lung. Most therapists opted not to do it because the procedure was difficult and caused the patient to gag and choke. They settled for breathing treatments and chest percussion instead.

My doctor was hostile and abrupt and we had a very difficult time communicating. From the very beginning, his attitude conveyed contempt and disrespect. He seemed to regard my fear of respiratory problems as foolish, and was too impatient to let me explain anything that had happened in the past.

He wanted to perform a procedure called a bronchoscopy, under general anesthetic, to help remove the fluid from my lungs. I said I would agree to the procedure as long as he promised I wouldn't have to be intubated. The long, frightening night on the respirator in the ICU was still fresh

Chapter Eighteen

in my mind, and I didn't want it repeated hundreds of miles from anyone I knew who cared about me. He said there was no reason that I should have to be intubated, so I signed the consent.

When I awoke after the surgery, I was on the respirator. The mechanical device was breathing for me, and, again, I was unable to communicate. I wondered what had gone wrong, and began to get frightened. There was no one to reassure me or explain what had happened. The tube was as uncomfortable as before and made me feel like I was choking. I reached up to try to adjust it, and immediately a nurse grabbed my arms and strapped them to the bed. My discomfort and anxiety caused me to shake uncontrollably, and I bit down on the respirator tube. They jammed a wedge-shaped piece of nylon between my back teeth so I would clench down on that instead. There was nothing I could do but wait. When they finally pulled out the tube, one of my molars fell out, broken in two.

After another day or so, I was paid another visit by the hostile doctor. "Well," he announced from the end of the bed, "you're getting worse."

It was difficult to decide exactly how to respond to such an observation. It had been my understanding that it was his job to help me get well, yet he seemed to be placing the responsibility on me.

I wasn't too sick to realize that I didn't like this doctor and decided to call my father in Seattle and ask him what to do. He asked the doctor's name and said he would call me back later. After speaking to a few people, and inquiring about my lab values, he returned my call, sounding surprised and somewhat panicky.

"Jesus Christ, Janet, you don't have enough oxygen in your blood to be alive," he exclaimed over the phone. "How do you feel?"

"Not too bad," I answered, "I've just been lying around in bed. My chest hurts a little."

After considerable deliberation, he decided to have me flown by air ambulance to Seattle, an expensive undertaking not covered by insurance. I arrived there weak and severely ill, with one lung completely collapsed.

Return To Chewelah

The pulmonary specialist who had taken care of me after my accident was called in. I idolized him in a way and credited him with having saved my life once already. He was compassionate, intelligent, and at times very humorous, but he was approaching this situation seriously. He wanted to do another bronchoscopy, but said he was not sure whether or not the lung would ever reinflate. This time, it would be performed under local anesthetic.

The procedure was simple and painless, a breeze. I couldn't believe what I had suffered through before for such a minor operation.

I was suctioned several times a day for the next week or so, coughed and vigorously pounded on by the respiratory therapists. They made me use an incentive spirometer to encourage deep breathing several times a day, and sat me up at the side of the bed. Fortunately, the lung reinflated, and I began to feel better after a few more weeks.

I wanted to go back to Chewelah; I now considered it my home. So I prepared to return, a little wiser, but with much yet to learn about managing my own health.

NINETEEN

By the time I returned to Chewelah, snow had fallen. It continued to fall until it was so deep we had to shovel a tunnel to the front door. The drifts were over six feet high, and it was beautiful, but very, very cold. The sub-zero temperatures caused our water pipes to freeze and break underneath the kitchen floor, and George had to plug his car in every night to keep the engine from freezing. The oil heater in our living room was no longer adequate for warming our drafty home, so we purchased a specially made wood-burning stove and installed it in the old one's place.

I enjoyed the snow at first, but didn't realize how long it was going to be before I'd be able to get out of the house in my wheelchair. The weekdays became lonely with George at work, and I began to realize I didn't have enough to do to keep from getting bored. For most of the day, I sat at the roll-under counter we had built in the living room and did artwork or listened to music. Cars rarely passed by our home on the outskirts of the town, and the blanket of snow outside made everything seem silent, as though the whole world were sleeping. My friends from high school were all busy, either with jobs or children, and virtually never stopped by to visit. I didn't understand why none of them came by to visit; I didn't even realize how much my life, and I, had changed. I was oblivious to the fact that I was just existing. Day after day I sat gazing out the window, as unproductive as the frozen ground outside. The way I looked at it, I was doing plenty. I was forgetting, and that was taking all the energy I had.

On the weekends, George took me to the ski hill with him. I had a warm-up suit which consisted of overalls and

Return To Chewelah

a matching parka, so there was no chance of getting too cold. While George was skiing, I sat in the trendy bar with my drawing pad and sketched the colorful surroundings. Most people assumed I was just a skier with a broken leg, so my presence didn't inhibit their enthusiasm for dangerous outdoor sports. The atmosphere was warm and friendly, and when George came stomping in, out of breath, with his hair and mustache frozen into icicles, I didn't miss skiing at all.

Christmas came and went, quietly and uneventfully; neither of us felt like making a big deal out of it that year. My family was scattered around Seattle, and I was still married to Mel, though we rarely spoke to one another. George's divorce had recently been finalized, and he'd lost custody of his son. The boy was almost three, and would continue to live with his mother in Spokane.

Although George and his wife were no longer a couple, they were still very much parents, attempting to share the responsibilities of raising the child. There was no way I could really take part in this, and it was very difficult for me to determine what my role should be. The little boy did not respond well to me, perhaps because of the wheelchair, or perhaps just because he was already confused from being passed back and forth.

George's ex and I were distant friends at first, but that began to change when she developed the practice of dropping the child off at a second's notice: whenever she had a date or felt like taking a vacation.

The reason I had decided against having children was because I did not feel I was in much of a position to raise them properly, yet suddenly I had acquired a child to care for. He was strong-willed, and very, very active, and I was at a total loss in knowing what to do with him.

Watching him while George was at work was a nightmare; I was physically unable to intervene when he did something wrong, and verbal admonitions bounced off him as though he were deaf. He quickly figured out my physical limitations, and stayed craftily out of reach. The days I cared for him were nerve-wracking, frustrating, and completely unrewarding.

Chapter Eighteen

George's ex-wife was attractive, and had an exceptionally nice figure. She always took care to dress up when she dropped off their son, and she often caught me in the middle of going to the bathroom, which embarrassed me greatly. I was envious of her beautiful clothes and hairstyles, her perfect figure, and her flamboyant lifestyle, and her visits left me feeling dumpy and depressed.

When the snow finally began to melt, we were so relieved that we had a huge party to celebrate. It was a Mexican potluck, and our small house was crammed with people, most of whom sat in lines on the counters in the kitchen passing a blender full of Margaritas. At the end of the night, we all gathered outside to watch people try to drive through the slush, which was two or three feet deep. The half-melted snow had an uncanny way of pulling cars off to the side of the road, and many of the guests had to abandon their swamped vehicles until morning. We got out all our extra blankets and the stranded guests spent the night on the living room floor.

Spring officially arrived with warm sunshine after five long months of snow. Once again, I was able to leave the house, and relieved the monotony and boredom of being stuck at home.

With my electric wheelchair, I was able to go to the bank, do my grocery shopping, and run errands. The town was completely flat, and surprisingly, most of the buildings were accessible. People honked and waved at me as I rolled down the highway, though most of them didn't know me personally. In a town as small as Chewelah, not many things go unnoticed.

George loved my cooking and wasn't at all picky about food. Unlike cooking for Mel, I was able to be as creative as I wanted with ingredients and spices. Cooking became my favorite pastime. I used an electric skillet for most of my recipes and a cutting board with a hinged knife which Steve had invented. Unfortunately, eating became my second favorite pastime, and soon the calories began to show. I had come to Chewelah much too thin, but by late spring could no longer tuck in my blouses. The extra weight was even quite noticeable on my face. It seemed that I had gained so much weight so fast that I went to the doctor to be sure there wasn't something wrong with me. He was brisk and unsympathetic as I tried to relate my insecurities about my body.

"The way you look is normal for someone with no stomach muscles," he stated impatiently. "Your arms and legs aren't too fat. If you try to lose weight, your stomach will probably still stick out, but the rest of your body will be too skinny. Just relax; there is no woman in this world who is happy with her figure." I reluctantly accepted the discouraging advice and tried not to worry about my appearance.

The doctor I was seeing in Chewelah had gone to the University of Washington for part of his training. I chose him because he knew who my father was, and I hoped that somehow this meant he would be a good doctor. He was young, and I felt comfortable around him. I hoped very much that he would be someone I could confide in, and rely on for advice and support, but he didn't seem to want to talk, or listen, much at all. The numerous problems I had been trying so hard to ignore would come to the surface during my visits to the doctor, but each time I approached the subject of my separation or my financial difficulties, I was cut short before I'd had a chance to say anything. He clearly was not interested in hearing about my situation, and I began to wonder if my feelings were even valid, or if I was a genuine pain-in-the-neck and everyone was sick of listening to me complain.

It was this spring that I developed my "stomach pain," a burning, incapacitating pain from my ribs to my abdomen. It occurred at random times, sometimes when I was home feeling bored and lonely, but also when I was out with friends, socializing and having a good time.

The only medication that seemed to relieve the pain was an intramuscular shot, a mixture of Talwin and Vistaril which I learned to ask for by name. The doctors were not at all reluctant to give me these shots, and, on one occasion, an older town doctor even made a house call in order to give me one.

After three or four hours, the effects of the shot would wear off and the pain would be gone. I loved receiving the

Chapter Nineteen

pain shots; they made me feel temporarily wonderful. The world seemed perfect under the influence of the powerful drugs. That allowed my mind to wander far away, skip pleasantly from thought to thought, and make it impossible to worry. It was a feeling like floating on a cloud, lighter than air.

The doctors didn't have any idea what might be causing the pain, nor did they seem interested in giving it much thought. The only explanations offered were that it could be phantom pain, a common problem with spinal cord injuries, or pain from an existing physical problem which had yet to be diagnosed. For the time being, the problem was solved by an occasional shot, so no further research was considered necessary.

My relationship with George was satisfactory in most ways, but not altogether perfect. He was entertaining, kind and supportive, and fun. We were good friends, and we rarely disagreed, but I just didn't have the deep feeling of belonging with him that I had shared with Mel. Although he cared for me deeply, living with me was difficult for him at times, a fact he didn't acknowledge until after we had broken up.

There were some evenings that I know I disappointed him by not wanting to kiss and make love. I simply wasn't able to be affectionate sometimes, and needed to be left alone. When this happened, I suffered tremendous guilt for not being able to make him happy.

We also had misunderstandings due to my faulty memory. I would sometimes forget entire conversations from the day before because of the large amounts of Valium I'd taken for so long; plans we had made or agreements we reached together were completely erased from my mind by the following morning. George had a tendency to take this personally, as though I just didn't think matters between us were important, and, although I didn't blame him for feeling that way, I didn't like being blamed for something I couldn't help.

It didn't occur to me to stop taking the Valium because it was prescribed by doctors whom I knew were good doctors, and I had been thoroughly convinced by the rehab hospital that I needed it to control my muscle spasms. The problem continued and became worse.

There were rare unpleasant occasions when George had to take care of my physical needs simply because he was the only one around, and he admitted later that, if he had been given a choice, he would have preferred not to have been involved.

One night, in particular, was an ordeal for both of us, one which I'm sure he has chosen to forget. I awoke in the middle of the night needing to go to the bathroom, and had to have him get me out of bed. The helper lived miles away at the top of the mountain and had no phone; it was just the two of us.

George had not previously been versed in any type of helper duties, so I reluctantly tried to explain what needed to be done, and he unwillingly attempted to cooperate. In spite of our efforts, nothing would work the way it was supposed to. George was at his wits' end; he had to work the next day, and there was nothing I could do or say to make things different. I distinctly remember the total frustration in his voice, as he asked God "why he was being tested" in this way. Sometime towards morning, we were finally able to return to bed. But each similar situation, each unexpected illness, each random episode of unexplained pain, chipped away at my self-esteem, George's confidence, and our happiness together. We were in over our heads, and didn't want to admit it.

That spring Grammie Hafer died of cancer. I had tried to visit her in the hospital, but she looked like a corpse by the time I got there and was totally incoherent. The nurses didn't let me go into the room, but just let me see her from the door. She was nearly unrecognizable, and obviously very close to death.

Her funeral launched me into a state of depression which lasted a very long time. I cried during the memorial service, all through the dinner afterwards, and for the next several days. My brother was visiting again, and he and George tried loading me into the car to drive the back roads in hopes of cheering me up. I sat in the car and gazed out at the wheat fields with tears streaming uncontrollably down

Chapter Nineteen

my face. The fields just made me think of Grammie, and I cried harder. Eventually they both just gave up and left me alone.

With Grammie gone, Chewelah just wasn't the same. Grandma had arranged for one of her friends to move in with Grandpa and take care of him after she was gone because she had known for so long that she was going to die. They married soon after Grammie's death. The woman was large and awkward, with ridiculous taste in clothing and furniture, and before too long the farmhouse was transformed into something resembling the interior of a camping trailer. The hominess, the warmth, the wonderful scents, the flower gardens, all of those things disappeared once Grammie was gone. I began to dream she was still alive, and visited with her in my dreams, but seldom returned to visit Grandpa and the farm.

Soon after Grammie died, George's wife went on an unexpected trip, leaving their son with us for three months. As always, I found the little boy impossible to manage, and felt completely out of control when he was in my care. He was very mischievous, and didn't listen to a thing I said. Early on, he figured out exactly how far away from me he had to be to avoid my getting ahold of him, and I was virtually helpless when he was misbehaving. I knew nothing about how to deal with difficult children, and didn't have the foresight to ask advice from any of my friends. I also felt I had been taken advantage of by his mother, and therefore was less willing to put a great deal of effort into parenting.

The child's favorite pastime was to lie on the dog's back and pull her tail until she growled. Our dog was a sweet, calm German shepherd, and I knew it was a serious warning sign when she began to growl, but often I could not reach well enough to keep the boy away from him. I definitely wasn't in a good position to be an effective baby-sitter, nor was I in the proper frame of mind.

One day the boy came down with a terrible cold and was so congested I felt he needed a doctor. It was an unusual day for Chewelah, with bucketloads of rain pouring down. I didn't have any choice but to take him to town on my lap in my electric wheelchair. I had an oversized umbrella which could be mounted onto the chair, so I bundled him up and drove him to town on my lap, sheltered from the rain by the huge umbrella.

It turned out that he needed antibiotics, so I was glad I had taken him in, but the office girls clearly thought I was nuts, or someone else was nuts to leave him in my care. His cold cleared up quickly with the medicine, so I tried to reassure myself I had done the best thing under the circumstances. The fact remained that the situation had been less than ideal.

The mother came home as unexpectedly as she had left, disrupting special plans we had made for the weekend, and left us feeling used and unappreciated. She and I eventually got into a nasty fight over the telephone, in which I told her I didn't think she was fit to be a mother because of her out-of-control social life. I deeply regretted having made this remark later, as it caused repercussions beyond anything I could have ever imagined. Her anger over the argument escalated into numerous threats related to George's visiting rights, and eventually into hysterical warnings that she would harm herself, or the child, if George ever allowed him near me again. The ensuing problems caused a rift in George's family in which most of his relatives sided with the mother, and so a bad situation was made even worse. We never managed to resolve the conflict.

TWENTY

There is one aspect of living with a spinal cord injury that is more humiliating than any other. It is a condition shared by most paras and all quadriplegics, and is seldom mentioned in the presence of able-bodied people because it is embarrassing. As some people may find it hard to relate to, I will describe a situation involving an able-bodied person which would be similar.

Imagine that you have just gone out to a romantic seafood dinner with a new date whom you are anxious to impress. For the sake of the story, we'll assume the unfortunate subject is a male.

You order raw oysters on the half-shell as an appetizer, followed by steak and lobster, with a bottle of the best champagne. So far, the evening has been perfect. You are driving her home, wondering if she is going to invite you in, and there is an accident on the freeway. All four lanes are jammed, and there is no possibility of moving any time soon.

Suddenly, you begin to experience severe abdominal cramps, and realize you need to find a bathroom. You glance around furtively and consider the possibility of leaving the vehicle, but you are surrounded by cars and people, and there is no exit in sight. You consider saying something in the form of an explanation, but she is gorgeous, and you just can't do it. She is talking to you, but you don't hear a word she's saying; you are concentrating on attempting to avoid the inevitable. Your mouth is dry and your forehead breaks out in a cold sweat, and, after several of the longest moments of your life, it happens. There is an audible cracking sound and warm liquid begins to run down the leg of your slacks; no explanation is necessary now. She is visibly shocked and embarrassed, and you know at this point that you will never be able to face her again.

If you can imagine yourself in a situation like this, you may be able to understand the way I used to feel when it happened to me.

It was George's weekend off and we were relaxing at home together. He was out mowing the lawn, and we had plans to go visiting later in the day. I was dressed in slacks and a loose-fitting top which I wore over the pants to disguise my stomach. I had begun to wear a girdle because I was so self-conscious about the weight I had gained.

I was sitting in the bedroom putting on makeup when I began to get goose bumps on my arms. I tried to ignore them, hoping they would go away. Instead, they became more intense, and shortly I broke out in a sweat which became so profuse it was rolling off my face and chest in small rivers. My head developed a dull ache, and with a growing sense of panic I realized that I was experiencing dysreflexia. Something was wrong, either with my catheter, or perhaps my bowels. My heart rate picked up as I imagined the worst case scenario: I needed to go to the bathroom, or perhaps was already going. I was home alone with George, and worst of all, I was dressed in pants and a very tight girdle.

I reviewed my list of friends in my head, realizing there were none loyal enough to be presented with a problem of this nature. I was feeling worse by the second. Warnings from the rehab hospital of patients having a stroke from untreated dysreflexia added to my sense of impending doom. I knew without a doubt that I didn't want to involve George in any more crash courses in nursing care.

Reluctantly, I went outside and quietly explained that I was having a problem and probably needed to go up to the hospital. George rolled his eyes as if saying, "Not again," as I asked if he could drive me there and drop me off. This turned out to be the right decision, even though it ruined our plans for the day.

By the time we got there, I was shaking and sweating so much that I could barely talk. The hospital staff was understanding and discreet; they were accustomed to seeing me there. They helped me get out of my clothes and took care of the problem, a major bowel impaction.

It took quite awhile to get me cleaned up and comfortable. I asked for a pain shot and was given one "to calm things down a little," in the doctor's words. I gratefully drifted out of reality, wishing I could stay out of reality forever.

While cleaning me up, the nurses observed poop in what they considered unlikely places. They feared I may have developed a recto-vaginal fistula, an opening between the two areas. This was a very serious condition which would require surgery to correct, and they decided I should go to Seattle for further testing.

It seemed that common sense and the laws of physics explained how poop had gotten in the wrong places; but they were the professionals, so I went along with their ludicrous theory.

At this point, I lacked the perspective to question why I was having unexpected bowel accidents, and failed to realize they might be preventable. All I knew was that it was a part of life that I absolutely could not accept.

My self-image plummeted to an all-time low, and I felt like a fat, disgusting pig. I blamed myself for eating too much and hated my body. The only time I felt at peace was when I was in the hospital, staring at the sterile white curtains and listening to the nurses come and go. At home I felt increasingly out of place, useless, and out of control.

A short time later, I was sent to Seattle to a hospital where I could be cared for by my old rehab doctor, Henk. It was good to be back in Seattle and reunited with my family. One of my best friends from high school called and asked if I needed anything at the hospital. I asked her to bring me a maternity blouse so I could cover up my stomach.

I had been gone for over a year. Mel had temporarily returned to Seattle and news soon reached him that I was back. We talked on the phone and arranged a time for him to come and visit.

Hearing his familiar voice over the phone was incredibly painful. When we spoke, it was as though nothing between us had changed. We had separated from each other physically, but in our hearts we still belonged together.

He agreed to come and see me the following day. Waiting for him to arrive, each minute seemed like an hour. I finally leaned over and folded my arms on the bed, put my head down, and closed my eyes to rest.

Later I heard footsteps and a pair of black leather gloves landed on the bed near my face. I sat up and there he was. Every ounce of love that I had ever felt for him came pouring back in a flood.

"Hi baby," he whispered, wrapping his arms around me. He held me closely for a moment and then stepped back. He was crying.

"Fucking hospitals!" I heard him say as he turned and wiped his eyes. After a few minutes, he regained his composure and told me I looked pretty. My hair was longer than it had been, and it had become very light from the sun. He told me it was beautiful.

"Let's go outside, Janet. There's something I want to show you," he exclaimed proudly.

It was a huge, gleaming Harley-Davidson motorcycle. He kick-started it for me, and it nearly broke my eardrums. I couldn't imagine how he could possibly own a motorcycle without killing himself or getting thrown in jail, but I didn't want to spoil the moment by telling him my thoughts. It was just too good to see him.

He had brought a bottle of peppermint schnapps to celebrate our reunion. We drank it straight from the bottle in the hospital parking lot, ignoring all boundaries of acceptable social behavior.

Mel wanted to take me for a ride on his Harley; he thought he could just strap my feet to the footpegs and it would work fine. I thought about the time I had tried to sit up on the horse's back, and politely declined the invitation, explaining it would be too hard. Finally, it started to get late and cold and he pushed me back inside, laid me down in bed, hugged me one last time, and left.

I fell asleep quite drunk and later couldn't be awakened by the nurses. They noticed my breath, took my vital signs, and left me to sleep it off.

I didn't see Mel again before I went back to Chewelah, but his visit had left me undeniably certain that he still loved

Chapter Twenty

me, that I still wanted to be his wife, and that we would never get back together.

I went through a series of tests which turned up nothing. The doctors determined that I did not have a fistula, and that the stomach pain I had been experiencing was probably phantom pain. This was a difficult condition to treat with medication, but they decided I should try an anti-depressant, Sinequan, along with an anti-psychotic drug called Prolixin. They explained that this combination had been found effective in some patients experiencing phantom pain. The drugs were to be taken in addition to the forty milligrams per day of Valium I was already taking.

After going through rehab, I didn't have much respect for the powerful medications or their potential side effects. The Prolixin pills were tiny and sugar-coated, and didn't seem to do much one way or the other. Sometimes I took them, and sometimes I just skipped it, too lazy to open one more pill bottle.

The Sinequan, however, was a different story. Right away I noticed that it made me extremely drowsy, and that when I took it before I fell asleep I slept very soundly.

I was no longer happy living in Chewelah, and I didn't know how to face it, so like everything else in my life I chose not to think about it. There was nothing for me to do there, but I was unable to see how empty my life had become.

I liked George well enough not to leave him, but the fact remained: I was deeply in love with Mel and actually still married to him.

Mel's girlfriend had somehow developed the idea that the farm, and Mel, belonged solely to her. Consequently, she assumed the responsibility of calling me on a regular basis to try to convince me to give Mel a cheap, no-fault divorce.

"It's really easy," she claimed. "All you have to do is order the kit through the mail, sign the papers, and it's finished. I've done it a couple of times myself."

Needless to say, I didn't think much of the idea. Not only was I unready for a divorce, I also was unwilling to give everything I had worked so hard for to her.

"What we do with our marriage should be between Mel and me," was my usual reply. In spite of everything that had transpired between us, I was still not ready to let go completely. Until I heard something from Mel, I had no intention of proceeding with a divorce. It made me uncomfortable to think about Mel living with someone else, but I calmed these feelings by assuring myself they did not share the same closeness he and I had.

My relationship with George had begun to suffer since the trip to Seattle, and it became increasingly more difficult to be intimate with him. Most nights, I wanted to be left alone, and usually had great difficulty falling asleep.

When I was asleep, drugged on antidepressants, Valium, and often alcohol, I was allowed to escape from the unhappiness which had become my life. I didn't realize that I was depressed, because I seldom cried. Instead, I just felt emotionless and blank.

The hours of the day stretched by endlessly as I sat in my chair, looking out the window at the willow in the corner of the yard. There were no cheerful visitors, no pleasant conversations, no creative ideas in my mind, nothing but the fragrance of the country air, and silence.

Some days the silence was disrupted by George's little boy, who remained obstinate and unmanageable in my care. One day he pulled the dog's tail so many times that he was truly in danger of being bitten, and it seemed there was nothing I could do to keep them separated. It was too hot and stuffy in the house to close the door and lock the dog outside; I yelled until I was hoarse; the dog was cowering, and the child was oblivious to my reprimands. I found myself silently wishing the dog would just get it over with and bite him. I finally took a swing at the child's behind, which he dodged with lightening speed, adding to my sense of frustration and helplessness. I went to the bedroom and took a couple Sinequan and a couple Valium.

When George got home from work that night, I was sitting with my head down on the drawing table, sound asleep. It was the first time I had ever seen George really angry. He shouted that I was supposed to be taking care of his son and that he had been relying on me to do a good job. I observed his anger in a detached way, mildly sorry that I had disappointed him, but too sleepy to care about anything much, except going to bed.

TWENTY-ONE

The flu was going around town, so naturally I caught it. Within a few days I was back in the hospital again, too sick even to think about getting out of bed.

The atmosphere within the rooms and halls seemed noticeably hushed and somber this time, as though there were some sort of emergency. The nurses were walking faster, and talking more softly. Rumors were going around that some of the older patients had already died from this flu, and, judging from the way I felt, I didn't doubt it.

The Chewelah Hospital was very small, and lacked the sophisticated equipment available in larger institutions. There were no respiratory therapists, blood drawers, or laboratories, just nurses and nuns. The rooms also lacked television sets and were adorned instead with quaint religious pictures. I had visited each of the rooms so many times that I had developed favorites. This time I was in the room with the picture of Jesus. He was wearing a halo and holding a cane. I wondered how they knew what he looked like when they made the painting. His hair was long and his eyes were blue, and there was something radiant about his face, so that when you looked at him you recognized him right away.

In order to save himself a little work, my doctor gave me an "as needed" order for my favorite pain shots, and I was allowed one every four hours. Since I hurt all over, I asked for one every four hours. I was unusually comfortable for someone with a severe case of the flu.

After lying flat on my back for a week or so, without getting up, I also caught pneumonia. It was first diagnosed by one of the youngest, but most intelligent nurses at the hospital.

"It smells like pneumonia in here now," she stated with confidence. "I can always tell what's wrong with a patient by the smell in the room." She took my temperature several times and vowed to tell the doctor. I saw the doctor a few times following her discovery, but he gave no indication that he had talked to her.

Several more days went by; I'm not even sure how many. Then, late one afternoon, I had my life's first, and only, claustrophobia attack. Unlike most people, I didn't feel trapped by the room itself; it was the oppressive silence that seemed to close in on me. It was a terrifying, suffocating feeling like drowning. I told the nurses I felt like I was going crazy and I needed to get out of there. They were sympathetic and looked as though they believed I was going crazy, but they also insisted that I was too sick to leave. After thrashing around in bed for about half an hour, unable to move much except my arms, the feeling of panic subsided and I was able to fall asleep.

The following day I had two visitors. The first was my doctor, who informed me that I was still running a very high temperature. He asked me how I felt and I told him that the bed had been spinning, but other than that, I didn't feel too bad. I wasn't throwing up or feeling any pain. He mentioned that perhaps the dizziness was a result of some of the medication I was getting, but I said I didn't think so; I didn't want him to take my pain shots away. At that point, I was dangerously close to becoming addicted to narcotics, and couldn't have cared less. Unfortunately, the doctor didn't care either.

A little while later one my best friends, Susan, came in. She was an RN and had been known during high school for her "spunk," in other words, her aggressive personality. "Jesus Christ, you look terrible!" she exclaimed wildly as she neared the bed. "You've gotta get up! How long has it been since you've had a bath? We're gonna get you up and wash your hair."

"I can't get up, Susie," I argued weakly. "I'm too sick."

"You're gonna be a lot sicker if you don't get out of that bed," she yelled, and began to pull back the covers. As soon as she got me into the wheelchair, the room went white,

Chapter Twenty-One

and I began seeing the little sparkling diamonds a person sees right before they pass out.

"I can't stay up, Susie, I'm gonna pass out," I gasped. I couldn't get enough air.

"If you pass out, I'll catch you, I won't let you fall," she argued. "Come on, we've gotta do this."

As the minutes passed, I wasn't feeling too much better. Susan kept telling me to take deep breaths, but I just couldn't get enough air. I must have been up a total of twenty minutes, but it seemed like hours. After washing my hair in a nearby sink, she put me back in bed and left me to catch my breath, saying that she would be back soon.

She was back in a matter of minutes.

"C'mon," she ordered, "You're going to Spokane."

I didn't have the energy, or the desire, to argue. She rode with me in the ambulance, taking my temperature and wiping my forehead every few minutes with a cold cloth. The drive took about an hour. She talked the entire time about the crazy things we had done in high school. High school already felt like light years away.

I was completely worn out and half asleep when we arrived at the hospital, but Susie had taken charge of the situation anyway. She waited until I was admitted, and comfortable in bed, before talking to the nurses. "Let's do something fast," she prompted them, "She's burning up."

My temperature was a sizzling one hundred and six point two degrees. The nurses put me on an icy-cold blanket and bathed me with ice water. They continued this procedure all afternoon and part of the evening. After Susie was satisfied that matters were under control, she went home, and I was there alone. By this time, George was so accustomed to my being in the hospital that he waited for the weekend to come and visit.

My new doctor wasn't irresponsible enough to keep giving me pain shots, but by that time, I was too ill to care anyway. Although I did have pneumonia, I was transferred to neurology, for unexplained reasons.

A few days later, while eating breakfast, I suffered a grand mal seizure. It was one of the most frightening, confusing things that had ever happened to me, including breaking my neck. One minute I was being fed breakfast by two friendly young nurses, and the next minute, I was in a room full of strangers. I couldn't remember who they were or how I had gotten there. They had to tell me my name, and where I was from; they told me the date and the year. I groped for familiar images, for something which would jog my memory, but the thoughts skittered out of reach. I remember feeling like it was unfair, as if something very precious had been stolen from me.

The nurses, however, seemed to be taking it all in stride, almost as though they had expected it to happen. After an hour or so, I was able to remember things without as much difficulty, but remained quite frightened. I wished my mother were there, in case it happened again. It wouldn't be so hard to recognize her. I was repeatedly assured there was nothing to worry about, and that everything was fine, but it was not easy to trust and believe people I didn't even know.

It took a long time to recover from the near-fatal flu bug, about six weeks altogether. If Susie hadn't come and rescued me, I probably would have died. Years later she told me that, when she had come that day to visit, I was completely blue from lack of oxygen. She added that I had been in the care of the worst doctor in history and that he was eventually forced to leave town by angry residents after several of his patients died.

The recovery was arduous and time-consuming. My blood pressure "bottomed out" every time I got out of bed, and I had to be put back on the tilt table because I'd been lying flat for so long. It didn't take as long to retrain my physiological responses as it had during rehab, but I was extremely weak, and much had been lost in the overall condition of my health.

My father reassured me over the phone that having a seizure was not extremely serious, but I still felt worried and frightened by it. I had completely lost faith in my ability to remain healthy. I no longer thought of myself as a "normal" person; my self-image was that of one who had become chronically ill.

After intensive breathing treatments, I once again be-

Chapter Twenty-One

gan physical therapy. I had lost about twenty pounds, and sitting up in the wheelchair was an exhausting task. At the beginning of my recovery, as I was being wheeled to the Physical Therapy Department, I caught sight of myself in a full-length mirror. I could not believe that the image reflected in the glass was actually me. The person in the mirror looked like a skeleton, or a tall, bony ghost. Her skin had absolutely no color, her face no expression. Her eyes were sunken dark circles, her hair was matted and misshapen. There were white bandages on her skinny, bruised arms, and a disgusting, embarrassing plastic bag of urine hung off the side of the wheelchair. The hospital nightgown drooped like a rag over the tall, awkward frame, and was much too short. It exposed long, atrophied legs, positioned awkwardly apart, too thick at the knees and much too thin in the calves. My bare feet curled over the end of the footrests, resembling bird claws. I was suddenly, silently grateful to be in a place where nobody knew me.

As soon as I began to think about going back to Chewelah, my "stomach pains" returned. I begged the nurses for pain shots, which were routinely denied. I was asked repeatedly to describe the pain. The more I focused on it, the more intense it became.

Whether it was phantom pain or not, it felt real. I knew that I had abused the privilege of pain medication in the past, but felt that I really needed it now. It was as if they were all conspiring against me, smug, confident, and condescending. I was to be pitied.

I was required to undergo an upper and lower G-I series before I could return home because of my repeated complaints of abdominal pain. For the lower G-I series, the patient is required to drink a large amount of barium, a substance with the capability of turning to cement in the bowels. After the test, the patient is given a bottle of magnesium citrate, which causes the barium to be expelled from the body. I was given an entire bottle of mag citrate to drink, and discharged from the hospital without any instructions or warning of what to expect.

George seemed like a stranger to me by the time I got home, and I'm sure he felt the same. After each one of my frequent absences, we had to get to know one another again, a process which took at least a few days.

I arrived home in the evening, and the next morning was greeted by a new helper. She had only been hired a few weeks before I left, and was still in the process of being trained. We were just saying hello when we heard a strange noise like a clap of thunder. As I sat up in bed, a virtual waterfall of some strange liquid cascaded over the edge of the bed, from the top to the very end. It took me a minute to figure out what it was, and my heart sank as I realized that it had come from me.

It was diarrhea, in gallons, bucketloads; more than I could have ever thought humanly possible. As I watched the pool expand, I apologized, and then began to cry. I watched miserably as she threw towels across the floor in an effort to stop the flood from running into the living room, and then went to get the mop. I cried the whole time she cleaned it up. The watery diarrhea had soaked all the way through the mattress pad onto the bed and ruined the mattress. She helped me into the shower and started a load of laundry. She was quiet, and made no attempt to console me. It was taking all her energy just to deal with the mess.

The incident sent me into a tailspin of depression from which I could not recover. All hope of a normal, respectable life had been wiped away. It was a disgusting, degrading existence from which there was no escape. It seemed as though I had no control whatsoever over my bodily functions. I was forced to rely on total strangers during these deeply personal, humiliating moments, drawing them into the disorder. I hated myself, and hated what my life had become.

After a few more days, George sat down to have a serious talk with me. He told me that I couldn't continue to live in Chewelah because I was "too smart to sit around with nothing to do." He thought we should separate, and that it would be best if I went back to Seattle.

All I heard of the conversation was that he didn't want to be with me anymore. Mentally, I added him to my growing list of people who could not stand to live with me, and rather than try to understand that he cared about me I told myself I was being rejected.

Chapter Twenty-One

When I told my brother Karl what had happened, he listened kindly and was genuinely sympathetic. However, I was in no frame of mind to be able to accept his honest response.

He tried to explain that it had been very difficult for George to care about me but not be able to help me, and that it was hard to be around someone who was so depressed all the time. I still felt rejected in spite of his logic.

When I tried to think through the details of moving again, it seemed impossible. For one thing, I couldn't think where I would go when I got back to Seattle. I had already tried living with Mom, and it had been a disaster. My dad was just beginning a new relationship and was living with his girlfriend. Going back to the farm was out of the question. I knew that I had taken a tremendous chance by moving off on my own, and now I had completely run out of options.

It was early evening and I was sitting in my bedroom, looking at my face in the mirror. I was twenty-seven, but nothing about my face looked young anymore. There was no happiness in my expression, no sparkle in my eyes. My gaze fell to the table where I kept my makeup and pills. I had just had my Valium refilled, so I had fifty of those, and about forty Sinequan.

After a great deal of thought, I decided that the best thing for me to do would be to kill myself. It looked as though I had enough stuff to do it with, and I had a pretty good plan. I would take them now, and then tell George I was tired and ask him to put me to bed; he was used to letting me go to bed by myself. Then, I would just die quietly in my sleep, and it would finally all be over.

I wasn't at all afraid of dying, although I was much too afraid of guns to shoot myself. With pills, it would be easy. I hoped that death would be like a long sleep without dreams; and I hoped I would not be able to remember what my life had been like.

I ran some water in the peculiar old bathroom sink, wondering how long ago it was put in and why they had made it so round and small. The water hit the bottom and splashed up over the edges onto my lap, as usual. I shut it off and returned to the bedroom.

Return To Chewelah

Starting with the Valium, I began to swallow pills five or six at a time, being careful to listen for footsteps so I wouldn't get caught. It wasn't as easy as I thought it would be. I got all the Valium down and started on the Sinequan. They were capsules, and started sticking in my throat right from the beginning. I must have been taking too many at once. I got down twenty or thirty and then gave up.

After checking my expression once again in the mirror, I called George in from outside, and he helped me to bed. I acted cheerful, as though nothing were wrong, said good night and fell asleep.

When I woke up, I was in the damn hospital again. And as if that were not bad enough, I also discovered that everyone was mad at me. My plan for dying wasn't even being designated a "suicide attempt;" it was being called a "drug overdose."

"And how are you feeling today?" the nurses kept asking, as though it were just another day.

"I wish I had died, actually," I would answer caustically. They didn't seem to understand. I tried rephrasing it ... "I wish I were dead!" I stated more emphatically, hoping to get my point across.

"Would you like some breakfast?" they asked next.

Oh sure, I thought bitterly, why don't you try feeding me some eggs and see if I have another grand mal seizure.

Then George came in to visit, looking all worked up like the time I was supposed to be baby-sitting and fell asleep.

"Don't you ever do something like that to me again!" I heard him say. I moved my eyebrows up and down, trying to figure out what he meant. I thought this was something I had done to myself.

"How do you think I would have felt if you'd died?" he continued angrily. "I would have had to live with that for the rest of my life."

Once again, the burden of everyone else's guilt rested heavily on my shoulders. Mel's guilt for surviving, and for not being able to accept my injury; my mother's guilt for things going wrong while I was under her care; and now, George's guilt for my desire to end my life. A deep feeling of regret closed in as I recognized how flimsy a plan it had been.

Chapter Twenty-One

When George had joined me in bed, I had tried to say something. My speech was so slurred that it alarmed him. He checked the pill bottles, and my suicide attempt was discovered. They pumped my stomach in the Chewelah Hospital and sent me on to Spokane. My heart was to be monitored for the night, and then I would be free to go.

The doctors didn't want me to go back to the house in Chewelah. My brother went home and packed some clothes for me, and we prepared to return to Seattle. They decided that I would live at my father's house for the time being.

It was only a few minutes drive from the hospital to the long, straight highway that would take us over the mountains to the coast. I didn't try to talk much. I stared out the car window and cried for a few hours, and then I must have fallen asleep.

The next day I woke up in the hospital in Seattle. I was greeted by my old friend and doctor from the rehab hospital, the resident with the Dutch accent. Henk had become a practicing physician during my absence.

After saying hello he asked me how I was feeling. I tried to reply honestly, and with tears streaming down my face explained that I still wished I were dead.

"I think you are depressed," he observed thoughtfully. I could always count on Henk to understand.

My father was to assume responsibility for my medical care until I was "all straightened out." The first thing he did was discontinue all the medications I had been taking, including the Valium. Surprisingly, I didn't have any withdrawal symptoms, though some of the drugs were addictive. It was quite a surprise to discover that none of them had actually been necessary. Very slowly and gradually I began to feel a little more like living.

A few weeks later I went home to the same house we had when I was in high school. The living arrangements were makeshift and temporary, the best my father could do under the circumstances. I was given the master bedroom upstairs, where my parents used to sleep. There was a bathroom in the upper hall which had to be remodeled for me, and everything else, including the kitchen and living room, was downstairs. It was only possible for me to enter the lower

Return To Chewelah

part of the house by going outside, down a steep hill, and back in.

Each evening Dad and his fiancé cooked dinner for me and carried it upstairs. We hired an LPN from the hospital to help with my personal care in the mornings, and Dad put me to bed at night. It was a difficult, inconvenient arrangement for all involved, and, once again, my dependency had a profound effect on the lives of my family members.

The changes had been very difficult. I felt like the lone survivor of a shipwreck, tossed around violently and washed ashore in some distant place. Each attempt I made to regain control of my course in life had failed, and now the ship had broken to pieces and sunk in the ocean, leaving me stranded here.

I took to heart the remark George made about making him feel guilty, and vowed not to become a burden on my father, who I knew was doing his best to help me. I lost weight, lacked ambition and stamina, and spent many hours in bed watching television, reading, and thinking. If I felt sad, I tried my hardest not to show it; I had put my family through enough already. I slept restlessly, uncertain of my future and unaccustomed to the new surroundings.

It was the middle of the night; I awoke to the eerie, fleeting sound of the train passing by at the beach below the house. An overwhelming sense of *deja vu* filled the darkness as I suddenly recalled the dream from Vashon Island. I was sleeping in this bed, in the room that had been my father's. Mel was gone, and somehow I knew we would never touch, or hold each other again. A foghorn echoed, deep and lonely, reminding me of the time we lay together in the cool sand with the smoke of bonfires and the salt of the waves in the air, his arms around me, my head resting on his chest, peaceful, protected, and loved.

But I was no longer his wife, and I would never be the mother of his children. I had asked God to let me die, tried every way possible to end my life, and the request had been denied. Why was I alive? There had to be a reason, a purpose I had been chosen to fulfill.

My deepest fears had become reality and I was being forced to face them; there would be no more convenient

Chapter Twenty-One

escapes, no more running away. I no longer had any choice but to accept whatever circumstances fate might bring, and go on with my life, alone.

EPILOGUE

PSYCHOLOGICAL EVALUATION:
Name: Janet Gretchen May
Date of Birth: 7-17-52
Date of Evaluation: 8-7-89
Referred by: William Anderson, VRC
  Division of Vocational Rehabilitation

REASON FOR REFERRAL:
Miss May suffered a broken neck in 1976, the result of a horseback riding accident. Since that time she has been a quadriplegic who has partial use of her hands and is able to turn while seated. She has approached the DVR for help in obtaining funds to outfit her with a van that has appropriate driving accommodations, as well as a wheelchair lift. Mr. Anderson is seeking a general psychological evaluation which is to include an Intellectual Assessment and Personality Description.

OBSERVATIONS AND IMPRESSIONS:
Miss May arrived at the evaluation at the appointed time. She is a single white female who looks her stated age of 37. She is an attractive woman with blonde hair, pleasant demeanor, and exuding a quality of pleasantness and cooperation. She was very forthright in answering the questions asked and was a good historian in that she was able to provide a well-ordered chronological history. There were no unusual habits or mannerisms noted.

Epilogue

RELEVANT HISTORY:
Miss May has worked at Swedish Hospital as a Cardiac Monitor Technician for the past ten years. This puts her in contact with nurses and other medical personnel on a daily basis and has brought her a sense of meaning and belonging, as well as a social life. She currently lives in an apartment which has been remodeled and tailored to her needs. This apartment is located above her father's home so he is nearby and has been essential in taking care of her.

Miss May was born in Chewelah, Washington, the second-oldest of five children. Her father was a physician who, at that time, was doing his residency. Mother stayed at home and took care of the children. She describes a pleasant childhood and a warm, functional home life. The family moved to the Seattle area and she grew up primarily in Seattle. . . Her parents separated when she was a junior in high school and during that time she lived briefly with an uncle in Chewelah. She graduated from high school in Chewelah in 1970. Then she moved to Bellingham and attended Fairhaven College and Western Washington University. She reports that she fooled around at school for most of the time for one year, picking up a few scattered credits, but was not very academically inclined. She fell in love, dropped out of school, and moved to Seattle where she attended ITT Peterson Business School. She got married shortly after the move, and her husband managed a boat propeller shop. She states that her marriage was okay other than the fact that she stayed somewhat a "little girl," and was quite dependent on her husband.

In 1975, after several years of marriage, they moved to Vashon Island and got two horses. Miss May had been a horse lover throughout much of her childhood. In February of 1976 she stated that she was quite tired, got on a horse bareback on a windy, stormy day, and was thrown off, resulting in the broken neck. Apparently it was a very serious broken neck, and she was immediately paralyzed from the chest down. In addition to being unable to walk, she lost bladder and bowel control and was unable to move her fingers. After being hospitalized for about a year, she returned to Vashon Island where her husband had remodeled their previous home to meet her needs. They tried to resume their former life, but eventually the many changes they faced became overwhelming, their sex life went bad, and pretty soon there was just not much between them.

Janet states that her husband was simply unable to adjust to the kind of chronic ailments she suffered at the time, and the constant nursing care that was required. They became separated in 1977. At this point, she lived briefly with her mother, moved back to Chewelah, and got a job as a medical transcriptionist, but there she found herself constantly depressed and physically ill most of the time. She spoke of having bladder infections, stomach pain, and pneumonia, and being in a constant fog from Valium, and later Sinequan. In 1979, she stated that she ate a large amount of both these medications in an attempt to commit suicide.

It was at this point that her father intervened, took her off all the drugs, helped her through the throes of her divorce, and got her living situation straightened out. By 1980, she had attended Shoreline College for awhile, and gotten a car that she could drive, but not get in and out of independently. Sometime later her father provided her with a remodeled apartment that she could function in. Her husband was killed in an airplane accident in 1984 on Vashon Island.

Currently, she describes her health as quite good. She states that many of the physical problems she had in Chewelah were due to the medications she was on. She also believes that her own lack of knowledge in regards to her personal care contributed to the problems.

She has no history of mental health counseling, nor does she have a history of problems with the legal system. She currently, as was previously stated, works part-time, and has an active but limited social life, due to having to have someone take her everywhere.

She states that she generally stays in good humor, but at times becomes depressed. Toward the end of our interview, she asked if she could see me sometime in a therapeutic setting if her depression mounted. She does her own cooking, watches TV, struck me as a quite realistic person, and a good manager of money.

INTELLECTUAL ASSESSMENT:

Ms. May was administered the WAIS-R in the normal manner. She earned a verbal IQ score of 113. The performance score and therefore full-scale IQ scores were not attainable due to her physical condition. The verbal IQ of 113 places her in the high average range of current intellectual functioning . . . Inspection of the verbal subtests indicate above average functioning on Comprehension, Similarities, and Digit Span subtests. This suggests that she certainly has the ability to assess common sense situations, understand the reasoning and social judgment required, that she is able to see the relationships with things and ideas and categorize them into logical groups, and through the Digit Span subtest demonstrated an intact short-term auditory memory and the ability to focus and hold her attention. Her lowest score was on the Arithmetic subtest. This score was consistent with her description of herself as not being a very good math student and particularly not liking verbal problems.

She approached the verbal test with confidence and demonstrated the ability to concentrate effectively and efficiently. She tended to be a bit impulsive and not very detail-oriented, but in general performed quite accurately. . .

The overall impression is of an individual of average to above average intelligence who has obvious limitations in terms of vocational functioning because of her physical condition.

PERSONALITY DESCRIPTION:

The interview materials and testing results are not suggestive of any mental disorder that I could discern. This young woman appears to be dealing with the constant difficulties of her condition rather well. She seems quite realistic, conscientious, and dependable. She states that the hardest part of being quadriplegic is that everything takes more time, particularly tending to her personal needs such as getting dressed, and having someone constantly load and unload her and the wheelchair from the car. The other issue she deals with is money. It's quite expensive to have the type of attendant care that she requires. She points out that the medical insurance provided for her by her job is essential, but despite her part-time income and insurance, her father still pays for her helpers and provides her with a place to live.

Certainly the trauma she suffered in 1976 had psychological implications as well as physical. It sounds like she struggled very hard both physically and psychologically for the first five or six years after her accident. Since then she has seemed to be functioning remarkably well, and has some very good ideas about what she would like to do. She may want more education so that she could be a therapist or counselor or some kind of consultant to disabled persons. It seems to me that she has the capability to do this if she so wished.

I found her quite a charming woman with a good sense of humor. . . she, at this point, wishes to obtain a well-equipped van which would meet her transportation needs and relieve some of her dependency. She also is considering going back to school for retraining as a therapist or consultant and I think this makes reasonable sense. It's clear to me that she feels she needs a change in her life and I think vocational counseling might be useful in helping her make a realistic choice. My overall impression is that she is quite a healthy, well-adjusted young woman.

If there are any questions regarding this matter, please feel free to contact me.

THE END

Acknowledgments

I would like to thank my dear friend Doug who made it possible for me to write this book. He taught me how to use a computer and his friendship gave me the strength to keep going when I didn't think I could write anymore. I would also like to thank my psychologist who guided me through the darkest moments of my life with extraordinary compassion. My father deserves credit for salvaging the remains of my life and giving me a chance to start over again. Finally, thank you to all the other members of my family and Mel's who offered love and support, and to my friends who were with me during the times I can't remember.